The
EX-WIFE
Syndrome

The
EX-WIFE
Syndrome

Cutting the Cord
and Breaking Free
After the Marriage Ends

Sandra S. Kahn

 RANDOM HOUSE ▪ NEW YORK

Library of Congress Cataloging-in-Publication Data

Kahn, Sandra S.
    The ex-wife syndrome: cutting the cord and breaking free after the marriage ends/
Sandra S. Kahn.
        p.   cm.
    Includes bibliographical references.
    ISBN 0-394-57678-0
    1. Divorced women—United States—Psychology. I. Title.
HQ814.K34 1990
305.48'9653—dc20   89-43546

Manufactured in the United States of America
9 8 7 6 5 4 3 2
First Edition

*This book is dedicated
to the memory of my nephew,
Richard Warner.*

ACKNOWLEDGMENTS

First and foremost, I want to express my warmest appreciation to Suzanne Lipsett for the professional skills, perceptiveness, sensitivity, and sense of accuracy that she contributed to this project. Her superb writing abilities added greatly to the quality of this book.

I would like to thank my assistant, Norine Siegel, for her total commitment in assisting me with all aspects of the manuscript. I am also grateful to Norine for sharing her personal experiences with me. They have been inspirational.

I would also like to thank Jack Kahn for his support and Bonny Barezky and Cindy Warner for reading and discussing the chapters with me as they developed.

I am forever grateful to Brenda Clorfene Solomon, M.D., for always being available to explore issues and offer encouragement.

To my agent, Barbara Lowenstein, goes my gratitude for her help and support and to Lou Weber my thanks for pointing me in the right direction. A special thank-you to my editor, Becky Saletan. This book has benefited greatly from her wise advice, skill, and enthusiasm.

Finally, I am grateful to the many women who cannot be thanked by name. These are the women who have shared their personal experiences and feelings with me. Their generosity and openness have contributed to this book.

Contents

Introduction

Slowly, like a building tidal wave, the figures on divorce keep mounting. In the course of the eighties, we were first dismayed and then alarmed to learn that fully half of all marriages in the United States would end in divorce. As we begin the nineties, the dramatic and troubling truth is that this figure is unquestionably here to stay.

The amount of pain, confusion, and emotional turmoil hidden behind that figure is absolutely staggering. But even more disturbing is the *duration* of the disruption. Most people, including many mental health professionals, would like to believe that after a year or so following divorce the crisis fades and the separated spouses find new paths to take, but the facts are often otherwise. As Judith Wallerstein and Sandra Blakeslee have written in *Second Chances*, their landmark long-term study of divorced families, the punches keep coming, consequences keep unfolding, even years after the divorce is final. Many people *do* recover and go on to more satisfying lives. But a large proportion of divorced people—a proportion we can only guess at, since it has yet to be measured—never quite mend.

This book is written to all women everywhere who are struggling to recover from the trauma of divorce, whether they went through it last week, last year, or a decade or two ago. It is not a book about *going through* divorce—although much that we will explore will be helpful to those who are in the midst of divorce, or even contemplating it. It is not about helping children adjust to divorce—although, again, it offers much concrete guidance on this subject. And it is not a book about how to live the single life—though it definitely contains fundamental information about that. Rather, the subject of this book is *completing* divorce—laying it to rest permanently and then moving on—no matter when the divorce itself took place. My goal, quite simply, is to help "ex-wives" wipe that label from their vocabularies forever and transform themselves into autonomous women deeply engaged in the business of living their lives—who *happen to have been divorced* some time in the past.

Like most psychotherapists, I often hear stories from different patients that resemble each other. Early in my fourteen-year practice, which has focused primarily on women, I began to realize that many of my divorced clients had strikingly similar tales to tell of their lives after divorce. The men, it seemed, rarely looked back after the divorce was final, but all too often the women, after an initial period of relief and hopeful anticipation, unexpectedly found themselves paralyzed, sitting in a room with the shades drawn—metaphorically, at least—and dreaming about how things used to be. Feeling fragmented and uncertain, they asked themselves why they couldn't pull themselves together.

These weren't simply women having a rough time adjusting to new circumstances. These were women who, one, two, three—even ten, twelve, fifteen—years after they'd gotten divorced, were absolutely unable to begin their lives anew.

Elizabeth is an example. The relief she experienced directly after her divorce quickly gave way to obsessive brooding on the old issues that had divided her and Charles during their marriage. He had always behaved with impeccable courtesy and apparent warmth toward her in public, for example, but at home he had clearly, if nonverbally, conveyed the message that he had no interest whatsoever in conversation with her—not about the children, not about the house, and above all not about money. Furthermore, he had made many decisions that directly affected her without breathing a word to her about them. In fact, midway through the marriage he had actually bought an apartment in town and put their house up for sale—with no mention to Elizabeth until after the fact. At the time she had been just as glad to be free of the anxiety she often felt around decision making, but now she replayed this and a dozen other incidents repeatedly. Each time she grew so incensed that the next time she saw Charles she'd immediately pick a fight.

Yet Elizabeth's divorce, five years in the past, was ancient history as far as she was concerned. She came into therapy because she felt her life lacked focus. But as she spoke she gradually revealed that indeed her life *did* have a focus. She never got very far into recounting an anecdote without making reference to Charles, and she rarely got through a therapy session without coming up against a brick wall—some unresolved conflict with Charles—that was standing between her plans for herself and her execution of those plans. Far from leaving Charles behind with the divorce, Elizabeth had virtually guaranteed him a central role in her current life.

The more carefully I listened to Elizabeth and my other divorced clients, and the more I compared their case histories, the more certain I became that in one way or another these women were still emotionally connected to their ex-husbands and that this unbroken, unexamined link was the source of both their paralysis and their extreme emotional distress.

There wasn't much in the psychological literature to illuminate what I was finding. There were empirical studies showing that "attachment"—the impulse to bond with others—kept many divorced people tied to their ex-spouses and that postdivorce attachment often resulted in emotional discomfort. But how, exactly, did such attachment express itself? How did it continue to function in the atmosphere, often downright hostile, that followed divorce? And most important, how would one go about ending such attachment to achieve *emotional* as well as legal divorce? None of these questions was answered in the literature. I started to see the work I had cut out for myself.

*   *   *

Gradually, over the course of my work with divorced women stalled in the process of emotional divorce, I began to discern a set of symptoms that accompanied the unsevered bond. Taken together, symptoms and bond formed a recognizable constellation—where the bond was intact the symptoms I had isolated were sure to be present to one degree or another. And yet, like Elizabeth, many of the patients I saw with this cluster of symptoms were completely unconscious of the connection that still gripped them. They turned to therapy because they were suffering from unexplained depression, a sense of meaninglessness, plummeting self-esteem, a loss of direction. For them, the divorce experience was something they had gratefully left behind; now they had other problems they were trying—in vain, to their consternation—to work through. But in case after case, when these women were encouraged to describe their current relationships with their former husbands, they brought buried issues to the surface that finally moved the therapy forward. In working with these women, I came to understand just how devilishly stubborn and enduring the effects of the divorce trauma can be, even in women who believe the experience is far behind them.

As the years went by, I developed a specific approach to therapy with divorced women who exhibited the pattern I had learned to recognize. The chief characteristic of this therapeutic approach was its *directiveness*; I found it was beneficial to urge these patients toward specific issues, a procedure that would have been out of place with patients whose problems were internal. For example, I would ask a woman to recount and study her current interactions with her ex-husband—even if she considered them completely irrelevant to her current concerns. Or I might ask her to think back to the dynamics of the divorce proceedings themselves—how, for example, had her attorney advised her to "play her part"? Time and again, when patients looked at these experiences with fresh eyes, I saw their faces light up with insight, *recognition*.

"All this time," one patient told me, "I've been doing everything to get my ex-husband and the whole mess behind me. Once the hell of the divorce was over I wanted it *over*. Sure, I have to see him twice a week, when he picks the kids up and then brings them back. And sure, we still argue every time—we might as well have stayed married as far as the arguments are concerned. But I never really saw before that perhaps I hadn't finished with the guy emotionally. I just turned my back and ran without knowing I was dragging him and all our baggage behind me. No wonder I've felt so horrendously tired for so long. I've got to stop and get rid of all that extra weight!"

Seeing my patients consider the possibility of an unsevered connection, wrestle with it, and then begin to see its relation to their current emotional troubles confirmed my hypothesis that a woman who remained emotionally attached to her former husband—by whatever feeling, from "love" to bitter hatred—was in for trouble in many aspects of her life. And if in addition to being linked emotionally, she was also linked biologically, through children, she would probably be in for a very bumpy ride.

Where the diagnosis fit, the light of insight cast the woman's marriage and divorce in a new light and opened the way for her to work with me on devising strategies to sever the bond and, equally important, begin to shape a new independent, single life.

I marveled at the success of this therapeutic approach. For woman after woman, insight into the dynamics of the problem proved to be remarkably potent—almost inevitably, action followed on the heels of recognition, and each successful attempt to neutralize the obsolete connection brought these patients closer to emotional health and autonomy. Though the work was often very difficult, and always required courage and determination, the results came as close to a surefire cure as anything psychology has to offer. One by one, my patients ended their therapy with renewed self-confidence and enthusiasm for life, two hallmarks of good psychological health.

As I grew more familiar with the symptoms and their underlying cause, it became clear that I had isolated a distinct psychological condition. I named the constellation of symptoms "The Ex-Wife

Syndrome" and began the work of describing it, precisely defining the symptoms, and refining my therapeutic approach. It has taken me more than twelve years to achieve these goals. In my practice to date, I have seen roughly two hundred women suffering from the Ex-Wife Syndrome. Most of these clients have been middle-class white women of somewhat similar life-styles. Once I began to see that I was dealing with a recognizable condition, however, I actively interviewed approximately two hundred more divorced women of varied backgrounds. My interviews confirmed my suspicion that the syndrome crosses all social boundaries. Wherever there is divorce, women are at risk for the Ex-Wife Syndrome.

In psychological terms, the formula behind my treatment for the Ex-Wife Syndrome was relatively simple and straightforward: *authentic insight followed by appropriate action yields improved psychological well-being.* This formula plus the somewhat directive psychotherapeutic style I had developed for use with my syndrome patients suggested to me that it would be possible, and valuable, to write a book describing the syndrome and guiding readers everywhere through the process of disconnecting with the past.

WHO SHOULD READ THIS BOOK

First and foremost, this book is for the woman whose divorce is in the past and who is experiencing emotional distress she cannot explain. This woman may feel that what were once vague and unnameable problems—a baffling indecisiveness, perhaps, or a feeling of being overwhelmed by life—are now coming to a head; she may be experiencing a new urgency in identifying and working on trouble spots in her life. But she may not necessarily believe she has loose ends to tie up concerning her divorce. In fact, the opposite may be true: she may consider the divorce to be a past event that has no bearing whatever on her problems. This is the woman just at the verge of examining and defining her current situation. She needs guidance in finding the root cause of her vague and building distress.

But the book is by no means limited to women with divorces in the past. As we as a society finally come to accept divorce as a fact of life, we are not only educating ourselves about its effects but are struggling hard to figure out how to do it *right*—to minimize the trauma and smooth the difficult transition from the married to newly single status. In this light, *The Ex-Wife Syndrome* will be valuable as well both to women going through divorce and to those considering it. Armed with a detailed understanding of how the process of disconnection can become stalled or stopped completely, these readers will be well prepared to prevent the Ex-Wife Syndrome from taking hold of them. Others will find here ways to urge troubled marriages onto a new foundation.

Finally, this book speaks to widows. Though their marriages have ended differently, and often more unexpectedly, than those of divorced women, widows face equal psychological and practical challenges in adjusting to the single life. Many widows suffer the Ex-Wife Syndrome, and in most cases the psychological dynamics of the condition are the same. Chapter nine addresses widows directly, but I strongly urge widowed women to read the book straight through. They'll find much that will help them recognize and surmount impediments to their healing.

EX-WIFE: A FOUR-LETTER WORD

To me personally, *ex-wife* is a four-letter word.

Yes, I know it has six letters, but as far as I'm concerned it falls into the bad-taste category. It's a term I'd like to see banished from courteous interchange altogether, an off-color tag as degrading and stigmatizing as "dumb blonde" or "easy lay," and replaced with the simple descriptive term *divorced woman*.

But in a professional context, I have the goal of seeing the Ex-Wife Syndrome listed someday in the *Diagnostic and Statistical Manual of Mental Disorders (DSM)*, the standard reference work that describes known disorders of the psyche. I hope that in the same way a person who washes his hands forty times a day is diagnosed as having obsessive/compulsive disorder, a woman who defines herself as an ex-wife will be diagnosed as having a clearly defined and treatable psychological condition.

If your sense of your self is in large part determined by your status as your ex's former wife—or if you have simply been mystified by your inability to move on in your life since your divorce, even if you don't see the connection—this book will be your guide out of the limbo of "ex-wifeness," a land where unmarried women still call themselves by their former husbands' names and look backward for direction. The program is based on the fact that a healthy, vital self-concept is rooted in the present, not the past, and is determined from within, not from the outside. It's a fair bet that you don't see yourself as a little girl anymore, you don't see yourself as engaged to that sailor who turned out to be a summer romance, and you might not even see yourself as "mommy" anymore if your children have reached a certain age. In that same way, with the help of this book, you will come to see—on the very deepest level, where your self-concept is formed—that far from living a dead-end life in the limbo of ex-wife land, you are a mature single woman with the experience, resources, and *power* to shape your life as you wish. If you've been through the difficult process of divorce, you've unquestionably earned your freedom. This book is designed to help you not only use that freedom but to *savor* it.

Part 1

THE SYNDROME

1

ORIGINS

One evening when I was in a city far from home attending a conference, I treated myself to a good dinner in a lovely restaurant. Though alone, I wasn't lonely, and I enjoyed my food undistracted, luxuriating in my leisure after a busy day. At the next table, within hearing distance, sat a nice-looking couple. They were both very sharply dressed, and there was a spark and tension about them that made it obvious to me that they were on a date and didn't know each other well. The man, in his midthirties, looked attentive and obviously pleased with the company. The woman, about the same age, was animated and excited—even, I thought, a bit nervous.

As a psychotherapist with a busy practice, I don't make a habit of listening in on other people's conversations. I hear enough secrets during the day to keep the most committed eavesdropper happy. But these two were less than three feet away from me, and I couldn't help hearing what they were saying.

He was asking her questions about her life—about work, children, and so on.

And she was telling him, in full color and minute detail, all about her ex-husband.

It was clear she didn't mean to do it. In fact, I'm sure she didn't *know* she was doing it. But although she began each response to one of his questions with a token reference to her current life, this beautiful young woman, who obviously had a gift for conversation and a very interested listener, couldn't seem to get far without making reference to the man to whom she had once been married and who was the father of her children.

Her companion continued to ask her questions and to smile and nod as she talked, but he began to look a bit perplexed, then even a little bored. Oblivious, she talked on.

I left my table to freshen up before my dessert came, and while I was in the ladies' lounge the young woman came in to use the phone. She talked into it with the same animation I had seen in her earlier—but with an added touch of urgency. She spoke of "the kids" and asked, "When do you think you can pick them up?" "They'll really be disappointed if you don't show," she warned, and irritation flashed from her eyes. It wasn't hard to guess to whom she was talking.

The question was, why had this woman, all dressed up and out on the town with another man, gotten up in the middle of a special meal designed to make her forget the everyday world in order to make a phone call to her ex-husband? More generally speaking, what would account for a woman's unconscious habit of sabotaging her current happiness for the man from whom she had separated physically and legally for all the world to see?

I'd been pondering variations on these questions for twelve years. In part the answer lay, I knew, in the very architecture of marriage as we know it in our society.

MARRIAGE: THE BREEDING GROUND

Lying beneath vows of love and fidelity within marriage are silent agreements about responsibility—who is to do what, who is to control both the everyday domestic scene and the overall direction of the family. To have responsibility is to have power, and when two people agree to assume the roles of husband and wife, they are implicitly agreeing to a distribution of power that is influenced to one degree or another by the culture. The energetic revolution of thought that was the women's movement of the sixties and seventies made it clear as nothing else had that the power distribution within conventional marriage is far from fair. In subtle and not so subtle ways, marriages typical of every social stratum reflect a similar structure: the man, with major responsibility for breadwinning, decision making, and worldly know-how, is *one step up*; the woman, chiefly responsible for the domestic and emotional health of the relationship and of the family, finds herself *one step down*.

Remember that I'm discussing *norms* here. Many couples refuse to conform to this structure and work hard day by day to keep the division of labor and power in the home equitable. But even in these "equal marriages," as recent research shows, maintaining a fairness over the long term is a challenge—a challenge that most often falls to the woman.

And there was never a harder challenge. Any woman who has ever returned home from lunching with a group of bright, talkative, fair-minded women friends knows there's often a gap the size of the Grand Canyon between knowing what is fair and just and practicing it at home. We all know some of those bright, fair-minded women who still talk baby talk to their boyfriends or husbands, we all know women as well as men who view child care and housework as exclusively women's work, and we all have our own difficulties in practicing what we know to be right.

Claudia, for instance, who was one of my interviewees, described her marriage as perfectly equitable, a fifty-fifty proposition all the way. She and George earned comparable salaries, both enjoyed their jobs, and they contributed equally to paying for household help. But when baby Angela came along, it was Claudia who arranged for child care, paid for it, and stayed home when Angela or the baby-sitter got sick. Claudia liked it that way, she told me. In fact, she announced that despite George's enthusiasm for Angela, she had never, ever "let" him stay alone with the baby until the child was past three. George washed the dishes and cooked on Sunday nights, but he never changed a diaper in his life.

Irene, a highly successful painter, also had a story that took me by surprise. She had recently flown back from Paris, where she had attended the opening of a one-woman show of her work, and was showing me around her apartment. I remarked that I was disappointed to see none of her work on the walls. "Oh," said this worldly woman, "Michael never lets me hang my work here. He never has." Michael was a successful novelist, and his books, which I had read, were scrupulously free of sexism. But there was that telltale word "let" once again—a clue to hidden power discrepancies.

We could all tell countless stories to the same effect, and all of them would attest to how monumentally difficult it is to buck not just a lifetime but a culture's whole history of sexual inequity. By the time we marry, all of us—women and men alike—have had years of indoctrination from our parents, the media, our schools, and our religious institutions in the distinctly different roles women and men are expected to play in a marriage. And these roles bring with them different and unequal amounts of power.

From very early childhood, most girls see their fathers as the authority figure who controls money and knowledge—and who gives protection. The father is *the boss*. We learned this not only from dad but in large part from our mothers too, if they turned to their husbands for protection and, in troubled times, rescue. "Wait until your father comes home," our mothers might have threatened. Or "Your father will take care of it—don't you worry." Families where this is not the case frequently view themselves as unconventional, going against the mainstream. Sadly, members of these unconventional families often consider their family systems weak.

Until very recently, of course, only men had free access to that mysterious realm where money and power, not food, shelter, safety, and love, were the common currency. Therefore, until very recently, nearly every authority figure a girl or boy was likely to encounter *outside* the home—police officers, politicians and government officials, principals, doctors—was male as well, until the numbers started to shift noticeably in the 1970s.

Both within and outside the family, most people dutifully act out their sex roles. Those who don't face a kind of confusion and social isolation that most people are unwilling to endure—the pain and risk of placing oneself outside the mainstream have always been powerful deterrents to nonconformity. So, as growing boys, males now over the age of twenty practiced and learned the language, postures, and gestures of men of authority and knowledge; girls learned the language, postures, and gestures of weaker beings in need of protection and, at times, of rescuing. Boys learned to look outward, to the world at large, to find their true work and self-fulfillment. For these rewards, girls learned to look to marriage.

Even where women have clearly moved out of the conventional "female" life-style, the traditional roles have proved amazingly stubborn. Women in my practice and interview sample who were working, even when they had attained the high ranks of their professions, tended to continue to play the traditional wife and mother as well, working a "double shift"—at their professions and as full-time homemakers. And we wonder why those we call superwomen become exhausted by their struggle!

For the real-life drama we call family life, then, there is this traditional context: the man's realm is the money and what can be done with it, while the woman's realm is the emotional and social well-being of the marriage itself (food, health, home comforts, clothing, and so on). As the primary wage earner, the husband serves as the lifeline, pure and simple. The homemaker/wife or the working wife who, bowing to convention, turns over her paycheck to her husband gives him the power to keep her and the children alive. By virtue of his position as breadwinner, their food, shelter, clothing—their very physical survival—are filtered through him.

In this simple fact is the origin of his power and her dependence.

If you don't believe that society and its institutions reinforce the second-class status of homemaker/wife, check out your old tax returns sometime and see who falls under the heading of "dependent." Along with the minor children, you'll find listed there the nonwage-earning wife.

Of course, the healthier the marriage, the more equal the two individuals are, both in theory and practice. It is not impossible for a woman and man to love each other and to take equal responsibility for the economic and emotional well-being of the family, whatever the work roles of each partner. The absolute requirement for such a fair-minded partnership, however, is *equal and mutual respect*. But the conventional family model is far from a fertile breeding ground for mutual respect.

What *does* thrive there, what feeds on the built-in inequality, are the strong and stubborn roots of the Ex-Wife Syndrome.

WHEN MARRIAGES COME APART: A TALE OF TWO WOMEN

One serious consequence of the one up/one down model is that men and women often enter marriage with differing, and conflicting, expectations. Whereas a man frequently sees himself as setting up a domestic base from which he can travel into the world to do his "real" work and express his "real" identity, women tend to see marriage as the *source* of their identity and ultimate satisfaction, even when they are actively involved in their own careers.

The consequences of these clashing expectations are dire enough in an ongoing marriage, but in one that's beginning to falter, they can be disastrous for the wife—while making withdrawal easier on the husband. His attitude means that a substantial aspect of his life remains intact despite a troubled marriage. But for the woman whose marriage is not only the source of identity but also her exclusive responsibility, the disintegrating relationship leaves her with an awful sense of failure and a ringing question: Who, apart from this man and this marriage, am I?

It's typical, as the marriage crumbles, for a woman vulnerable to the Ex-Wife Syndrome to lay the groundwork for what I call The Official Story, which casts the woman's marriage, her husband, and herself as the marriage "keeper" in a healthy light. To the public, everything is "just wonderful." Below the surface, the relationship, which it has been her role to care for and to nurture, has gone awry and the woman is alone, without an ally.

Gloria's eighteen-year marriage was so deeply troubled that she and her husband, David, barely spoke when they were alone. Their sex life was nonexistent, no warmth passed between them, and yet Gloria carried on her role as "earth mother" to a large extended family. She entertained for Thanksgiving every year and threw birthday parties, anniversary parties, and showers. When David finally admitted to being in love with someone else, the marriage collapsed, but Gloria used all her strength to downplay the trauma and reassure those who were concerned about her. By day she managed to maintain the cover-up. But evening found her at home with the blinds drawn, mute with despair.

Gloria had expected marriage to "complete" her, and for many years she'd felt that it had. But then David retreated from her and eventually broke away completely, and she felt not only loss but also shame and embarrassment. In withdrawing, he diminished Gloria (in her eyes) and left her once more "incomplete." After the divorce, she did what she could to keep her old image intact among her relatives and friends, but alone in the house she acted out her self-image as a person who was less than whole.

What was Gloria thinking as she sat at home staring past the soaps on the TV screen? She was reminiscing about the good old days—days that had never been—when she and David were happy and in love, the children were young, and the future was rosy.

Such is the power of the myths we are raised with—they not only shape our experience, they shape our memories as well.

Had she been recalling those days accurately, Gloria would have been thinking about the late nights she spent dealing with the children alone after a long day, David's complete indifference to domestic matters—especially those concerning the children—and her own nagging suspicions that he was being unfaithful on his endless weekend business trips and that he had a growing drinking problem she wouldn't be able to conceal much longer.

Instead, Gloria spent her time "remembering" a handsome David glowing with sex appeal who was a responsible breadwinner and an attentive father. With these distortions dominating her memory, she had little chance of making a successful transition to the role of single divorced woman. Myth and fantasy competed in her mind to cloud her vision, not only of her ex-husband and her marriage but of herself as an independent person. What Gloria saw when she looked in the mirror was a pathetic and hopeless *ex-wife*.

One evening about a year after the divorce was final, Gloria was once more staring into the mirror, this time trying to make sense of what she had done the night before.

David had come by to see the children, but they were out.

He hadn't knocked. He never did. After all, he had lived in the house for eighteen years.

He had come upon her in her robe, fresh from the shower.

It was a Friday night and she was so lonely she had been crying.

"You look tired," he said.

She did look tired—she *was* tired, all the time. But to Gloria, David's remark sounded like the most insightful, most intimate observation anyone had ever made. In fact, who else knew her well enough to make it? To everyone else Gloria put on a bright, happy face. To David, coming upon her by surprise, she appeared as she was.

It's still true, she thought as she looked at him. I can be myself with him. He's still the person who knows me best, still the one I shared my life with.

"How about dinner?" he asked softly, and she melted.

They went to a place that had been a favorite of theirs in the old days, and throughout the meal Gloria felt better than she had in months. She gossiped, she laughed, she even felt pretty. She almost forgot that when David dropped her off he'd be driving back to his girlfriend.

"Feel better now?" he asked her as he pulled into the driveway. Then he leaned across her and flipped her door handle. "Listen, it's Pam's birthday next week. Could you tell the kids I'll just see them the week after?"

She cried for an hour facedown on the bed, sick with the knowledge that she'd let herself slip into make-believe.

Next morning, in the light of day, Gloria stared at herself in the mirror, appalled. How could she have forgotten all the pain leading up to the divorce? Was she so starved for affection she was willing to let him back into her life, pain and all, whenever he could spare the time? What was going on?

Gloria was playing out the secret that lay behind The Official Story. She was still linked to David; without him she felt she had nothing, not even herself. She knew of no other way to regain her sense of who she was but to slip back, if only for a moment, into her familiar role as his wife.

Women like Gloria, who have spent the major part of their adult lives in a conventional one up/one down marriage, often have had little or no experience living as single women and will often endure a great deal of adversity and even humiliation to make themselves feel safe. Without the skills to function independently, many women fear for their very lives—fear they simply won't make it in the world at large on their own.

Like Gloria, they crave the *familiar* above all. A painful though telling analogy can be found in any courtroom in the country on any given day. A little child, perhaps covered with bruises and cigarette burns, is deemed a ward of the court and separated from abusive parents. As the parents leave the courtroom, the child cries, "Mommy, Daddy, don't leave me, I love you." To this child, an unimaginable future is more terrifying and seemingly more life-threatening than any amount of abuse in the familiar surroundings at home.

The same is true of the ex-wife who cries—literally, or silently, in her heart—"Honey, honey, don't leave me, I love you." Like a frightened child, this woman is kept by self-doubt and a lack of experience from seeing her situation clearly—from seeing that she can indeed live life on her own. But neither self-doubt nor inexperience is irreparable; both are improved by the gentle and supportive exposure to new information. There is some chance, at least, that the child separated from abusive parents will wind up in a loving and nurturing new home. Chances for the divorced woman, once she begins looking forward, are much greater, for with practice, determination, and courage, she can choose her own path through life.

But what of the woman who is accustomed to taking on the world directly, the woman whom experience has taught the habits of autonomy and self-assurance? Is she, too, vulnerable to the Ex-Wife Syndrome in the wake of divorce?

Sylvia was a highly successful financial adviser whose clientele respected her aggressive investing philosophy. She was smart, knowledgeable, and sure of herself—and at the collapse of her marriage she found herself absolutely consumed with hatred for her ex-husband. James was a prominent cardiac surgeon, well known in the city, and the two had had a glamorous, exciting marriage based, Sylvia believed, on equal and mutual respect. But James had left her suddenly to take up with a young woman of no apparent skills or interests. He set up house quite happily with this young woman and never looked back. "So, where was all our wonderful 'mutual respect'?" Sylvia asked me bitterly when she entered psychotherapy. "It was just a sham. He didn't care about how smart I was, he didn't care that I was successful. All that stuff he told me he loved about me didn't mean a damn to him. The bastard *lied* to me, and I'll hate him for it all my life."

Sylvia had begun therapy not because she was furious but because she feared she was losing her drive. Both her energy and her attention for her work were flagging. She had terrible insomnia and was losing her feel for the market. She'd made some expensive mistakes, and her confidence was faltering.

But as Sylvia told and retold her story, seeking its deepest meaning, I suggested she consider possible links between her diminished performance at work and the trauma of her broken marriage. Her hatred flared and burned—not unlike Gloria, whose "love" for her ex kept her paralyzed in her life, Sylvia was captive to her hatred. Like a grieving person who refuses to cry, Sylvia was staunchly refusing to acknowledge or feel the pain behind her hatred and trace it back to its source. She saw herself as too tough a cookie to be hurt by the loss of a man—she could only hate James for betraying her trust; she couldn't grieve for the loss of him.

But the real loss Sylvia had yet to acknowledge was not the loss of her husband's presence; it was the loss of his approval. There weren't many men whose opinion of her she cared about at all, but there was one whose opinion meant everything. Without James's respect for her, Sylvia had none for herself.

It took a long look backward and much self-exploration before Sylvia could see that in her marriage, in her world, James had stood one step above her and that her self-acceptance depended on his continued approval of her accomplishments. Deep within Sylvia, in a secret place so dark even she didn't know of it, lived a highly dependent woman who, through hatred alone, was holding fast to her sole support. And that buried woman had none of the outward trappings of success or autonomy about her. She was a pure ex-wife, and she was running the show. Not until Sylvia came to terms with this secret part of herself could she begin to rely on herself for the approval and respect she needed in order to carry on.

Dependency, whether hidden deep below the surface or formalized in a conventional marriage, is the fuel that feeds the Ex-Wife Syndrome. It leaches a woman's power from her just when she needs it most. But what stacks the odds against her as she struggles to find a foothold is the fact that society itself, *history* itself, reinforces her dependency. Everywhere she looks—in the work force, where a woman still earns sixty cents to a man's dollar; in the media, where single women are portrayed either as sexual prizes or pitiful throwaways; even, perhaps, in her family, who may consider the collapse of her marriage her own personal failure—a woman can find reinforcement for feeling "one down." And nowhere is that reinforcement so explicit as in the proceedings that lead to divorce itself.

GAMES LAWYERS PLAY

Once the slow, creaking wheels of the divorce machine begin to turn, two new characters emerge on the scene of the domestic drama. These are the divorce attorneys, his and hers, whose job it is to battle out the divorce settlement point by point.

I have interviewed many, many divorce attorneys in my research into the Ex-Wife Syndrome. The similarity of the information I have gathered from them and from the women I interviewed has suggested to me that certain generalizations can be made about the divorce transaction and its effects and that these generalizations can be extremely useful to those who have passed through the transaction. And let me say at the outset that there are many fine divorce attorneys; in fact, I keep a file so I can make referrals to my patients. Many attorneys, however, promote the destructive strategies identified here. It is absolutely imperative that you know who you are working with and are certain your trust is well placed.

Think of the divorce attorneys as directors in the family drama. A significant part of their job is to coach their clients to adopt a certain stance—play a part—to increase their chances of receiving a favorable settlement. Unfortunately, the "casting" tends to be strictly defined by gender.

While men's divorce attorneys groom their clients to assume an aggressive, no-nonsense stance, women's attorneys usually coach their clients to roll over on their backs and wave their paws. Their objective is to prevent the woman from seeming strident, demanding, *difficult*—that is, powerful enough to fend for herself in the world: "Just stay calm, let's not upset the cart, let's concentrate on what you *need*," the attorney might croon. Behind his words lies this silent message: "You're weak, you're in need, you need to throw yourself on his mercy." Quick translation: "You're about to become an ex-wife, and just as dependent as ever—maybe more."

The underlying message isn't lost on the woman—quite the opposite. Even a woman well versed in worldly matters can find it difficult to maintain a distinction between "stance" and reality, and women who lack experience in the business world may feel uncertain or intimidated when a professional they have hired directs them to behave in a certain way. Perhaps I *am* needy, they muse. Perhaps I *should* throw myself on my husband's generosity. Perhaps I *haven't* got the resources to make it alone in the world. As you don't need to be reminded, it takes a strong sense of self to assert your own desires against a chorus of opposing voices.

Over and over again, attorneys I interviewed told me that in a divorce case it was easier by far to represent a man than a woman. Except in rare cases, the man was already in control of the estate. The man's objective, even where the amounts of money involved are modest and even if support of the children is one of his goals, is to protect his money. What helps the attorney in this regard is the client's known ability to pay his legal fees.

Not so with women. The lawyers generally see them as weaker and as poor risks for toughing out a difficult court battle. Why? No money. In chapter seven we'll get into the symbolic meaning of money in a family. Here it is sufficient to state an obvious truth in our culture: money is power.

This book is not about divorce per se, but in assessing the impact your divorce may still be having on you, even years afterward, it's important to realize that many women drop drastically into a lower socioeconomic level the minute the decision to divorce is reached. During that first phone call, many lawyers advise their male clients to get all their money out of any joint accounts and cancel their wives' credit cards. And this is the case even where the money is legally considered jointly owned, as it is in those states with community property laws.

But the women in my practice and interview sample, if they took any initial financial precautions at all, tended to secure *half* the money in the joint account to get them through the period before a judge set temporary support payments. And if their attorneys advised them financially in the initial stages, they generally suggested leaving the money untouched in order not to antagonize the man. Generally, the legal stance was, "Let's let the judge decide."

As no one needs to be reminded, the amount in the bank at any one time is often negligible. So even where the woman makes an effort to secure some money for herself, her financial situation is almost always altered greatly, as the man's often is not, with that first decisive phone call.

The irony, then, is that with the divorce decision, the woman almost always becomes *more* dependent on the man she is divorcing than she was when they were still trying to sustain the marriage. This means that even after the judge has set temporary support payments, the woman without her own financial resources—and that includes career women who deposit their paychecks into joint accounts—doesn't have the money to maintain her own and her children's former life-style.

In *Second Chances*, Judith Wallerstein and Sandra Blakeslee cite these figures from a landmark study by Harvard researcher Lenore Weitzman: *"On average, women with minor children experienced a 73 percent decline in standard of living during the first year after divorce whereas their husbands experienced a 42 percent increase in their standard of living."* The woman's shocking and frightening decline begins at the moment of the decision to divorce.

With the husband and his lawyer in a position of power, the implicit goal during the divorce trial becomes to *break the woman's spirit*. Temporary support payments are often set at alarmingly low levels, and in the year or so it may take for the litigation to run its course, the woman may be forced to go through any number of humiliations and fundamental financial struggles. I have had clients from affluent neighborhoods who have had their phones or utilities cut off for delinquent payment. These are terrible experiences for everybody, particularly the children, and they contribute to a general erosion of a woman's confidence. Such experiences tend to confirm her worst fears about what sort of head of household she will make. After such tribulations, many women lose the sense of righteousness necessary for fighting the good fight. At the point where a settlement is offered, they are willing to take *anything*.

I could cite many stories, but two from opposite ends of the financial spectrum will suffice as dramatic illustrations. Meet Pauline, who was married for nine years to a very wealthy man. Stuart was a flamboyant businessman, and it wasn't until many years had passed that Pauline discovered that much of Stuart's income came from illicit drug dealing. By that time Stuart was using cocaine as well as selling it, and he had become unpredictable and both physically and mentally abusive. After two trips to the hospital, once with broken ribs, once with a broken cheekbone, Pauline asked for a divorce. Stuart became furious, threw a tantrum in which he hurled glasses around the room as their young son watched, and finally slammed out of the house—directly to his attorney's office, as it turned out. When Pauline went to cash a check at the bank the next day, she was told the account was empty. From that moment on, despite the Mercedes she drove and the big house she lived in, Pauline subsisted at poverty level. As is routine, the judge based her temporary support level on her husband's *reported* income—the result was $225 month in child support, period.

Pauline's new life-style and her level of financial anxiety weren't very different from those of Judith, who had been married to a policeman for fourteen years. Bud was an insecure man who needed to prove his worth constantly, and all too often he did so at Judith's expense. He was a "good old boy" on the force but hypercritical at home, and Judith's life was miserable. However, it wasn't until she realized he was an alcoholic who would never acknowledge his problem and seek help that she was able to decide to divorce him. When she told him of her decision, he laughed, told her she was fat and ugly and a terrible wife, and after taking all the money out of the joint account . . . *quit his job!*

Judith was destitute. She had two young children in her care and had to go out to find a job—after initiating the grueling search for full-time child care. Her attorney's advice? "His infidelities won't gain you a dime in court. I advise *against* going to court."

Judith was outraged. She disregarded her attorney's advice and pursued the case. The trouble was, Bud played the role of poor, hurt, out-of-work policeman in court, and even *Judith's* attorney responded to him as the sympathetic character in the case. Judith won virtually no support.

This interpretation of what happened during her divorce was not at all clear to Judith at the time. She was of course angry and hurt, but she had put her fate into the hands of this particular attorney and felt she had to trust him no matter how uncomfortable she might feel with the passive, compliant posture he recommended. Still, the desire to go to court plagued her, and she found the strength to resist his attempts to persuade her to settle. That struggle over, she found herself way out of her depth in the world of litigation and felt she had to rely on his judgment about how to respond to Bud's case. The idea that the attorney's own preconceptions resulted in his colluding with *the other side* never crossed her mind. But in fact the passivity, softness, and "nonstrident" tone that many women's divorce attorneys urge them to take play into the ex-husband's main objective—to maintain control of his estate.

One more strategy surfaces all too often during the negotiations and jockeying for position that make up a good part of the legal battle. That strategy is summed up nicely by a terrifying comment one interviewee overheard her husband's attorney make as they headed into the courtroom: "We'll scare the hell out of that bitch and go for custody."

Remember that lawyers in lawsuits often see themselves, not their clients, as the principal opponents. They are seeking an advantage, a strategy that will win them the case. In the cloudy realm outside the courtroom, they are not above urging their clients to use psychological weapons in the form of threats even where there is no substance behind them. Thus, a typical strategy is to urge or allow the man to voice a threat—"My attorney told me we have grounds for custody"—even when there are no such grounds. The lawyer won't say it . . . but who needs the lawyer to say it? If the idea is to break the spirit of the opposition and keep her weak and dependent, even an empty threat regarding the children is potent enough to scare the fight right out of her. Too many women, terrified at the prospect of losing their children, remain unaware or unconvinced that the likelihood of the father winning custody of the children is still extremely small.

In helping you to understand the origins of the Ex-Wife Syndrome, it is not my intention to drag you through a painful rerun of the crisis during which your divorce agreement was forged. But it's important for you to recognize that unknowingly you may have been "directed" by outside forces to play a weak, dependent character and that somewhere along the line you might have begun to believe in the "character" you were asked to play. Indeed, the stance your attorney advised you to adopt as a strategy during the divorce proceedings may *still* be influencing your behavior and your feelings about yourself. If that is the case, and it has been the case with many of my patients and interviewees, you need to know about it.

Did your attorney urge you to calm yourself, tone down your demands, and take care not to upset your husband?

Did your attorney urge you to dress differently and project an image more demure, more childlike, and more "innocent" than you normally do?

Did your attorney agree that your husband had some goods on you that could cost you your rightful support and even your children? Did you take his or her word for it without getting a second opinion or doing some research on precedents in your state?

Did you, in the end, feel that your attorney considered your case hopeless, an irritation, an opportunity to do some charity work, or some other imposition on his or her valuable time?

If you have answered yes to any of these questions, it is important that you *yourself* review your relationship with your attorney *and* the terms of your divorce decree. As I will make clear in chapter five, it is crucial that as a divorced woman you have legal resources readily available, particularly if you have children. In that case, your ex-husband will likely be in your life forever, and it is imperative that you have the means to define or redefine your relationship legally whenever the need comes up. To depend for this function on a lawyer or attorney who knowingly or unknowingly undermines the stance *you* choose to take, the goals *you* set, and the model of expression *you* adopt in pursuing them is to defeat your purpose before you begin.

THE EMOTIONAL EXPERIENCE OF DIVORCE

I don't have to tell you that divorce is warfare or that the stakes are often high. Where a divorce is being litigated, there is a brutal contest going on for children, for support, for property, and the sense of competition between the spouses is continually pumped up by the lawyers, who ride point in the actual confrontations.

The only hope for each side is to remain fully armed, psychologically as well as practically. And yet women who step onto the battleground are in danger of being *dis*armed in ways that men are not. By the culture, by the conventions of marriage itself, and, as I have shown, by their attorneys, women are taught, urged, cajoled, conditioned, all but *forced* into a position of weakness. The very process of divorce is designed to turn them into ex-wives.

The pitched battle can go on for weeks, months, sometimes years, and in the course of the war the overriding atmosphere is one of emotional chaos. Issues of custody arise one day; a week later, after days of furious preparation, the husband cancels his deposition and an anticlimactic tedium sets in; next day comes his wife's shock at discovering that her assets have been frozen; a day later he sends a letter threatening to prove her an unfit mother. All hell seems to be breaking loose.

In such emotionally chaotic situations, the struggle to maintain a sense of righteous independence is often lost to emotional exhaustion. Most of my patients and interviewees have reported that they wound up hoping simply for the ability to keep some semblance of control over their day-to-day lives. For while war rages, life outside the battlefront goes on—there are still children to raise, livings to earn, and households to run. It's no wonder that litigants in a divorce set their sights with grim determination on settlement day.

When it comes—when the settlement has been pounded out and the judge hands down the decree—*relief* floods the hearts of the most fiercely dedicated combatants. Meet Celeste, for example, who escaped occasionally from the confusion of the divorce by day-dreaming about the celebration she would give herself on her official divorce day. When the decree came in the mail, she had already given a lot of thought to the restaurant she wanted to go to, the people she wanted around her, and even the wines she wanted to order for her "freedom party." She had already lived for six months on an inadequate temporary support arrangement and knew she had to economize permanently, but she felt this party was important enough to justify the expense. Getting the decree was a true rite of passage, and after the hell she'd been through, she was determined to launch her new life in high style. She had been worn down daily for months; the party would mark the point at which she would begin to turn herself around.

Even with all her advance preparations, when the divorce was final Celeste was unprepared for the elation she experienced. "I'm happy, I'm reborn, I'm *free!* The monkey that was my lousy marriage is finally off my back—along with *its* monkey, that putrid divorce!" Celeste's party was a great success, with warm and festive toasts all around. She drove home from the restaurant feeling blanketed in the loving kindness of her friends and ready to take up her real life again. It was only the practical matters that faced her now, she told herself: find a job, fix up her place the way she wanted it, then maybe stick her toe into the dating world again. "It was a long haul," Celeste told herself, as she opened her front door, "but I made it."

Euphoric but emotionally exhausted, freed of continual assaults to her self-esteem but psychologically wounded, Celeste faced more than practical decisions as she turned the key in her lock. She was about to begin an extended period of emotional healing from the divorce trauma itself. The direction that healing would take, based on the inner resources still left to her, would determine a great deal—nearly everything—about the course of her new single life.

The divorce experience is almost always traumatic, and the damage the combatants sustain can be very deep. Far too many women, unaware that they can gain control of and ultimately direct their gradual healing, simply remain, paralyzed, at this crucial juncture. But for the woman intent on understanding not only what she has been through but how she wishes to grow and where she wishes to take her life, the first step toward complete recovery begins with taking a fresh look at just where she stands.

2
____

WHAT IS
AN EX-WIFE?

No matter how awful the marriage, no matter how traumatic the divorce, when the decree is handed down and the dust begins to settle, the newly divorced woman has experienced loss. A marriage is over, a whole way of life—with its good points as well as its bad—is gone. Finished too is the role of wife as the woman has played it throughout the marriage, with its satisfying aspects as well as its frustrations. As many writers on divorce have pointed out, in large part recovering from divorce means mourning and ultimately accepting those losses. Not until she goes through the natural grieving process can the newly divorced woman turn expectantly to the future.

In many ways, the postdivorce healing period is identical with the grieving that occurs after the loss of a loved one. Both processes play themselves out in a relatively predictable amount of time, and in both cases, when sufferers move through the process too quickly or fail to reach acceptance within the predicted time span, psychologists become alert to the possibility that the process has become stalled or has gone awry. The normal mourning for the death of a loved one can last up to two years. The range for normal recovery from divorce is approximately six to eighteen months after the divorce becomes final.

THE NORMAL RECOVERY PROCESS

Healing from divorce takes place on three different levels simul-taneously—emotional, practical, and intellectual. On the emotional level, where grief is felt most intensely, the divorced woman, like the widow, mourns the loss of attachment, a phrase that means exactly what it says; after divorce, as after the death of someone close to us, we miss the connectedness to another that human beings crave, and we must come to terms with that loss. Sadness, lone-liness, and feelings of uncertainty are perfectly natural and are expected during this healing period. In the healthy recovery pro-cess, the acuteness of the sense of loss recedes with the passage of time.

Then there are the practical matters Celeste anticipated as she turned her key in the lock. Gradually, through practice, the newly divorced woman comes to terms with the logistics of being a single woman and head of household. At first, she may feel that she is going through the motions, but gradually she starts learning or relearning the ropes with respect to friends, dating, work, sexuality, the handling of finances, making child-rearing decisions on her own, and finding nonexplosive, painless ways to deal with her ex-husband in her unavoidable encounters with him. When all goes well, the progress she makes on the emotional level spurs her recovery on the practical level, and vice versa: a problem arises, she solves it as a single woman, and her newly emerging self-concept as a single woman becomes more clearly defined. Small successes in daily living nourish the new identity; the new identity eases the chal-lenges of daily living. In this way, the woman gradually shapes and comes to accept her new way of life and her new view of herself.

The third critical aspect of healing takes place in the divorced woman's mind. Again and again, she thinks through the events leading up to and including the divorce itself—to find their true meaning and ultimately to accept it. In the thick of battle it was impossible to reflect on and interpret the war, but now she has the freedom to replay her mental videos as often as necessary to reach a final understanding of what she's gone through. Again and again, she reviews, rehashes, replays. "I practically drove myself crazy with thinking about it," a woman will say. "I was obsessed with understanding what had happened. I just couldn't let it go."

Exactly! Understanding is the prerequisite to acceptance, and acceptance is the prerequisite to moving on. An extended period of intense *thinking* about divorce is natural and necessary, and it allows the healthy woman eventually to develop a final interpretation of the collapse of her marriage and the subsequent divorce that satisfies her need to understand. As the answers to initial questions—"What went wrong?" "Who was to blame?" "What could I have done differently?"—fall into place, the emotional integration of the experience progresses. As questions regarding the past are answered, one by one they recede from her consciousness, and she is able to turn her attention to the present. By the end of the normal six to eighteen months (though, remember, this is an average, not a strict rule), the healthy woman has laid the experience to rest.

WHEN RECOVERY GOES AWRY

But what of the woman who is unable to arrive at answers to her questions, whose mind and emotions are constantly stirred up by unsuccessful attempts at interpreting and laying to rest what she has been through? And suppose this woman—call her Alice—is making every attempt to come to a final interpretation by struggling with who was to blame, what she could have done, and what caused the initial rift while *simultaneously* doing continuous battle with her ex-husband over the children, support payments, and their conflicting attitudes regarding the divorce settlement. Suppose, too, that Alice finds the loss of attachment unbearable and her loneliness frightening in its intensity. Finally, imagine that Alice is plagued by deep but unarticulated beliefs that a woman without a husband is incomplete, that a divorced woman has failed at her job as the keeper of the marriage, and that she'll never feel intimacy with another man again.

Alice is stalled in the recovery process. Her frequent encounters with her ex-husband only add to her unanswered questions about what she's been through, since they inevitably end in arguments even more vicious than those that led up to the divorce. Far from achieving an interpretation of her recent past that she can live with, Alice feels ever more isolated by a haze of anxiety and depression. She's fearful of the intensity of her emotions and furious at herself for her inability to pull herself together.

Months go by, then a year, then two. They are marked by continual encounters with her ex-husband that Alice dreads, endures, then reels from in the aftermath. The divorce is in the distant past, but the issues that provoke conflict, mostly involving the children, just keep coming. Between periods of emotional chaos, feelings of anxiety and depression keep Alice cut off from the outside world. Luckily, she loves her work in a marketing firm and comes alive there temporarily, but the world at the office has a sense of unreality for Alice, as if she were merely playacting there. At home the continual possibility that her ex will show up and another argument will break out hangs over Alice like a threat.

Far too confused to understand that the healing process is being continually interrupted by the ongoing encounters with her ex, Alice begins to question her ability to manage her own life. She's bewildered by her inability to focus, by her terrible irritability, and by her eternal restlessness. Exhaustion dogs her; she has no energy, and her house falls apart around her. She can't seem to take an interest in her appearance any longer; she can't seem to take an interest in anything. She gains weight and eats poorly, binging for comfort, then fasting for days to the point of starvation. She's terribly lonely, and knows she should get herself out of the house and involved in some social activity, but she turns down every invitation from concerned coworkers, and eventually they stop inviting her out.

Another year passes, and Alice is still collapsing after work on the couch, waking at eleven to eat a TV dinner, and then crying herself to sleep. With misery increasing daily, she finally does what she meant to do a long time ago: she asks her friend at the office for the name of her therapist. "Can you tell me a bit about why you are seeking therapy?" the psychologist asks when Alice calls. After a long silence, Alice tells her, "No, I really can't. I'm not myself. I'm not anybody. I just don't know who I am or what I'm doing anymore." So speaks a woman three years divorced, her recovery gone awry, leaving her trapped in the limbo of ex-wife land.

THE EX-WIFE SYNDROME

Sufferers of the Ex-Wife Syndrome are prisoners who are blind to the walls surrounding them, blind to the fact that they are held fast. With their divorces final and the whole world before them, they assume their newly single status with the idea that they will live full, productive, enjoyable lives. But after a time they find themselves unable to transform their lives and move on. The question of why this is so is the greatest mystery of these women's lives.

When they enter psychotherapy, such women present a cluster of recognizable symptoms and describe a set of specific feelings and behaviors that can safely be described as self-destructive. Most of these symptoms, feelings, and behaviors are familiar; many are associated with psychological distress in general. It is the combination of symptoms and the circumstances in which they occur that determine the diagnosis of the Ex-Wife Syndrome. In general, the symptoms are these:

- depression and anxiety
- sleep and eating disturbances
- low self-esteem and the self-devaluing thoughts and behaviors associated with this state
- behavior that is an effort to compensate for a poor self-image (for example, overprotective parenting, extreme workaholism,

highly rigorous dieting and physical-fitness programs, a slavish
effort to be fashionable)
- difficulty in forming social relationships
- fear of and resistance to intimacy
- suicidal thoughts based on undefined shame and self-disgust
- psychological paralysis—the inability, despite the desire, to "get
moving again"
- a tendency to sabotage any potentially positive life changes
- a tendency to be secretive, giving out an "official story" while
keeping the real story to—though more often *from*—oneself
- an ongoing connectedness to the ex-husband that the sufferer
unknowingly but fiercely nurtures and protects regardless of the
man's indifference or downright hostility

The most pervasive of these symptoms are intense anxiety and
debilitating depression, as is the case with most psychological conditions arising from an unresolved inner conflict. But to say that
an inner conflict causes the anxiety and depression is not to say
that the sufferer always understands the connection between her
pain and this inner conflict. In fact, in most cases my patients enter
therapy because their psychological and emotional pain have become unbearable but the reasons for it remain mysterious to them.
They are haunted by questions they cannot answer. If you have
troubled to read this far out of concern for yourself, I suspect you
have asked yourself these same questions at one time or another:

Why do I feel anxious and depressed so much of the time?
Why am I unable to sleep and eat—or to do anything but sleep and
eat?
Why am I plagued by thoughts of revenge? of unbearable jealousy?
of suicide?

For the women in my practice, these questions are the starting
places for psychotherapy. But in every case of the Ex-Wife Syndrome I see, it isn't long before the patient is focusing in therapy

on symptoms farther down the list. Now they ask such questions as these:

Why, when I'm feeling so lonely, do I shy away from new relationships, especially ones of potential intimacy?

Why, when I am so deeply dissatisfied, am I sabotaging the good things about my day-to-day life and any chances I might have to change it?

Why, when I know intellectually that my family and friends wish me well and can be my support during the transition period after marriage, am I keeping secrets, giving out Pollyanna stories, and suffering alone and in silence?

Why, when my marriage is over and my ex-husband has moved on to a new life, is he still the central figure in my life? Why can't I *let him go*?

Two more questions keep arising, often as "throwaways" at the end of an hour or in a very hushed, sometimes shamed voice after a long silence:

Why, with the marriage over and the divorce final, am I still having sexual fantasies about my husband?

And sometimes: *Why*, oh why, did I go to bed with him last night?

TWO TELLTALE SYMPTOMS

Few women with the Ex-Wife Syndrome make the conscious connection between the emotional distress that brings them into therapy and their connectedness to their former husbands. Typically, these women begin therapy by focusing on generalized symptoms—anxiety, depression, furious bursts of uncontrollable anger, lack of focus, plummeting reserves of energy, indecisiveness, and so on. But eventually, as the interpreting process proceeds, two distinct symptoms emerge and absorb the woman's attention: *self-sabotage* and *a secretiveness—from the self*. These two symptoms have been present to some degree in every case of the Ex-Wife Syndrome I have treated. In essence, they serve as markers, and studying them in detail reveals the nature of the bond to the past that lies at the heart of the syndrome.

Eve, a bright, beautiful, and highly successful interior designer had been divorced for three years. Because her husband resented her flair for business, her marriage had been a deadening experience for her. Richard didn't actually "forbid" her to work, but he made it clear that he couldn't be happy if she did. For years, Eve dutifully stayed home and played "wife." Then Richard began to complain of boredom. His restlessness quickly escalated into a constant stream of criticism that Eve found abusive and, finally, intolerable.

As soon as she understood that Richard's behavior change was permanent, Eve filed for divorce and went back to work. She specialized in the design of office spaces and other commercial properties, and her business grew by the month as word of mouth spread. In fact, things were happening almost too quickly. Eve knew she had to move the business out of her home and into an office and hire a business manager to run it. But the very idea of taking these steps exhausted her. She kept finding reasons not to take them, and the details of running her business began threatening to overwhelm her. She was so snowed under with administrative work that she had to stay up all night to do her designs.

Complicating things further was Manny, an attorney who cared deeply about Eve. He wanted to help her find an office, even offered to look around himself. As for their more intimate relationship, he was clear in his desire to marry her. But knowing she was still bruised, he was willing to proceed cautiously. Still, he wanted some reassurance that he stood a chance with Eve. He knew she liked him, but could he hope for a commitment some time in the future? Was she serious about him, or was he just wasting his time?

Eve *did* care for Manny, and she assumed they would probably marry someday, but she felt incapable of talking about their relationship. In fact, Eve froze whenever Manny pressed her on how she felt about him. Soon they were hitting the same snag in every conversation:

"Look, Manny, you know I care for you. Why do I have to say it?"

"Because I *don't* know. And it makes me nervous to see that you can't bring yourself to say it. Let me know I'm not wasting my time here, will you?"

"Don't put words in my mouth, Manny. Please."

Eve *couldn't* say it, and in therapy it became clear why: because the energy and attention required for intimacy were already reserved—for Richard, the ex-husband who had given her so much grief. It wasn't love she felt for Richard; it was a powerful anger and a continued, unabated need to argue with him mentally and vindicate herself. As we will see, love is only one possible manifestation of the emotional connection that ties the sufferer of the Ex-Wife Syndrome to her ex-husband.

Though Richard had long since remarried, Eve was still—internally—talking to him, arguing with him, battling with him in her mind over every move she made. His voice, his attitudes still dinned in her ears as she contemplated the steps necessary to keep her business thriving. In a sense, it was a question of orientation: how could she open to Manny when she was still turned back toward Richard, doing battle? Though Eve was unaware of it, she was still being faithful to her long-gone partner.

Eve's deepest feelings centered around Richard. Thus engaged, she sent Manny to the sidelines—and she lost him. He acted on his intuition that Eve wasn't able to love him. Her sadness at this loss and her bewilderment at her own behavior brought Eve into therapy.

Eve's is a story of sabotage from within. One way to view her seemingly self-destructive behavior is as a means of telling herself a fundamental truth that she has been unable to admit into conscious awareness. In a very real sense, Eve *was* unable to take full responsibility for her business and *was* unable to love Manny, or anyone, until she had resolved the inner conflict between her past and present. As a first step, she had to see that she was psychologically connected to Richard and that the connection, like a chain around her ankle, was holding her back from life.

It took Eve some hard work in therapy to understand that she was still linked to Richard, still viewing herself and behaving like an ex-wife. Although to a large extent the link to her former husband was determining how she acted and felt, on a conscious level she was unaware of its existence. I call this stubborn, buried connection the "secret from the self."

Eve thought of herself as a capable, self-reliant woman with the ability to succeed in both the professional and personal realms. She had many reasons to hold this view of herself and few reasons to doubt it. Eve knew she was in no way a loser—and yet in a matter of months her business had faltered under her indecisiveness and, for the same reason, a good man had withdrawn from the scene. It hurt Eve to look within for an explanation, but eventually, in the supportive psychotherapeutic environment, she was able to see the secret attachment to Richard she had been keeping from herself.

Looking inward at this secret is *always* painful, and the more self-reliant the woman, the more shrouded the secret and the more painful its unmasking. Where the Ex-Wife Syndrome is present, the secret remains outside conscious awareness, so it finds expression in two ways: through *feelings* (the characteristic depression, anxiety, anger and rage, low self-esteem, suicidal thoughts, and often shame) and through *behavior*. Behavior consists of self-sabotaging actions and actions performed consistently and compulsively to keep the connection alive.

An example of a strong woman sabotaged from within in this way is Joanne, a patient in my practice who managed to keep her secret from herself for many years. Her story is of particular interest because while she was unknowingly suffering from the Ex-Wife Syndrome, on the surface she seemed to be glorying in her freedom from her husband and actively and energetically ensuring her autonomy.

She had been married to a prominent psychiatrist for twenty years, but, like the cobbler's barefoot children, she had never received from Harry what he gave generously in his work—empathy and understanding. The relationship was a battleground, and Joanne, who wanted the spontaneous affection and support that Harry couldn't give, was the perpetual loser. When her daughters had grown up, they urged her to leave the marriage, and she did, only to become embroiled in one of the angriest, longest-running property battles in her city's history.

Joanne and Harry's litigation went on for years and years. During this time Harry remarried and began a new family, severing his biological connection with Joanne and establishing a new biological family unit. The litigation was a pesky subtheme in his life that he allowed his lawyers to handle.

As for Joanne, far from languishing, she spent all day on the phone, in the library, and in meetings with her attorney defining her settlement terms. Still, beneath the activity and assertive talk, Joanne was stuck. The court battle had become life itself. It consumed her time and energy and all her best thinking. Friends, potential suitors, even her daughters took a backseat to her work with her attorneys and the constant paperwork she did for the case.

For nearly ten years, Joanne kept up the fight. In her eyes, and in those of her family and friends, she had changed her circumstances drastically by divorcing Harry. But in truth she was maintaining the battle that had characterized her marriage for as long as it lasted. Deep within her was the fear of the freedom she had ostensibly sought. She steered clear of freedom and change by continuing to swim in familiar, if turbulent, waters.

In therapy, Joanne wrestled for months with the wisdom of pursuing her course. What was fueling her taste for battle? What was preventing her from settling the case and, after all these years, getting it out of her life? In our sessions, I urged her to consider these questions again and again, asking her to try to answer as if for the first time. We talked a lot about the dynamics of the marriage and about the meaning of marriage vows in general. What had attracted Joanne to Harry all those years ago? What expectations did she bring to the marriage? What, specifically, were her disappointments, her satisfactions, with the way the marriage evolved? I asked the same about the divorce: What satisfactions, what dis-

appointments, had Joanne experienced from it? Gradually, in returning periodically to my questions, Joanne began to see that she
was still emotionally attached to Harry and, in her way, loyal to
him. As long as the battle that was their marriage raged in Joanne's
heart, she was still Harry's ex-wife. There was no room in that
heart to accept anyone else—not even a revised image of Joanne
herself as a single, divorced woman with an eye to the future. The
marriage to Harry—the *emotional* marriage—had yet to be rooted
out.

LIGHTING THE INNER LANDSCAPE

You may ask yourself how the book in your hands can substitute
for months, sometimes years, of face-to-face psychotherapy. The
answer is that it can't; nothing can substitute for face-to-face psychotherapy, and this book doesn't pretend to try. However, it does
offer an effective cure to the Ex-Wife Syndrome that *always* works.
Because the Ex-Wife Syndrome is largely rooted in the secret from
the self, once that secret is brought to light with the famous "aha!"
that accompanies a true, transforming insight, a woman who has
been stalled in her recovery can reach a final interpretation, complete the severance of attachment to her former husband, and move
on.

But how to achieve that famous "aha!"? How to cast the beam
of light that illuminates the inner landscape? The therapist helps
the patient achieve illumination by restoring a function the patient
has lost—the blocked interpretive function. This doesn't mean that
the patient describes her life and the therapist explains it. Rather,
it means that as the patient recalls and recounts her experience, the
therapist *urges her toward* interpreting it accurately—that is, toward
finding the true meaning in it that has been obscured by misunderstanding, inappropriate thoughts, and distortion.

The psychotherapist effects this "urging" with a word here, a
question there, as the patient speaks, to encourage her to pause
over a shadowy memory, a too glib anecdote, a family joke, and
seek its true significance with respect to the current emotional pain.

This book is designed to serve a similar function: to urge you toward self-understanding by guiding you toward the issues central to the Ex-Wife Syndrome. Here and there, I will offer you sets of questions designed to point your attention toward shadowy areas that I know, from experience, have significance for the Ex-Wife Syndrome. I encourage you to read these questions with pencil in hand, pause over them, write down answers. If you are a journal keeper, you may even be inspired to take notes on any new ideas they bring to mind as you work to see with fresh eyes your marriage, divorce, and current relationship with your ex. The goal is a gradual illumination, as insight follows insight and the path that led you to your current circumstances becomes clear. I liken the process to turning up a dimmer switch: awareness gradually grows to clarify the influences on your behavior and feelings.

AM I AN EX-WIFE?

These questions are not a precise diagnostic tool. Instead, they are meant to direct your attention to matters that may have remained outside your awareness in your day-to-day life. There is no "score." "Yes" answers to any of these questions could indicate an unbroken attachment: many "yes" answers would suggest that the man you are legally divorced from still plays a major role in your life and attracts an inappropriate amount of your attention.

1. Do you feel controlled by your ex-husband in any area of your life? For example, with respect to child-rearing, finances, your home, your livelihood, your work, your social life. In what area or areas?
2. Do you find yourself talking about your ex to friends, family, or any new men in your life? Is it difficult for you to stop referring to him even after you have resolved to do so?
3. Does your ex still have the power to hurt you?

4. Are you still "in love" with your ex? If yes, list the three qualities that most draw you to him.

5. Do you harbor fantasies of any type about him (getting him back, seducing him, killing him, seeing him poverty-stricken or hurt)? What are they?

6. Is he capable of making you doubt yourself? Recall the three most recent instances.

7. Does it seem to you now that being married to him was easier than being divorced from him (even if the marriage was awful)? If yes, why?

8. Do you feel a sense of impending doom without any apparent reason? In what circumstances have you recently felt this way?

9. Do you wake up feeling anxious when you know you are going to have contact with your ex?

10. After you speak to your ex, do you feel strong emotions? For example, excited, sick, scared, depressed, or angry?

11. If your ex becomes upset with you, is your day or week ruined? Think of recent instances.

12. Is your ex often in your thoughts? In what context?

13. Do you feel that you are stuck or trapped with your ex for the rest of your life?

14. Do you care whether your ex thinks you are a good person? If so, why?

15. Is it important to you to get even with your ex?

16. Is it important to you that you look good if you bump into your ex?

17. Do you regret getting a divorce?

18. Do you feel that divorcing him made you a loser?

19. Do you feel that your life has no meaning?

20. Do you feel that *his* life *does* have meaning, and does it inspire jealousy in you?

BATTLING DISTORTION

In therapy, one comment comes up again and again: "Sure, I know the divorce was traumatic, but divorce is hard for everybody. I'm just at loose ends, that's all, can't get my life in order. But I don't see why I have to rehash the damn divorce again."

The response to this objection is quite specific: *defense mechanisms*. This term refers to psychological phenomena that protect us against excessive emotional pain. Defense mechanisms work by distorting reality to make it, in the short term at least, more bearable. But in the long term, these distortions account for our inability to recover from emotionally painful experiences and move on. Simply stated, it is impossible to come to terms with an inner conflict and resolve it without focusing directly on the conflict itself. But defense mechanisms often stand between our conflicts and our clear perceptions of them. It is defense mechanisms that keep from us any secrets we have buried from ourselves. In the case of the Ex-Wife Syndrome, it is often defense mechanisms that convince a woman she is finished with a man to whom she is still vitally and destructively attached.

There are many defense mechanisms, but those most relevant to the Ex-Wife Syndrome are these:

- **denial**—the conscious attempt to suppress or screen out of awareness an unpleasant reality by refusing to perceive it or face it. For example, Bette continues to believe that her ex-husband loves only her and will return to her regardless of the fact that he has told her he's seeing a woman seriously and is thinking of remarrying. Bette is denying reality and basing her behavior on the distortion resulting from that denial.
- **suppression**—a form of selective memory, which filters out unpleasant or unwieldy facts. For example, Colleen grieves relentlessly after Ed's death, deeming all other men unfit to replace him and committing herself to perpetual widowhood. Her closest friend would tell you, though, that Colleen is suppressing her memories of Ed's continual diminishment of her and his

constant carping and snapping. Again, Colleen's reality is distorted by her suppression, with the consequence that she is unable to complete the grieving process and move on to begin a new phase of her life.

- **fantasy**—a form of escape that gratifies frustrated desires but takes the person out of reality and into an imaginary world. Ruthann, for example, hates her ex-husband, Phil, and spends much of her time alone fantasizing about killing him. The danger here is not that she will do it—although in an extreme case, where other psychological adjustments were awry, this *would* be a danger—but that she will never see and act on the truth: that she must take the initiative in breaking her bond to him, which is reinforced by her anger, and in learning to live on her own.

- **rationalization**—the attempt to prove that one's behavior is justifiable and worthy of your own or others' approval. An example here is Angela, who justifies her constant calls to her ex-husband, Mike, by insisting that their financial life is just too complicated for her to resolve alone. She argues that their mutual investments are her chief interest when she calls, whereas in reality those investments merely serve as a pretext for her continual involvement with Mike.

- **intellectualization**—acknowledging hurtful situations but defusing them of their emotional charge by means of logic. Beverly, for instance, met her husband's constant infidelities with a fierce commitment to "open marriage." The two had agreed on an open arrangement before they married, and Beverly knew that if she showed the slightest jealousy her husband would leave her. Instead, she talked a good line about the right of every man and woman to "live and love as fully as possible in a lifetime." The toll she paid for fostering this distortion of her emotional reality was a growing sense that her life was an empty shell.

- **displacement**—assigning the blame for one's negative feelings to a person other than the one responsible. As an example, Deborah and Paul had an "amicable" divorce, and Deborah was proud of the fact that both had conducted themselves as civilized human beings. She was nonetheless increasingly convinced that all men were fools and could hardly contain her impatience in any interactions with a man. Deborah's irrational prejudice, a generalization that distorted life as it is, prevented her from expressing and resolving her terrible anger at Paul and "protected" her from ever having a meaningful relationship with a man again.

ANXIETY AND DEPRESSION: SIGNPOSTS OF CONFLICT

Defense mechanisms distort reality and keep our deepest secrets from us, and they can function ably for a long, long time. But they never work perfectly. Psychological distress continually leaks through the barrier of denial or repression, fantasy or excessive intellectualization, and pervades awareness. And the forms this distress takes most often are everybody's worst enemies, anxiety and depression.

Depression, which is really unexpressed anger turned inward, and anxiety, which is simply fear, well up to haunt us as we attempt to ignore or evade unresolved internal conflicts and simply go on with our lives. For women who work smoothly through recovery from divorce, the difficult patches in which these feelings surface are inevitable but relatively brief. But for sufferers of the Ex-Wife Syndrome, in whom the connection to the former husband remains both stubborn and vital, depression and anxiety can become a way of life. These distressing feelings are the direct results of the discrepancy between distortion ("The divorce is behind me") and reality ("I am still deeply connected").

An analogy drawn from daily life demonstrates how this works. Suppose you hear the brakes on your car grind—not once, not twice, but every time you step on the pedal. But suppose you don't have the money for a brake job and contemplating the dilemma triggers a feeling of despair over your financial difficulties. Denial—a resistance to thinking about your brake problem at all—kicks in.

However, your brakes keep grinding, and every time you hear them, energy goes toward suppressing the truth while anxiety at the possibility of brake failure clouds your consciousness. As the cycle continues, the anxiety, not the underlying conflict, becomes the major focus of distress. "Why am I so jumpy all the time?" you ask yourself. "Why can't I relax? Why does my back hurt? Why do I dread leaving my house and entering the outside world? I'm a weakling, a coward, a failure at life." Denial of the brake problem, then, not only distorts your perception of the state of your car, but it fills your perception of reality with a nagging, generalized anxiety and a heavy fog of depression.

In the chapters to come, I will recount many anecdotes and case histories to help trigger your recognition of secrets you may be keeping from yourself. And should you discover in the light of new insight evidence of an unbroken connection holding you to your former husband, you will find here many practical strategies and guidelines for severing that bond and changing your behavior permanently. I cannot promise you that this book will bring you complete freedom from unhappiness stemming from life's contingencies, for example, from financial worries or your children's school problems. But I do promise that as you disengage from your ex-husband, the anxiety and depression that have been masking the true impediment to your moving on will lift.

But, a warning is in order. Cutting the cord is a *process*, not a single act, and each step can elicit psychological discomfort. Again, this discomfort usually takes the form of temporary anxiety and depression, the all-purpose signals that deep psychological conflicts not yet resolved are active beneath the surface.

Seeking and acting on the truth about yourself is never easy. Fearfulness and self-doubt arise often in the face of the unknown. Forewarning you to expect hard patches should help you cope with them and understand their part in the process, and at every stage I will make a point of alerting you to potential difficulties. In chapter five you will find some guidelines for easing short-term anxiety and depression. Suffice it to say here, however, that although in a sense I *do* promise you a rose garden (at least as compared with the Ex-Wife Syndrome), the path you will travel toward self-renewal as an autonomous single divorced woman will not always be smooth and sunny. There will be waves of fear; there will be discouragements and setbacks. But Pollyanna-type happiness is the dream of little girls; the more realistic goal of grown women is to embrace life as it is here and now.

FACE FACTS/TAKE ACTION

You will free yourself of the Ex-Wife Syndrome when you sever the connection between yourself and your ex-husband. You will not accomplish this overnight but as a gradual result of the interplay between new insights and practical action. Throughout this book, I use the phrase *face facts/take action* to stand for this process, and the book is structured to reflect the increasing interplay you will experience between insight and practical solutions. The description of the syndrome presented in these first two chapters is meant as a grounding in the psychological facts. More and more, as the book goes on, I will suggest ways of taking practical steps to act on the facts you face. The ultimate aim is to help you shape a life for yourself—and your children, if you have them—that reflects your and their *personal* needs, desires, pleasures, and goals. And within the bounds of these rather broad objectives lie some more specific goals I hope to help you achieve:

- learn a *new way* of relating to your ex-husband, as someone who is no longer a member of your inner circle
- learn to recognize and resist his treatment of you as dependent on, responsible to, or intimately connected to him
- eliminate the *emotional charge* that the new obsolete relationship with your ex-husband still carries for you
- redefine any feelings of "love" you may have in light of their power to bind you to your ex-husband
- stop playing the role of victim, laid to waste by the loss of your marriage
- recognize and eliminate typical ex-wife fantasies ("I'm incomplete without him," "He still loves me," "He'll come back to me

when he's through sowing his oats," "I could never love another man," "No other man could ever love me," "The marriage wasn't that bad")
- control the impulse to overcompensate for blows you've sustained to your self-esteem by behaving like superwoman and supermother
- recognize and eliminate dependent behavior in yourself
- learn the skills necessary to function effectively and with satisfaction as a single woman and single mother
- focus on your own power, knowledge, and decisiveness rather than assigning these qualities to men—especially your ex-husband and especially regarding your children and your finances
- understand, enforce, and enjoy your right to privacy, which means ending your ex-husband's access to your home and your life
- negotiate issues regarding the children while continuing to maintain the boundaries around your private life
- assess your current social and sexual needs and cultivate new relationships that meet them

I hope this list gives you a taste of the growing sense of renewed energy that will come as you learn to embrace the present—a vitalizing change after the sadness and frustration of focusing on the past. The "cure" for the Ex-Wife Syndrome is based on this shift in perspective, and the following pages will help you make it.

FINDING YOUR OWN PACE

In the next two chapters, we turn to the bond itself, and I present a wide array of case histories of women struggling to recover from the Ex-Wife Syndrome and study them as a research scientist studies slides from many different subjects. The result is a microscopic view of the bond to the ex-husband in all its manifestations. The goal is to provide you with a panorama of women with whom you might potentially identify and whose stories might trigger recognition and new insight into your own past and current life. However, before turning to the very heart of the Ex-Wife Syndrome, I must caution you to go easy, to have patience, and to restrain yourself from acting on impulse rather than on a foundation of understanding and psychological readiness.

You cannot wake up tomorrow and begin making strong assertions—"Get out and *stay* out!" You must first achieve true insight into the buried secrets and distortions that have been holding you to your past. It's important to know that the process of disconnecting *doesn't work when you fake it* (what does?). Jean Piaget, the great and pioneering developmental psychologist, echoed Shakespeare in pointing out that "readiness is all," and this quote wouldn't be out of place on your refrigerator door.

When readiness comes, it's unmistakable. I've seen it expressed hundreds of times in therapy, and each time it confirms my belief in the process of self-exploration. A client comes in after many weeks or months of looking hard at the problem and trying to figure out the first or the next step to take. Perhaps she suddenly sees she can no longer allow her ex-husband to call her at work. With a lot of effort, she has identified the kinds of interactions that keep her emotionally connected to him and has realized that his upsetting phone calls increase the emotional charge between them. "I'm going to tell him not to do it; I'll tell the switchboard to screen him out. Here's how I'll say it, and I'll only say it once. *Yeah!*" she says. "I'm going to *do* it!"

When the issue—and the solution—becomes that *real*, the deed is all but done. From that moment on, I know this woman is at a new level of strength. Her voice, her resolve, and her actions are all authentic, and their authenticity gives them authority.

In working toward healing with the aid of this book, how will you know on your own when you have reached a new level of strength? In exactly the same way my patients know in therapy. After all, I don't deem a patient "ready" and then "pass" her to a new stage of healing; I observe and sense the authenticity of her progress along with the patient herself. Readiness occurs when an idea or insight understood intellectually is fully integrated into the woman's emotional reality—a roundabout way of saying when she fully faces the facts. Throughout this program of self-cure, you will be internalizing and integrating new insights into your own emotional experience. This process in turn will enable you to push through the inevitable anxiety surrounding new, untried behavior to take the actions you come to recognize as necessary. When it all comes together and it's time to act, you'll feel a sense of *rightness* so clear it will shine.

3

THE BONDAGE
OF CARING

In therapy, Laura leaned toward me and spoke intensely about the experience that had turned her life around. Like many transformative situations, Laura's had taken place in a fairly mundane setting—a Thanksgiving Day conversation with a distant cousin she had not seen for many years. The woman, Gretchen, was about Laura's age, and Laura and she had been good friends as children before they lost touch. At the family gathering, the two women found a quiet place after the meal to catch up on their lives over coffee.

"Naturally, we exchanged war stories from the divorce front," Laura recounted, "trying to make them funny, trying to entertain each other. But I saw pain on her face, and while she was quipping away about what a jerk her ex-husband was, I could see plain as day that she was still in shock over the thing. She just couldn't let him drop, couldn't even stop talking about him. 'Oh, Jon would never—' or 'Jon would always—' she kept on saying. It was so clear she was aching for him; she couldn't accept that she had lost him. All the while she's saying what a relief to be rid of him, to have the whole thing over, I'm seeing that Jon is still everything to her; she can't describe her life, her world, except in relation to him.

And it's four years already, almost five.

"And I say to myself"—here she took a deep breath and pushed the hair back "—I say to myself, my God, that's *me*."

Once Laura had perceived the persistence of Gretchen's connection to her former husband, years after her own divorce, she experienced a sudden, transforming shift of perspective on herself, a shock of self-recognition—"My God, that's *me*!" From that point on, she turned her attention to working to break her *own* connection to her former husband in order to move on in life.

Very often our perceptions of ourselves and of the meaning of our inner experiences are blocked or blurred by our own emotions and the distortions created by our defense mechanisms. Providing ourselves with an opportunity to identify with others is a productive way of distancing ourselves from whatever inner confusion we harbor. Like Laura, we may be able to see in another what inner turmoil has obscured in ourselves, and the *real* facts and issues in our lives may crystallize in consciousness for the first time. The personal accounts in this and the following chapter are meant to afford you such an opportunity. Once you have been able to see exactly how you have remained connected to your former spouse, the work of breaking free will follow swiftly and inevitably.

A BOND OF MANY STRANDS

When I work with a woman I suspect of having the Ex-Wife Syndrome, I listen hard for clues that will tell me not only that she is indeed still linked to her ex-husband but also what *type* of emotional connection may be binding her. Although the connection itself defines the syndrome and is responsible for its symptoms, in different women different emotions predominate, in turn triggering differing sets of behavior. In all, there are eight distinct types of connection, each dominated by a particular emotion:

1. "love"
2. loneliness
3. guilt

4. excessive sympathy
5. self-pity
6. anger and rage
7. jealousy
8. fear

By the time it has become evident that the woman is still bound to her ex-husband, the patient and I have a pretty clear idea of the type (or types, where more than one emotion predominates) of connection holding her. This knowledge allows us to isolate and focus on the problem areas the woman needs to work through in order to break the connection. This process is central to the task of resolving the Ex-Wife Syndrome.

Until you see clearly the emotional patterns that are influencing your current interactions with your ex-husband, the idea of the connection will remain an abstraction for you. But once you recognize those repetitive emotional patterns and clearly perceive them as the cause of your psychological pain, the Ex-Wife Syndrome will become a reality—you will see it, believe in it, comprehend its destructiveness, and inevitably determine to break the connection and learn new ways of interacting with your ex that will establish and protect your autonomy. With recognition comes determination, and with determination comes the turnaround: the readiness to take the actions necessary to free yourself.

In some women, the connection linking them to their ex-husbands is dominated by what I call the "caring" emotions, feelings that can be characterized as relatively passive in nature and that often involve elements of self-blame and self-devaluation. The emotions on the list of types that fall into this category are "love" (the quotes are significant, as you will see), loneliness, guilt, excessive sympathy, and self-pity. When women are bound to their ex-husbands by connections of these types, they may experience their emotional bondage, however confusedly, as concern, warmth, and even affection. It should come as no surprise that because these warm feelings are rarely returned, these "caring" types of connections are often associated with an intensification of the depression that is symptomatic of the Ex-Wife Syndrome.

In other women, it is a furious rage, bitter jealousy, or a fierce terror that keeps them emotionally bound to the men they have divorced. These are harsher, more sharply agitating feelings than the caring ones, and in women who experience connections of this type it is the syndrome's characteristic *anxiety*, always present to some degree or another along with the inevitable depression, that is typically intensified, sometimes to a nearly unbearable degree.

In this chapter, we will examine connections dominated by the "caring" emotions—love, loneliness, guilt, excessive sympathy, and self-pity. In the following chapter we will turn to women held back from life by the fiercer, stormier feelings—anger, jealousy, and fear.

At the end of each section you will find a set of questions designed to help you determine which of the eight types of connection may be binding you to your ex-husband. As you answer the questions, you will undoubtedly find yourself answering "no" many times and perhaps checking an occasional "yes" here and there. A cluster of "yesses" indicates a problem area. A "yes" to virtually all the questions in a given category or categories suggests that you have identified the type or types of connections that bind you to your ex. Don't lose heart at this evidence! Congratulate yourself on having moved that much closer to self-understanding and to embarking on life as you've dreamed of living it.

ENDLESS "LOVE"

The emotions that masquerade as "caring" can be every bit as potent as raging hatred and certainly every bit as blinding. Jessica, for example, had been married to Rob for nineteen years and divorced for eight when I met her. Her story was one of paradoxes: although she told me she had loved Rob deeply throughout the marriage, finally she had been unable to live with him, for he had simply given her no peace. He was a nervous man who needed a scapegoat, and throughout their marriage he had berated her constantly in private. But he had also taken good care of her—the life he provided was built on the best that money could buy. In public Rob was a model gentleman; women adored him for his courtly manners.

Jessica was so used to thinking of Rob's temper tantrums as the part of her life that was nobody's business that after the divorce she began to forget them. Slowly she came to believe—like Rob's many female admirers—that Rob's public image was indeed the real Rob. Whenever she saw him she was completely seduced by his charm and consideration. Almost as soon as the divorce became final, she began to wonder why she had let him slip away. "He made my life worth living, and without him I have nothing," she said. "What can I give myself? An apartment, a lousy job? It's nothing. Everything I valued I threw away when I lost him."

Jessica's friend Margie often double-dated with Rob and his new girlfriend, and Jessica always called Margie early in the mornings after these dates to find out all she could. Breathlessly, she'd beg for details, and as she fed her pain and her sense of loss, she simultaneously fed her connection to Rob. The more she knew, the more tightly she was chained to her ex-husband and her past. She suffered constantly from the feeling that in divorcing him she had made a fatal mistake that had destroyed her life. Her only relief from self-hatred were the romantic and sexual fantasies she allowed herself to spin around Rob. When she came to me she described herself as "hopelessly in love with my ex-husband. I love him more now, when there's no chance I can have him back, than I ever did when we were engaged. I'm flat-out stuck on the guy for life."

I wasn't convinced. The obsessive quality of Jessica's feelings for Rob suggested that her very survival depended on her pumping life into old, obsolete emotions. Despite her protests, the frantic obsession Jessica described was something other than love.

But if not love, what was this feeling? Consider this explanation by psychologist Stanton Peale:

> We often say love when we really mean, and are acting out, an addiction—
> a sterile, ingrown dependency relationship with another person serving as an

object of our need for security. The interpersonal dependency is not "like" an addiction, not something analogous to addiction; it is *an addiction. It is every bit as much an addiction as drug dependency.*

The key word here is *dependency*: "a sterile, ingrown *dependency* relationship with another person serving as an object of our need for security." Compare this with the feeling psychologists recognize as healthy love: a mutual caring, in which the well-being of another is as important as one's own welfare. Clearly the key word in this case is *mutual*, and it contrasts sharply with the notion of dependency. In healthy love, two autonomous, self-respecting people whose identities are intact experience warmth and concern for each other; the essence of their interaction is mutual caring and sharing. In the addictive, often obsessive "love" many ex-wives feel for their former husbands, maintaining the emotion seems essential to their very survival.

At least that's how it *feels*. In fact, whatever security such loving gives these women is false. Although it is possible for two people to experience such dependency on each other, in the postdivorce period such love is by definition unrequited. Why, then, does the feeling persist? How is it possible that a woman can gain from unrequited love a sense, however false, of safety?

The answer is *through familiarity*.

Though the love is unrequited and the man has moved on to a new life, loving him is known territory. In this feeling the woman finds a sense of history, a past that makes sense of the present. Above all, in loving him the woman locates her place in the spectrum of known emotions. Outside the circle of the familiar lies a great and frightening range of unknown feelings and practical challenges. In the separation and divorce experiences, she has had a first, unpleasant taste of that unknown, and it has motivated her to center herself in familiar territory and stay there.

In therapy, Jessica came to see that through her feeling of "love" she was holding on to Rob—an idealized version of him, at that— for dear life. Focusing on her feelings for him had enabled her to hold at bay the overwhelming fear she had at the idea of "being alone" after the divorce. "Facing the world like that, on my own, with no one standing beside me," she said, in the therapy session in which she touched for the first time on her fearfulness, "it makes no sense to me, it makes me feel as if my life is completely meaningless. Without loving somebody, without being loved, why try? My love for Rob, seeing him when I can, dreaming of our getting back together someday—*that* gives me something to hang on to. I can't see giving it up."

We had many discussions about the fear of meaninglessness that lay behind Jessica's "love" for Rob, but one had particular significance in bringing her closer to change. On this day, I had asked her to consider how much her attention, how much her very consciousness, was taken up with thoughts of Rob. She looked at me in silence for a moment and then said, almost in wonderment, "Good Lord, I've left no room for anything, for anyone else. I think of Rob so much I simply haven't *time* to consider another man, even to *remember* another man!" In a burst of insight, Jessica realized that although her greatest fear was being alone for the rest of her life, her unrequited love for Rob was standing between herself and any chances for new social and sexual encounters. In effect, her "love" for Rob virtually guaranteed that her fear would be realized. It was a sober realization, one that led her to see for the first time that her connection to Rob, masquerading under the name of "love," was holding her back from life.

In time Jessica came to see that she was playing out one side of a love affair while Rob moved on, oblivious and uninterested. She was waiting for crumbs, all the while knowing that even were

1. Do you carry your ex-husband's picture in your wallet or keep it in your house? Do you look at it frequently?
2. Do you cry over him?
3. Do you fantasize about telling him how much you love him?
4. Is he still your hero?

5.   Do you fantasize about having sex with your ex? Do you have sex with him?
6.   Do you feel you will always be his "real wife"?
7.   Do you feel no one else could ever love him as you do?
8.   Do you feel someday he will realize what a mistake he has made and come back to you?
9.   Do you listen to old songs or deliberately go places that remind you of him?
10.   Do you compare other men to him, and do they inevitably fall short?
11.   Is he in your thoughts on a regular daily basis?
12.   Do you try to imagine what he would think or say before you make a decision?

he to toss a few her way they would never nourish her. Seeing herself as dependent for scraps on a man who had walked straight out of her life was a lot different from seeing herself as a loyal ex-wife "stuck on the guy for life," and that dependent image of herself didn't sit easily with Jessica. But further than that, as she described and redescribed her marriage, it became clear to her that she was nourishing a love completely rooted in fantasy—slowly, slowly into her consciousness came the memories of Rob's awful outbursts of terrible temper and his need to blame her for his mistakes. Focusing on the *facts* helped her see the need to break free. Bad enough to see one's life go by while one pines for an indifferent lover, but when one realizes that the lover is a mere figment of the imagination, the need to break free becomes all the more urgent.

THE "SAFETY" OF LONELINESS

Above all, Jessica feared loneliness, and she held off her most feared demon by trying to blow life into her obsolete love for Rob. But loneliness itself can create its own binding and destructive connection, sending a woman back into her past to try to escape its power to sap her vitality and love of life.

I have described the great wave of relief that is almost inevitable once the divorce is final and the chaos of the preceding months or years recedes. Remember Celeste, who sustained herself through the emotional chaos of the divorce period with daydreams of a party to celebrate her freedom? The party was all Celeste had hoped it would be, but back in her own home that night, though she had been living on her own with her children for nearly a year, there was a new quality to her feeling of aloneness. She would have described it more as an emptiness. To Celeste's astonishment, as the night wore on and she was unable to fall asleep, an unfamiliar sense of sadness overtook her, something she had never felt while she was anticipating the divorce. For the first time she felt alone in the world, alone in a way that could never be assuaged by the presence of children, friends, or family. And that feeling of aloneness seemed to threaten to go on forever. Sometimes in the small hours of the night Celeste cried herself to sleep.

While all women feel loneliness once the first blush of relief that the divorce is over has worn off, women who move smoothly through recovery soon begin looking for ways to ease it. But Celeste sank into the feeling—the cold, meaningless existence that Jessica held at bay with pumped-up feelings of "love" became Celeste's private world. For a time, Celeste went through the motions of living a normal life, keeping her loneliness secret. But eight months after her freedom party, she got the flu, and four weeks after recovering from it she caught it again. Sick in bed with a fever and feeling completely unloved in the world, she put in a call to her ex-husband at work. When he called back, she sobbed out her pent-up misery—she had no one to care for her, no one to talk to, no one who knew her the way he did.

Alarmed at the intensity of Celeste's sorrow and at the state of her health, John offered to leave work and visit her, stopping to shop for her on the way. Readily, almost greedily, Celeste accepted the offer. But fifteen minutes after John handed her a cup of chicken broth and sat down on the edge of the bed, they were having a full-blown argument. It was almost as if the divorce had never even taken place. And half an hour later, John stormed out of the apartment, leaving Celeste to face the four walls in despair.

An evening or a Sunday spent alone with no visits or phone calls to break the solitude can have a romantic poignancy that some of us might even enjoy. But if we feel lonely for any length of time, the emotion takes on an intensity and a seriousness that make it difficult to shake off. Loneliness seems to stem from our deepest selves, and if it goes on for too long it can drain the very meaning from our lives. Life seems empty, dead. We begin to wonder why we are even alive.

A glance at the literature on the psychological mechanism of *attachment* can help to shed light on the tremendous power loneliness can have to hurt us. Human beings require the presence of an attentive, caring individual from the moment of birth. Psychologists have studied infants' attachment to their mothers and other caretakers and have determined that it is through this initial attachment that the baby learns to trust and eventually to interact with others. Over the course of childhood, the child gradually learns to trust that he or she can play, go to school, or stay with a baby-sitter without losing access to the mother forever. In adolescence, the teenager experiments with and practices independence, finally pulling away permanently at the end of the teenage years.

In the time that follows, most people seek another attachment figure in the outside world, someone they hope and trust will satisfy their lifelong needs for security and comfort. When people marry, they assume that marriage will guarantee a permanent attachment with their chosen spouse. And when that expectation goes unmet— when the marriage ends, through divorce or death of the spouse— terrible disappointment is often one result. But a more certain result is profound loneliness, the emotional experience of life without a significant other to provide security, comfort, and the sensation of being loved. For many people, the postdivorce period is the first time ever that they have had to face life alone, without a significant adult attachment. In healthy recovery, time itself mutes the painful loneliness that ensues as the woman finds ways to turn outward for relief in new, if frequently temporary, attachments. But many women whose recovery is stalled reach back in their distress to the man who was once the source of their emotional security and comfort.

Although a woman with the Ex-Wife Syndrome can experience her loneliness as a pervasive and emotionally paralyzing longing for her ex-husband, what she is missing is in fact the *attachment* itself, not the man. It is an understandable error but one that can only cause her pain, for, like Celeste, she reaches for comfort to a man who is no longer there. And what does she find when she does so? A busy man, involved with his own life, perhaps showing initial concern but eventually losing interest—if she's lucky. If she's not so lucky, the man she turns to could move quickly from irritation to exasperation to outright hostility. And it won't be long before the unresolved conflicts that led to the divorce have risen to the surface like hungry sharks. Far from finding the comfort she longs for, this woman will find herself in the thick of the bloodletting once more.

But one more result is even more certain and perhaps more destructive. For as long as the woman turns to her ex for relief, he will stand between her and any other attachment opportunities. In this way, loneliness itself functions as the bond that holds the woman to her dead past. As long as Celeste viewed her loneliness as a problem that only John could solve, she remained bound to him as tightly as when they were married, but with none of the benefits of marriage. When John slammed out of the room that night, Celeste found herself trapped not only in her sickbed with the four walls looming but, more dangerously still, in the limbo of ex-wife land.

Celeste did not realize that her very loneliness kept others away, for one person and one person only could assuage it. In shutting out others, this yearning after John actually kept Celeste safe—safe from other contacts that could possibly go awry and give her pain. On a very deep level, Celeste was protecting herself from the inevitable risks of rejection, failure, disappointment, and other forms

1. Do you actively miss your ex on a daily or weekly basis, wishing you could be with him?
2. Does your life seem empty and lonely without him?
3. Do you feel empty if you have not made contact with him for a while?
4. Do you constantly wonder what he is doing or who he might be with?
5. When you see him is it painful?
6. When he leaves you do you feel empty and lost?
7. Do you fantasize about the happy times in your marriage?
8. When you date other men, do you still feel a kind of emptiness or discontent that you believe only your ex can extinguish?
9. Do you feel lonely while in the company of other people (coworkers, family, and friends)?
10. Do you feel there was something special about your marriage—a kind of spiritual "rightness" or a sense that it was ordained?

of psychological distress that go with the territory when one ventures out into the world in search of potentially meaningful relationships. Deep within her she was choosing the known, "safe" pain of loneliness over the unknown ones that lurked outside her room. In fact, however, Celeste was only safe in the sense that a paralyzed person in a wheelchair is safe from stubbing her toe. The sole benefit of her loneliness was the guarantee that nothing would change and that she would remain in the limbo of ex-wife land.

DOING TIME: GUILT

"I feel terrible about what I did to him," says a patient. "He just can't seem to recover from the shock of losing his family. When he calls me, I feel like a criminal—like I stole his chance for happiness. I try to tell myself it was either him or me, but I feel as if a better person would have chosen him."

Women who view marriage and the well-being of the family as their sole responsibility often view divorce itself as a crime. If such a woman initiated a divorce, she often sees that act as despicably self-indulgent, shamefully self-serving. Once the divorce is finalized, guilt at "doing this to him" can arise to blind her to her own right to hope for a decent, satisfying life. Her distorted version of the divorce is that the man is a victim and she herself the perpetrator of a life-wrecking crime. Very often, this interpretation is reinforced from the outside by the ex-husband's disavowal of all responsibility. "I never wanted this divorce," he'll say. "I never understood why we couldn't just work things out and stay married. *You* were the one who wanted out."

It's no wonder that most women who see themselves as fully responsible for seeking their divorces are unable to move on to the next phase of life. The guilt inherent in this view sends them rushing back to their ex-husbands constantly—to help, to fuss, to ease their burden of emotion by trying to "fix" the men's lives. What could be a clearer expression of the bond to the former husband than this habit of constantly returning to him, mentally or physically, to try to make up for the "mistake" of divorce?

Gina and Burt were high school sweethearts. After graduation they married and bought a small gas station. But Gina hated working in the gas station, and as soon as they could afford to hire an employee, she enrolled in the local college and studied commercial art. Gina showed a true talent for her studies, and after she received her B.A. she was hired by a graphic design firm in a city forty miles away. She loved the job, and going to work in the city was like going to another planet—exciting, sophisticated, endlessly interesting. But the more Gina loved working in the city, the harder it became to go home to Burt and their quiet life every night.

Increasingly, Gina spent time with her city friends, people with whom Burt felt tremendously uncomfortable. Four years after beginning work in the city, Gina realized that the breach between herself and her husband was unbridgeable. The two had no common interests, nothing to talk about, no friends in common—and all Burt wanted to do, day or night, was hang out at the gas station and work on cars. Gina realized it was time to strike out on her own. She filed for divorce.

The divorce went smoothly, and Gina was sure she had done the right thing—but she couldn't get Burt out of her mind. Her happiness was in her grasp, she knew all she had to do to secure it was move to the city and immerse herself completely in her new life. But she couldn't bring herself to make the leap. She moved out of the house she shared with Burt and took an apartment a few blocks away. She worried constantly that he had nothing in his life, nothing but the gas station. She believed it was her responsibility to get him interested in something, even find him new friends, perhaps even a girlfriend, before she could feel free to enter her new life completely. She worried, she fussed, she lay awake at night blaming herself for being too audacious, too self-centered, too ready to leave her husband and pursue her own happiness.

Her feelings of uncertainty and concern grew particularly acute when a coworker began to ask her out and she felt a growing interest in him. And she'd left Burt with nothing but the gas station! The promise of great fulfillment was ruined for Gina by her sense that she'd shrugged off her responsibilities and run.

Gina was allowing her concern for Burt's happiness to outweigh her interest in her own and to hold her back from her future. Initially, her view of reality had been clear enough—she had recognized the deficiencies in her married life and the great value of venturing out into the world. But her clarity of vision extended only to herself and her own possibilities. When she looked at Burt, she saw *his* life as a job she had left unfinished.

Gina's guilt hinged on her denial of a central fact: Burt was perfectly happy. He never complained about losing Gina, he had agreed fairly readily to the divorce, and now he did exactly what he wanted to do, what he had *always* wanted to do: hang out at the gas station and work on cars. There were ways, in fact, in which

Burt was downright relieved to be finished with a marriage that had made him feel he ought to be trying to be something other than what he was.

In therapy, Gina discovered that her guilt was masking uncertainty about her new direction, uncertainty that, through denial, she was screening out of her conscious awareness. A clue was that her guilt grew more intense as her coworker's attentions became more serious. In assessing the guilt feelings in the context of the whole picture, Gina perceived that it was anxiety about the unknown, not concern for Burt's happiness, that was linking her to him and keeping him central to her life.

Ferreting out the origins of emotions in this way is difficult in the best of circumstances. But, when outside forces are intensifying guilt feelings, seeing things as they really are becomes even more challenging, as Linda's story shows.

Linda grew up believing that divorce happened to other people. In her own family it had never happened. So when it became clear that her marriage to Howard had deteriorated past the point of recovery, Linda's parents encouraged her to make the best of it. For ten years she went the route of marriage counselors and relationships workshops, trying to make things work. Through it all she did everything she could to avoid the obvious: that this was a bad marriage from beginning to end, that Howard was abusive to her and the children, and that he could only feel good about himself by making her feel small. At her most discouraged, she tended to suspect that Howard had married her because she was pretty and easy to push around. What he wanted was a maid; what he needed was a human ladder, somebody to stand on to make himself feel big.

Howard had always made a point of being sweet to Linda's parents, and throughout the marriage she had carefully kept his real nature a secret. Her efforts were so successful, in fact, that she felt satisfaction whenever her family talked about what a great guy Howard was and how lucky she was to be married to him. When she wasn't believing them she was congratulating herself on her loyalty.

After ten years, though, the strain broke Linda's resolve. As their children grew bigger and Howard's raging and ragging at them began to spark full-blown battles, Linda realized that by protecting the image of their "happy home" she had in some way extended Howard a license to abuse them all, or so he seemed to believe. After two more years of doing secret battles, she saw that her own mental health and that of the children was at stake. She made the decision to sue for divorce.

Howard roared. He cried, he begged, he pleaded to "have my family back." He moved into the YMCA although he could well have afforded an apartment, and he made a second career of visiting Linda's parents, brothers, and sisters to plead his case and enlist their support. He was the "innocent victim"; Linda had "kicked him out." Linda began to get phone calls from her mother: "What you've done to this man you cannot imagine. He is bereft without his family, absolutely *bereft*."

Soon Howard's pathos turned to anger. He took to calling Linda and openly accusing her of wrongdoing: "You broke up my family. You took my kids from me. You think only of yourself—you're selfish and disgusting." Her family echoed these sentiments, though in somewhat milder form. It made no difference to anyone that although Howard had open visitation and could see the children as much as he wished, he limited his contact to dinner in a restaurant once a week.

The real trouble was that Linda believed him. Her guilt at initiating and pursuing the divorce, and at failing to reconcile after the divorce, was nearly unbearable. She felt she had failed as a wife, mother, and woman, and everyone whose opinion she cared about—her parents, brothers, and sisters—seemed to agree. Divorce wasn't for *them*; they were tougher than that, a family that always saw things through. By divorcing, Linda felt she had lost not only her immediate family but her parents and siblings as well. She saw herself as a pariah.

The only times Linda felt any relief at all from her oppressive guilt were when Howard was mean to her. Indeed, she found herself deliberately antagonizing him in order to justify and rejustify the actions she had taken. The result was a continuation of the very misery that had prompted her to act to save her sanity—abuse, ridicule, and excessive and bizarre criticism. What Linda needed was another divorce to sever her *inner* connection with Howard. Three years after the divorce, the link through guilt was as binding and painful as ever.

---

1. Do you always feel you're wrong?
2. Do you find yourself apologizing frequently?
3. Do you feel you are to blame for problems your children are encountering?
4. Do you feel you never should have gotten a divorce?
5. Do you feel responsible for your ex-husband's unhappiness or anger?
6. Do you feel responsible for your children's unhappiness or anger?
7. Do you feel you have destroyed other people's lives by getting a divorce?
8. Does your ex have the capacity to make you feel you've been wrong or irresponsible for having sought a divorce?
9. Do other people (family/friends) have the capacity to make you feel you did the wrong thing in seeking a divorce?
10. Do you feel that you are a bad, weak, or selfish person?
11. Do you feel that other people find you unlikable?
12. Do you feel guilt-free about getting a divorce only when your ex is clearly being mean or obnoxious to you or your children?
13. Do you believe that if it hadn't been for your selfishness your family would still be together and everyone would be happy?

SYMPATHY—FOR THE DEVIL

Many women find that after the divorce they simply cannot let go—not because they "love" the man or feel they've done him wrong but because "he needs me, he just can't run his life without me." These women are swept with sympathy, even pity, for their ex-husbands at the thought of their trying to make it on their own in the big, bad world. On the surface, the mechanism of this emotional bonding may seem similar to that of guilt, which keeps the woman returning to the ex-husband to repair the damage she perceives she has done to him. But an overblown sympathy for the ex-husband grows not from a sense of having done wrong but from the reluctance to relinquish the form of control—often the *only* form of control—the woman could wield during marriage.

Andrea told me she was haunted by the idea of Ben sitting in his little apartment watching television: "From the very beginning of our marriage, I did the social life for both of us. He had a couple of friends from law school when we first got together, but they were sort of nerdy guys and after a while they dropped out of our lives. My friends were so great, and Ben seemed to like them. Pretty soon he was just doing whatever I arranged for us both. I can't remember him ever seeing anybody on his own—you know, calling somebody up for a drink. Now I think of him turning into a couch potato in that dreary little one-bedroom and I could just cry. He's so grateful when I ask him to stay to dinner when he drops Tracy off. God, what have I done to him? I feel like I've wrecked his life—and he finds ways to let me know he feels the same way."

Here's a footnote to Andrea's concern: two years after we had this conversation, she was devastated by Ben's announcement that he was to be married. And he wasn't marrying a woman he had met at a lonely hearts' meeting either—not by a long shot. He was marrying his secretary's sister, someone he'd known for years before he and Andrea had divorced. What Andrea hadn't realized—or hadn't faced—was that while she ran the social life within their marriage, assuming he was incapable of doing so, Ben had been cultivating his own secret social world. Andrea began to see that poor, pathetic Ben had had a few numbers to call from the phone by his TV set, and facing that fact enabled her to cut him out of the picture. But when Ben's engagement broke up and he came crying to Andrea for sympathy and support, Andrea was in danger of backsliding once more, for in her eyes Ben's tears turned him into a hurt child whom only she could soothe. This distinction gave her a sense of power over Ben that she found difficult to relinquish.

In women who are held to their ex-husbands by excessive sympathy, the nurturing impulse has gone berserk. Such women are often the ones who initiate the divorce because they can no longer stand the burden of their husbands' dependency—never realizing that they are feeding and sometimes even creating this dependency themselves. But because they understand themselves as women largely in terms of their role as comforters, soothers, and nurturers—in short, as the mothers of young children—the same cues still trigger their responses, divorce or no divorce. He complains and she responds by attempting to "fix it"; he expresses a need and she responds by attempting to fill it; he cries and she drops everything to put him to rights, a competent, expert mama running to look after a child.

Whatever the structure of your household was, whatever the rules of your marriage with respect to control and power, the agreement has been rendered invalid by the divorce decree. In fact, dissolving the rules of the marriage is the primary function of that decree. But women who remain attached to their ex-husbands by excessive sympathy and the impulse to comfort continue to operate in accordance within the rules of the dismantled marriage. What they haven't faced is that the old ways of responding not only nurture the man but strengthen the bond as well.

Jim was a man for whom the word *loser* was coined. After his divorce from Irene he lost his job, his friends, and one apartment after another. He seemed to be eternally falling backward, just about to hit the ground.

But hopeless as Jim seemed, he was far from harmless to Irene.

In a fog of self-pity, he often disappointed the children, forgetting promises he had made them. Time and again, he borrowed Irene's car—the car they had once shared—and time and again he brought it back late, out of gas, overheated, or dry as a bone. He was often late with support payments, telling sad stories about a mix-up in his checking account or the terrible month he'd had in his business. It wasn't surprising that the children's affections for their father seemed to cool over the years. This cut Jim to the quick, and he often cried to Irene about the fact that "the kids just don't love me and I'd do anything for them."

Those tears got to Irene. Every time Jim berated himself for letting the kids down, she found ways to comfort him, then feed him, and cajole him back into his sad-sack version of cheerfulness. But Irene paid for the care she gave him—she paid in the anxiety and depression that became the hallmarks of her life. Her surges of sympathy were undermining her attempts to keep her new household running smoothly, to keep her children feeling secure and safe within a predictable environment, and even to keep herself available to her new male friend, whose affections were growing important to her. Each time she gave of herself to Jim, she was wrenching herself away from the present and the woman she was becoming. Much as she tried to make a new life for herself, her pity for Jim was keeping her in place—as Jim's ex-wife rather than as her own woman. Either anxious that Jim would call or deeply depressed at having responded again when he did, Irene remained connected by guilt to the man she had left "forever" many years before.

Irene's pity—like Andrea's—masked a secondary gain to herself. Irene's excessive—one might say compulsive—nurturing of Jim was actually expressive of her power and control over him, the sole source of power and control that she had been allowed in the marriage. By responding to Jim's needs, she was able to have a distinct, and sometimes dramatic, impact on his life, for example, by raising his spirits enough so that he could make it to work in the morning. Just as a mother takes complete care of—and control over—a sickly baby, so Irene continued to assume responsibility for meeting Jim's emotional needs. And just as the mother whose baby grows up and goes away must find another means of expressing power and competence, so Irene needed to face the fact that her marriage was over and her worth must be measured in ways other than caring for Jim. It isn't easy to break an attachment to this source of power, and Irene had to face the possibility of feeling weak and at a loss until she found a healthy outlet for her energies, one that returned to her a sense of herself as a powerful woman with her own place in the world. But such discomfort is one of the prices to be paid for the greater possibilities that exist outside the familiar and destructive patterns of relating to the ex.

A woman who feeds her self-worth through her nurturing in this exaggerated way faces another risk too—that once recovered from the marriage she will go on to choose another "sickly" man needing excessive attention. Any woman who has felt the need to bend over backward for her ex rather than for herself needs to monitor her attraction to other men closely once she has reentered the social world so she doesn't repeat the pattern. If she doesn't manage to find another source of self-worth, her love affairs with these needy creatures will be more of a burden to her than a source of richness and pleasure.

1.   Do you think your ex has an awful life?
2.   Do you consider him a poor soul without the resources to make a good life for himself?
3.   Do you feel it is your responsibility to take care of him in some way?
4.   Do your children feel sorry for him?
5.   Do you feel sorry for him because he has so many problems?
6.   Do you feel he needs you to be happy?
7.   Do you feel he needs someone to take care of him?
8.   Do you feel a moral responsibility to do what you can to make his life easier?

9. Do you invite him to family gatherings during the holidays?
10. Do you portray him to others as a "pathetic guy," even at the expense of looking like a bad person yourself for having left him?
11. Do you try to hide his faults from others (children, family, friends)?

POOR ME: SELF-PITY

Self-pity is one of the most stubborn emotional connections to break in the period following divorce. Given the many losses sustained— of the husband, of the married state, of life as it used to be—self-pity has valid origins and few women escape it altogether. Many women move smoothly through this inevitable phase as they become accustomed to a new way of living and begin to experience the first small triumphs of building a life from the inside out. Some nonetheless succumb to self-pity and its chief danger: the temptation to return to the ex-husband for confirmation that they are indeed pitiable souls.

Three years after her divorce from Bill, Terry was still suffering actively. Day and night, she was haunted by thoughts she never had while she was married. "It's a couple's world," she would tell those friends who still stuck around to listen to her. "There's just no way a woman can be happy in this world of twosomes. I'll never figure out how to do it. I'm trying to make a life on my own, I really am. But it doesn't seem real to me to live this way. I really hate it."

Beneath Terry's complaints was the awful suspicion that because no one wanted her she was unwantable, because no man loved her now she had no value whatever. She had been raised to believe that a woman without a man was "incomplete" and pitiful, and she was suffering the consequences of that prejudice now. She felt so unlovable she never even dared to accept an invitation out, assuming in every case that the invitation was motivated by pity at her "failure as a woman and a wife."

On a particularly hard day, when she had stayed home from the office too depressed to work, Terry gave in to her curiosity about how Bill was doing and dialed his number. "I'm really low," she told him, "feel awful. How've you been?" He had time to talk, and they spent an hour on the phone, filling each other in. This phone call made Terry ecstatic—for days afterward she was buoyed up by the feeling that she might really be okay after all. Furthermore, the phone call set a precedent for her calling Bill whenever she felt like it. (He never telephoned her, but he never refused her call.) Soon they were meeting for dinner, and one thing led to another. . .

"I don't know how it happened," Terry told me in therapy. "I just know we're having this sort of affair. Every time I see him we wind up sleeping together. The funny thing is, it feels illicit, like we're getting away with something, and I'm walking around anxious that we're going to be found out. But when he walks out the door, he's headed back to his women and his stereo and a job he loves. Every time he leaves I can hear his footsteps down the path saying, 'Bye-bye, you're alone, bye-bye, you're alone.' And that's when I start to cry—I always feel afterward that I'm more alone than before he came over. The whole thing's all wrong, but I don't have the strength to change it. You need somebody in your corner to make a change. I can't do it all alone."

I pointed out to Terry that sleeping with Bill seemed to intensify her feelings of aloneness. "Yes, that's so," she answered. "But, like I said, I gave him up once. I just don't have the strength to do it again."

Any woman clutching at the remnants of her ex-husband's attention in this way has her work cut out for her: to recognize and accept the fact that she's living a fantasy. Do you feel that without your ex-husband your life has no meaning? Look again: face facts.

If he is responding to your pleas, he may be doing so merely out of the overdeveloped sense of protectiveness with which many men relate to women. Harsh though it sounds, protectiveness in this sense is a formality. A policeman on your local beat could give you a more consistent, and probably more genuine, sense of safety than an ex-husband who tosses crumbs your way when his real life allows him the chance.

Stan had initiated his and Laurel's divorce eight years ago, and never once did Laurel stop "loving" and actively missing him. Nevertheless, she managed to keep her feelings to herself. Three years after the divorce, however, she had to have major surgery, and with the operation imminent she told Stan that she needed help cooking for herself. "Please, I have no one else," she told him, and given her extreme attachment to Stan—despite his long-term involvement with another woman—unfortunately it was true.

Slowly, though, as Laurel recovered her strength, *she* began cooking for *him* on Friday nights. This "temporary" arrangement turned into a ritual—one that revitalized and reinforced the connection between them. Needless to say, Stan's girlfriend hated the arrangement—for two and a half years, she never had a chance to see Stan on a Friday night, "Laurel's night." But even a hint of ending the ritual brought on such tears and pleading from Laurel that Stan simply let things go. He was frightened at the unspoken but constantly suggested possibility that Laurel, in her extreme unhappiness, would take her own life. So three people were held captive by Laurel's self-pity and the web of the Ex-Wife Syndrome.

A woman like Laurel, who feels that without a man she can make nothing of herself, has a large investment in feeling sorry for herself. Not only does it drain her energy away from taking those inevitably scary experimental first steps toward complete autonomy, but self-pity itself often draws the concern and even pity of the ex, as it did with Stan. By getting her ex to feel sorry for her, the woman keeps the relationship alive *and* confirms her hopeless view of herself. The result is a kind of helplessness that no single woman can afford to adopt.

But the damage doesn't stop there. Though people bogged down in self-pity usually fail to realize it, other people take a cue from their behavior and come to see them as pathetic. In this way, their self-pity actively sabotages any possible new relationship that could serve as a pathway out of the emotional cul de sac of loneliness. Self-pity, though a convenient hook to hang their hats on, becomes an isolation chamber.

1. Do you feel sorry for yourself most of the time?
2. Do you feel your ex is to blame for your distress?
3. Do you feel better when your ex is sympathetic toward you?
4. Do you feel that this misery is your fate in life and there's nothing you can do about it?
5. Do you believe that without your ex life is difficult to manage?
6. Do you feel your life has lost its purpose?
7. Do you feel that your ex doesn't understand or care that you are suffering?
8. Does what he thinks about your situation really matter to you?
9. Do you frequently find yourself not feeling well?
10. Do you ever exaggerate your symptoms when you're not feeling well?
11. Do you feel that without your ex you can never be happy?
12. Do you fantasize about him coming back to you some day when he really understands your situation?
13. Do you feel shame at being alone?

All the women described in this chapter considered their divorces old, finished business when they entered therapy and initially reacted with impatience at my suggestion that we discuss them. But as therapy progressed, every single one of these women came to see that she had been keeping a continued dependency on her ex-husband a secret from herself. Not until each woman had expanded her frame of reference to include the divorce and her relationship with her ex did she understand how that relationship itself and all the unresolved conflicts attending it were sapping her motivation and undermining her every attempt to improve her life. Compare yourself to these women, and to those in the next chapter, and look for the similarities between their stories and your own, and you will learn how to place a frame around your relationship with your ex and see with new eyes how it impinges on your current life. This is the first step toward recovery.

4

THE BONDAGE
OF BITTERNESS

While the emotions associated with caring and concern sap a divorced woman's power and spirit, the darker, stormier emotions distort a woman's self-image in other ways. Far from conceding the fight and settling into the cloistered, life-stifling role of the ex-wife, women whose connection to the ex-husband is dominated by anger and jealousy are often totally *consumed* by the fight, and women bound by fear are continually attempting to flee from what terrifies them. Ironically, the battling, the running, or the continual desperate attempts to avoid battling and running have the same effect as the "caring" responses—that of feeding the emotions, strengthening the bond, and pressing ever further from the surface of the secret of dependency.

A WOMAN SCORNED:
ANGER AND RAGE

By far the most common sufferers of the Ex-Wife Syndrome I see in my practice are women whose emotional life is dominated by a burning anger toward their exes, which they have often kindled—

by contact with the ex-husband—into a white-hot rage, and some-times an all-consuming hatred. Like other sufferers of the Ex-Wife Syndrome, women with this type of connection generally enter therapy for reasons unrelated to their divorces, but scratch the surface and there lie the intense emotions and the behavior patterns that are impeding their well-being.

The initial source of this anger is often the betrayal of the promise inherent in marriage. While some women react to the loss of at-tachment with deep disappointment and self-blame, others rise up swinging, furious at the loss of security and comfort they had assumed would be theirs forever. This initial reaction is com-pounded many times over by the warfare of the divorce itself.

Divorce is a contest that almost always results in a winner and a loser, and the man is the most frequent winner by far. Recall Lenore Weitzman's startling figure on the wide discrepancy be-tween the man and woman's standard of living one year after di-vorce. The woman who sees her ex-husband walking away happy while she is staggering under new financial difficulties—and perhaps the vast responsibility of children as well—gets angry and often stays angry. The anger is understandable and generally justifiable. But unless this furious woman finds a way to defuse and resolve her anger, justifiable or not, it will keep her ex-husband at the center of her life.

More problematical still is the hatred that solidifies after a month, a year, an entire adulthood of frustration. If a woman has been thwarted all through her marriage—by her husband's indifference, lack of intimacy, or more explicit forms of abuse—and if she sees her efforts at looking out for herself in the divorce blocked as well, her frustration is likely to spiral into full-blown hatred. Such a woman might find herself fantasizing catastrophes in her ex-husband's life, even wishing for his death. She may be unable to work and to concentrate on her children's needs. Day and night she is consumed—by him! Where in such an emotional life is there room for the first tentative steps at, say, rearranging the apartment? Or going to a party with a friend? Not until the anger is resolved will it stop its wasteful consumption of awareness. And without the freedom to ruminate, to reflect, to think about one's own life free of the obsessive refrain of unresolved fury, novel and creative possibilities simply have no way of surfacing. Anger, rage, and hatred bind just as tightly as love—many divorced women who have recovered from the Ex-Wife Syndrome might even say *more* tightly!

To begin to understand how these intense emotions actually impede a woman's recovery process, picture Lynn, who is lunching with her best friend at a restaurant. In walks Peter, her husband for twenty-one years, her ex for three, and his beautiful new wife. He looks happier and healthier than Lynn has ever seen him—he is absolutely glowing with pride and well-being. Lynn feels sick; her stomach begins to burn, her face flushes hot, she is nauseated. She turns away from the sight and to her own surprise as much as her friend's, out pours a bitter diatribe about Peter and the marriage. In twenty minutes Lynn has revealed two decades' worth of family secrets, information she has long withheld from everyone.

The feeling that motivated this outpouring is familiar to Lynn—since the divorce she has experienced waves of rage without warning. She calls them "fits" and worries about what they mean. Is she crazy? Can she trust herself not to do something irrational, even violent? Her language, when the anger overcomes her, is uncharacteristically crude. Her body shakes, her eyes narrow—she doesn't know herself. Now she twists the napkin in her lap until she tears it clear through, and when she can finally stop talking she is swept by a hopeless feeling of failure.

Since her divorce, Lynn has done some dating, and when she's involved with a man, she notices that her rages at Peter are not so intense as when she is on her own. At the time of the luncheon, she is not involved with anyone, and the anger brings Peter front and center for her once again. As much as she hates Peter, unconsciously her emotion brings him to life for her and to some degree satisfies her strong desire to "have a man in her life." And once the anger has brought Peter back into play in her emotional life, she may well choose it over the less intense feelings new men in her life might inspire. In this way, the anger not only keeps her connected to Peter but blocks potential relationships with other men from developing.

Unless and until Lynn comes to see that the intermittent "fits" bind her to Peter, keeping him alive in her inner world, she will continue to be Peter's ex-wife, with little chance to live her own life.

Anger arises when we perceive ourselves to have been unjustly treated—when someone unfairly accuses us of lying, for instance, or smashes into our car by driving recklessly. *Rage* is anger raised to such a degree that we have to give it a different name—it is really a kind of *crazed* anger. Rage arises when someone has tapped into and stirred up an unresolved internal conflict deeper than the one occurring on the surface. Put the enraged person into a series of frustrating encounters with the object of her rage and inevitably the intermittent waves of intense emotion will even out into a constant state of hatred. Rage and hatred, then, are intensifications of the root emotion, anger.

When her ex-husband provokes anger in her after the divorce is final, a woman generally reacts in one of two ways, depending on her personality type. The woman I call The Fighter expresses her anger immediately, in which case an argument ensues. The woman I call The Suppressor remains silent, holding her feelings in. Each of these reaction styles has different consequences for the woman attempting to resolve her anger, break the connection with her ex-husband, and move on.

The Fighter

Postdivorce arguments are rage machines; one or both of the combatants can be counted on to reach into their ammunition bags and sooner or later let fair play go by the wayside. Here are Adele and Fred, divorced for five years, getting together for a meeting to discuss their daughter Shelley's college plans. After twenty years of marriage, Fred knows that Adele is highly sensitive to the fact that she has difficulty making friends. But the issue is tuition, not Adele's social life, so she's shocked and instantly infuriated when Fred says, "It would be three times as cheap if she stayed in the state, but you keep on discouraging her. Look, Adele, give me a break. You only hate the university because you had such a crummy time there, but Shelley's nothing like you. She'll love it there. She's much more outgoing than you ever were."

"What are you talking about, Fred? I'm not discouraging her from anything."

"You don't have to say it. You just pull that gloomy crap whenever the university comes up. Come on, lighten up. You're trying to break me here just because you never got into a sorority."

Adele is outraged. "Why the hell are you bringing *me* into this? This is Shelley we're talking about, not my freshman year in school."

"Because you're out to get what you can off me in this, that's why. I can see it a mile off."

"Damn it, what are you talking about?" she cries. "I'm trying to figure out how to do the best for Shelley, you moron. What do you think you *have*, Fred, that I'd ever *want* to 'get off you' anyway?" She scrapes back her chair and storms out before she breaks into tears of pure rage.

Back at home, Adele feels anxiety fill her mind and body as she tries to think through the problem. She has to meet with Fred again, has to confront him again—there's just no avoiding it; they've got to work this out. Sick at the endless parade of arguments that seem to stretch before her, Adele lies awake until the early hours of the morning.

The Suppressor

"You're just going to let him go down the tubes without doing anything about it?" yells Harold over the phone. "I mean, the kid doesn't try in school, he's a wimp on the baseball field, he looks like he's slept in his clothes. And you're just going to let him go along like that until he starts hanging out on the street all day long? Are you sure he's not on drugs or something? I bet you don't even know. I bet you haven't even thought of it."

Laverne takes a deep breath, waits for the fury to pass, and then answers in a soft voice. "I sent you that brochure on the tutoring service, Harold, don't you remember? You said it was too expensive, so I've been helping him as much as I can myself—"

"You? You couldn't do his math when he was in the second grade. What good do you think that's going to do?"

Laverne absorbs the barb, remembering the many nights she sat with her son over his homework, trying to boost his confidence and wracking her brains to think of ways to make him enjoy the math he hated. "I was just hoping that maybe you could sit down with him. You're so terrific at math, it comes so easily to you and everything. And then maybe practicing a little out in the yard with the baseball so he's not so scared at practice?"

"There you go with the nagging, Laverne. I mean it. I take the boy to good restaurants every week, I took him to get a watch for his birthday. I got him the cleats, the mitt, what are you telling me? I'm not doing enough?"

"No, no, I'm not saying that at all—"

"That's *exactly* what you're saying. You're saying I don't do my part."

"Oh, not at all, Harold. He looks forward to every Wednesday so much when he can be with you. I was just hoping that maybe this week before you take him for dinner, could you sit down with him for half an hour and look over his math?"

Maybe Laverne is hearing her mother whispering in her ear, "You know, you can get more bees with honey than you can with vinegar." It's a saying that's as shaky in its psychology as in its zoology, but it's one that many, many women subscribe to. Many women *experience* anger and rage but *express* nothing when their husbands or ex-husbands indulge in controlling, power-mongering behavior—ostensibly because getting furious back is unladylike, which they consider the most extreme form of unattractiveness in a woman.

Beneath the concern for appearances lies a more valid rationale: men are often significantly larger than women and most have been socialized in our society to puff out like blowfish when they get angry. Men yell; sometimes they pound tables with their fists. Even their footsteps, approaching aggressively, can be intimidating.

Young girls learn both to fear and to worship the sheer physicality of men—in a sick twist on nature, our media promote a positive association between male violence and virulence. In short, for many women, when he gets mad, she gets scared, and in a self-preserving impulse, she assumes a submissive stance.

Such a woman brings with her to marriage the ability to conciliate and smooth things over. "Don't provoke him, don't provoke him," warns a voice inside. In the event he does get angry, she has her techniques for neutralizing his anger, and there's an urgency to do it. She believes she *has* to "make it better—quick" to protect herself.

But after divorce those techniques don't work. When the ex-husband gets mad, she can't make it better any more because her strategies involved the currency of the marriage itself: food, sex, special treats, indulgences of his particular preferences, and the soft, compliant manner Laverne had down pat. After divorce, these currencies are inappropriate—although many women with stubborn cases of the syndrome continue to attempt to use them. Using sex, food, or conciliation to soothe an ex-husband can only result in drawing out the agony by perpetuating the connection. As before the divorce, so after: the suppressor keeps suppressing, and her anger can make her sick.

Growing agreement in the medical world points to complex links among body, mind, emotions, and environment. Where environmental stresses and emotional difficulties continue unabated, the body responds with physical symptoms. Debate continues over how these external factors contribute to the more serious medical scourges such as heart disease and cancer, but there is no doubt whatever that they cause and exacerbate many symptoms—anxiety, for example, with its attendant palpitations, headaches, backaches, chest pains, and stomach pains. The possibility of colitis or ulcers developing is high where anxiety continues unabated.

Although anxiety is particularly intense when a woman is connected to her ex-husband by anger, depression is inevitable when the anger is suppressed. The dynamics aren't hard to understand. If you miss your chance to express your anger or choose to swallow it—perhaps your ex-husband unjustly calls you irresponsible or ridiculous and you let the name-calling go by without a word—in the privacy of your home when you mull the moment over, aren't you bound to think to yourself, "Why the hell did I let him get away with that?" Soon enough you will have worked yourself into a froth about it: "How *could* I? What an idiot I am!" Self-loathing invades your spirit, and that old gray screen, depression, falls between you and the world.

Perhaps it's true, then, that you catch more bees with honey than with vinegar—but with all that buzzing around *inside* you—isn't it inevitable that you will be stung?

---

1. Do you feel hatred for your ex on a daily or weekly basis?
2. Do you fantasize about bad things happening to him?
3. Do you find yourself telling anyone who will listen how much you hate him?
4. Do you find yourself telling anyone who will listen all the horror stories involving things he has done (and is still doing) to make your life miserable?
5. Does thinking about him actually make you sick?
6. When you know you are going to see him or talk to him, do you feel angry and upset all day before the encounter? After the encounter?
7. Can he make you feel violent?
8. Do you hate the feelings he is able to stir up in you?
9. Do you find yourself transferring your feelings of anger and rage for him to other people you care about or who care about you?
10. When he stirs up feelings of anger and rage, do you feel you don't recognize yourself?
11. Do you hate yourself for what you feel?
12. Do you often feel out of control?

THE GREEN-EYED MONSTER: JEALOUSY

When women admit to feeling jealous with respect to their ex-husbands, I am alerted to the need to identify the true roots of the complex set of feelings to which the word *jealousy* refers. Is the woman jealous of *him* for coming out the winner in the divorce? Or is she jealous of another woman whom she sees as "filling her place"?

When a patient reports jealousy, then, my first task is to determine whether she is in fact feeling jealousy or the variation on that theme known as envy. Jealousy is based on the intense desire to keep something considered personal property from being taken away by another person; envy is rooted in the desire to *possess* something another person has. Both feelings are accompanied by feelings of anger, fear, and anxiety, and both flourish under the same conditions.

Both jealousy and envy are derived from a fear of losing something. That something, or someone, can be a woman's ex-husband, her place in the community, her self-esteem, or even her self-definition. Feelings of personal worth are very much at issue when jealousy or envy is a problem. People who feel good about themselves, who are self-confident and emotionally secure, rarely experience jealousy or envy; conversely, those who suffer from feelings of inferiority and inadequacy are likely to have these feelings.

Some women go out of their way to activate these emotions. They look for threats to their sense of ownership (or deserved ownership) and store up their complaints against those who threaten it. Subconsciously, exciting jealousy and envy is a way of holding off more painful feelings, for example, abandonment, rejection, or humiliation. In this context, jealousy or envy become distractions from emotions that seem literally unbearable.

My first task, then, when a woman speaks of jealousy, is to determine whether she suffers from true jealousy or envy. In the latter case, her feelings might be triggered by these perceptions: "He's the winner, I'm the loser. If I had gotten his end of the settlement, I'd be looking great and having a terrific time too," or "The children love him more than they love me. He can afford to show them a good time and be the good guy all the time, since I'm the one who worries about raising them right," or "I'm the fifth wheel everywhere now, since he walked away with all our friends."

These perceptions, clouded as they are with emotion, are more likely than not to be accurate. You don't need to look far to know that the man nearly always come out the winner in divorce. Certainly men suffer their own losses, the custody of their children chief among them (though not every father counts this as a loss). But as the figures show, the quality of most men's lives does not remain stable following divorce, it improves dramatically. The reverse tends to be true for women.

For many women, the feeling of bitter envy engendered by these circumstances is enough to keep their ex-husbands continually in the forefront of their minds and of their lives. Compulsively, a woman keeps going back to examine the wound, counting and recounting *his* blessings. No repetitive emotional pattern is more effective in turning a woman with great potential for living into an anxious, highly agitated, and hopelessly bitter ex-wife.

Envy

Caroline often stood up and paced in our therapy sessions as she obsessively recounted the terms of the divorce settlement that had been handed down four years earlier. "I look at his life and I think, 'Why him? Why not me?' It kills me how well off he is. I can't get past it. Thinking about how he lives is like going through the Sharper Image catalogue over and over again in my mind. It turns me completely green."

Caroline had worked as a lab technician to put Jack through medical school and to help him through the first years of his practice. Just as she was about to quit her job, he announced his intention to marry a young doctor he had met in medical school. He had been carrying on a clandestine affair, he admitted, for five years.

When Caroline recovered from her shock and the initial devastation, she pulled herself together for the divorce battle. She did her best to show that she deserved support from Jack so that she could go back to school to upgrade her skills—just as she had sent Jack to school in the early years of their marriage. The judge denied her request, and she struggled along in another low-paying clinic job. But her fury at the unfairness of the ruling gave her the energy and courage to return to court—only to be shot down a second time. Still, she couldn't let go. Caroline looked at Jack's luxurious life—built on two physicians' incomes, one of which she had made possible—and vowed to vindicate herself. But even more terrible than the price she had already paid in financial security and education was the waste of her current opportunities. As she paced and swore, paced and swore, life was passing her by.

For Caroline, envy was generated by a deeper emotion, a righteous, wholly justifiable anger at the way things had turned out. But in order to recover, the problem she needed to solve was how to resolve the anger, not how to justify it. What Caroline needed to see was that *the emotion itself* and her constant comparing of herself and Jack were holding her to him like clamps. Having lost twice in the courts, her only healthy course was to stop pursuing "justice" and a painful comparison and find other ways to climb out of the hole Jack and the judge had dug for her.

Sexual Jealousy

Nothing is more necessary for a healthy recovery from divorce than the sincere belief that you are worth the effort to save yourself— and nothing is more vulnerable to destruction on the divorce battleground. But when a woman is bound to her ex-husband by sexual jealousy, her self-esteem, already chipped away by the divorce experience, is fatally at risk. Here the sense of rejection can completely blind a woman to her own value. As a result, she can come to view herself as not only a loser but a washout, too defeated to imagine herself ever participating in life again. She concedes her old role to the new woman and voluntarily steps into the dead-end role of ex-wife.

Sharon's story illustrates the process. Unable to suppress her avid interest in every detail of her ex-husband's life, she watched him go through five years of short-term love affairs (while she had none of her own) and began to feel fairly confident that he, like herself, would remain permanently unmarried. She was taken completely by surprise when he announced his engagement—to the children, not directly to her—and at the news she experienced a sense of loss far greater than that she had felt when they divorced. In a panic, she set about learning everything she could about Matthew's fiancée. All Matthew's relationships had fallen apart before; Sharon was sure she would soon be able to identify the weakness in this one.

Sharon did some sleuthing and found out where the woman lived, and soon she was driving there every night after work and parking across the street from the woman's apartment building. She watched as the woman came home from work; later Matthew arrived, and late in the evening the light in the third-floor apartment went out.

The new woman was young and beautiful, and far from being assuaged, Sharon was dogged night and day by terrible jealousy and an awful, doomed sense of love for Matthew. The feeling kept her in a permanent state of distraction—she imagined the two together, fantasized about meeting them and causing a scene, imagined her responses should the woman be rude or insensitive to the children. But each time she saw the couple together, she felt less able to believe in the old myth that had kept her going for years: that no one would ever be able to put up with Matthew and take care of him as she had. Here was a lovely woman with a career who had not only hung in there for longer than the others but had agreed to marry Matthew.

Finally, Sharon's self-esteem bottomed out completely—the fact that Matthew's fiancée had qualities Sharon herself believed she was missing made her feel she had no value at all. Sharon began to see herself as a shell of a woman filled to the brim with nothing but anxiety, obsessive fantasies, and jealousy.

Jealousy arises naturally in the postdivorce recovery process, and healthy recovering women find ways to wait it out—to let the wave break over them and lose its power. Sharon, however, rode the wave as far as it would take her and in the process lost all self-regard. "If he can replace me so easily, I must not be worth much," she concluded. A true ex-wife, she turned back to her ex-husband to gain a sense of her value. When he never even bothered to look her way, she took his lack of interest as confirming evidence of her utter lack of value as a human being. In a sense, she went out of her way to undermine her self-confidence by knocking on a locked door.

Actually, what Matthew was doing had nothing to do with her. She could easily imagine her sister, her daughter, or her best friend breaking off a relationship and beginning another without thinking of *replacing* the person consigned to the past. But she viewed Matthew's revitalized social life as reflecting on her value as a person rather than as an expression of the legal right opened to him by the divorce.

The notion of replacement is a bogus one—it suggests that we choose our attachments as if we were casting a part in a play rather than because we are drawn to specific qualities in a specific person. But all that Sharon could see was that Matthew's fiancée had replaced her in the *role of wife*, and her yearning for the man who belonged to someone else was really a longing for attachment, not for Matthew.

If Sharon's mistake had stopped there it would have been serious enough. But her sexual jealousy set her to compare herself obsessively with the new woman and inevitably find herself falling short. Sharon learned that the new woman had a career, knew her way around the financial district in town, and lived on her own in an expensive high-rise apartment. In Sharon's mind, these points toted up to a very high score; on the other side of the scale, Sharon's suburban existence, now seriously compromised by her postdivorce drop in income, plus her complete lack of work experience seemed inconsequential.

Sharon knew she had strengths in the domestic categories. While the "other woman" had no children, Sharon (and Matthew) knew that she herself was a terrific mother, cook, and domestic administrator who had managed to keep things going miraculously during some very shaky years early in the marriage. But these positive points paled in the face of the points of comparison Sharon considered really important: age and physical appearance. In every one of these categories, Sharon lost out . . . predictably so. Though Sharon was a very attractive woman who kept herself fit, she saw herself as out of the running in the presence of a younger, slimmer woman with a drop-dead wardrobe.

And no wonder: research shows that most women consider themselves overweight and their physical appearances in need of significant improvement. In a recent study, for example, 70 percent of a sample of teenage girls picked *themselves* as the least attractive girl in their class. In another, 60 percent of both normal and anorexic women overestimated their own body size. Such results are typical of a wide range of studies. The conclusion we can draw is that when women start comparing themselves to other women, they almost always develop distorted perceptions.

When Sharon looked at herself in the funhouse mirror of jealousy, she saw an image of a woman who didn't measure up, one who had been banished to the sidelines and replaced. In short, she saw nothing more than Matthew's ex-wife. The danger was that, with sexual jealousy holding Sharon as tightly to Matthew as Matthew was holding his girlfriend, Sharon would never again see herself as she really was—as a woman worth freeing and sending into the world to create a full life for herself.

1. Do you find yourself seeking out as much information about your ex as you can get?
2. Are you especially hungry for information about his social life?
3. When you find out he has gone on a vacation or made an expensive purchase are you enraged?

---

4. Do you find yourself angry at him because the children love him?

5. Do you feel that your children love their father more than they love you?

6. Are you upset when the children spend time with him?

7. Are you upset that he's dating?

8. Are you upset that he looks good?

9. Are you upset that he has clearly been able to move on with his life?

10. Do you hate the fact that he's remarried, if he has?

11. Does it seem to you that he has no problems?

12. Are you plagued by fantasies of him making love to someone else?

13. If he's remarried or going out with someone, do you feel that he's ashamed to have been married to you?

THE WAGES OF FEAR

Newly divorced women have many fears:

"How am I going to handle the finances?"
"How am I going to reenter the social world?"
"How will I run a household by myself?"

These fears and the many others that arise once the marriage is over are related to practical problems, and to a large extent a woman can allay them as she gains information and experience.

But deeper, more destructive fears assail the divorced woman:

"He'll hurt me, as he did in marriage."
"I'm afraid I can't live without him—no one will love me or take care of me as he has."

"I'll be alone forever if I let go of him."
"He'll turn my children against me and I'll have no one."

In marriage, a woman afraid of her husband has some investment in giving in to her fear: "If I don't listen and behave, he will abuse me, scare me, hit me, hurt me, kill me, *won't love me* . . ." But giving in to the threat of punishment is a child's stance: "If I'm a good girl I'll get what I want and I won't get hurt." Where fear is present, the marriage contract keeps the woman in bondage; only her "good behavior" makes the marriage work. Where fear persists after divorce, the fear itself keeps the woman in bondage—and no other way of life has a chance to take hold. All that remains is the bondage, and the woman is trapped between two worlds—her past and the new life she deserves.

Kathy and Donald had had an awful marriage—he had cheated on her constantly and every time she had confronted him with her suspicions he'd flown into a fury and hit or pushed her. Twice he had hurt her badly enough to send her to the hospital.

During the divorce, Donald was extremely clever in burying his assets. He even convinced Kathy to use a lawyer from his own attorney's firm "to save money." Given Donald's creative income reporting and the ambiguous loyalties of her lawyer, Kathy wound up with a minimal support settlement. And even though Donald hadn't wanted the divorce, he quickly picked up the pieces of his life and was soon living with a new girlfriend, while Kathy, at near poverty level, struggled to support their six-year-old son.

Every week Donald called to ask the same breathless questions: "Do you miss me? Do you love me? Won't you reconcile? We could have such a beautiful life together now that the air is cleared, and you wouldn't have to struggle. Why won't you sleep with me? Why won't you give it a try?" Kathy was in a constant state of anxiety and dread, expecting to hear his voice every time she answered the phone. And each time he called she went into a state of super-alertness, for she feared that her rejection of him would trigger his rage and endanger her meager funds. She knew he was legally bound to pay, but a late support check could wreak havoc with her life, and twice when she had stood up to Donald he'd been two weeks late with the check.

But Kathy's fear of her ex went deeper than her concern about money. Below her consciousness, this fear was fed by a terror at facing life on her own. Her fear of "making it on my own" was proof that she had swallowed whole all the negative messages she had received about herself from Donald and, as a child, from her parents. She was terrified that she was inadequate, incapable of taking control of her life. And as long as she remained connected to Donald by a dependence born of fear, she would be *proving* herself incapable and inadequate to the task.

In short, Kathy was always afraid—under her fear that Donald would cut off her support lay the old fear of his hurting her. She was so wary of him and so convinced that her survival depended on him she could not see how *he* needed her. The point of view her own defensive attitude imposed on her had her locked into the role of Donald's ex-wife, a powerless woman still looking to him for support.

We all know that children can't make it alone in the world; they need protection and guidance. A divorced woman in the posture of a fearful child can expect neither from her ex-husband; his marital obligations to her end when the divorce decree is handed down. But what many divorced women don't realize is that not only is there nothing to gain by remaining fearful, but there is also *nothing to lose*. The marriage is over; it no longer requires protection. A woman's impulse to placate an angry ex-husband is *always* obsolete. It takes courage to face down fear, courage that may require a great deal of time and concentration to develop. There are a great number of tools and strategies for overcoming fear, and I will discuss many of them in part two. But by overcoming fear I do not necessarily mean eradicating it. To triumph *in spite of* fear a woman must see very clearly what she is missing out on and what she stands to gain. For Kathy and other women with the Ex-Wife Syndrome, the wages of fear are a life lived on the sidelines in the shadow of the ex-husband; the rewards are freedom, a life of one's own, and deserved self-respect.

Maryanne was a tenured law professor—extremely bright and firmly ensconced at the top of her profession. Her journal articles had earned her an enviable reputation among her colleagues nationwide, and her lifelong financial future was virtually secured because of her own hard work. She and Brad, a history professor, had been married for sixteen years, and their childless marriage had always been invigorated by a sporty competitiveness. But the marriage went stale after Brad had an affair, and Maryanne decided she would be better off alone. Without trust and the lighthearted fun they used to have, what was the good of saving the marriage?

Throughout the divorce proceedings, Maryanne felt secure in the course she was pursuing. Brad didn't seem too upset by the divorce; he hadn't tried hard to dissuade her from it. Given their relative earning power, the divorce proceedings were calm and businesslike.

After the divorce, Brad was honored with a chair at a prestigious British university. He began to prepare for a new life abroad. Maryanne panicked. She hadn't counted on Brad's vanishing. For two years after he left, Maryanne was consumed by the feeling that she had been abandoned, that there was no one to love her, no source of emotional nourishment open to her in the world. She took to drinking alone in the evenings and then calling Brad overseas. During these terrible phone calls she almost always humiliated herself by crying.

In therapy, Maryanne revealed the bleak vision of the future that had overtaken her. She would have no one ever again. An image of herself living and growing old alone turned her cold with fright and kept her in a constant state of anxiety. She became so anxious at social gatherings—she shook, her palms sweated, her voice trembled, she felt sick—that she stopped going anywhere except to classes and back home. She felt she simply didn't have the skills even to carry on a conversation.

Unknowingly during the marriage, Maryanne had given Brad sole jurisdiction over her emotional well-being and sense of connectedness; for instance, he initiated and planned all their social activities. Once he had withdrawn, she discovered herself to be completely unskilled in meeting her own emotional needs or reaching out to others in an effort to fulfill them. Her complete surrender to the sense of abandonment she experienced after the divorce bound Maryanne tightly to Brad, distant as he was physically and emotionally, and every phone call bound her tighter.

In our therapy sessions, smart, well-respected, professionally secure Maryanne came slowly to face the fact that she had assigned Brad sole responsibility for making her happy. She saw that now she must come to care for herself emotionally. Terrible as it seemed, she had to give up the midnight phone calls. Frightening as she found it, she had to acknowledge—and renounce—her reliance on a man who was no longer there. The most terrifying challenge of all was to risk entering the social world alone.

1. Do you feel anxiety when you know you're going to see or speak to your ex?
2. Do you avoid certain situations because you're afraid he might hurt or embarrass you?
3. On days you know you will be seeing or talking with him, do you wake up anxiety ridden?
4. Do you avoid answering the phone in case it might be him?
5. Are you afraid to ask him for anything even though you are right or entitled to ask?
6. Are you afraid to confront him?
7. Are you afraid to set limits that will exclude him from your life?
8. Do you feel that anything you do involving him could endanger you financially?

9.   Do you have difficulty making decisions that might affect
     him?
10. Do you look for and find ways to say no to him?
11. Do you feel physically ill when you see or talk to him?
12. Do you feel you must do everything you can not to
     endanger your support arrangement?

I hope that with the stories and questions I've presented in these
chapters, you've begun to recognize the specific nature of your own
bond to the past and to identify the behaviors and feelings that are
holding you back. I know that this process is painful, especially at
first. But difficult as it is—and different as the emotional "types"
I've described may seem—all of the women whose stories I've told
have this in common: they all had "happy endings." Once these
women had brought themselves to the point of self-recognition,
they were able to begin to take the actions that would unshackle
them from ex-wifehood and allow them to work toward living as
they wished to live. Every one of them made a full recovery from
the Ex-Wife Syndrome.

Of course, I'm not saying they all went on to get spectacular
jobs, marry the men of their dreams, or inherit a million dollars.
No "cure" can promise that. In fact, as they recovered, these women
found they had to pay special attention to their Achilles' heels, the
particular vulnerabilities—jealousy, self-pity, bitterness, and so
on—with which the syndrome had left them. But having faced the
essential fact that despite being single they still weren't free—and
having seen exactly *how* they were keeping themselves from being
free—these women discovered that there were concrete actions they
could take to sever the bond and liberate themselves. It is these
strategies that we will turn to in the next part of the book.

Part 2

STRATEGIES

5

RULES OF ORDER

As we've seen, the first step in breaking free of the Ex-Wife Syndrome is to identify what type of connection is keeping you bound to your ex-husband so that you can focus on the particular emotional and behavioral patterns that are blocking your recovery and causing you psychological pain. Once you have recognized these destructive emotional and behavioral patterns, the next and obvious step is to stop them cold.

But how? After all, the emotional ties we've identified are very strong and highly complex, and as I've shown, their roots in a woman originate deep in the psyche. Any substance abuser knows that resolving to break dangerous, even life-threatening, habits is one thing and carrying out that resolve quite another, and the connection to the ex can be as stubborn—and destructive—as any chemical addiction. How does one overcome months and years of habit to take that first unprecedented step in breaking free?

The question is valid, and the answer quite specific: *by radically shifting the perspective from which you view the relationship to your ex.*

Alcoholics and drug abusers who enter recovery programs learn that they must rebuild the foundations of their relationships to friends, family, and others if they are to become permanently free of their addiction. This is no less true of those who suffer from the Ex-Wife Syndrome, even though these women have not yet benefited from the same degree of public and professional recognition of their disorder. Fortunately, however, there is a model familiar to us all that provides an excellent paradigm for rebuilding the relationship to the ex-husband.

THE BUSINESS MODEL

The model I propose is the business relationship. Businesspeople don't have to like, love, hate, or feel anything at all about those they interact with to get their jobs done. A complex emotional relationship has no place between, say, a city planner working out a joint deal with a contractor or a real estate broker and a potential buyer attempting to come to terms on a property sale. In fact, quite the opposite is true: emotional involvement often impedes the business relationship, where the objective is to accomplish a stated goal—no more, no less. To that end, communication must be efficient and unambiguous and subjective considerations are understood to have no place.

If you're a typical syndrome sufferer, this sort of relationship probably couldn't be further from the kind of interactions you're accustomed to having with your ex-husband—or even the kind of relationship you're accustomed to *fantasizing* about having with him. But if you've read the preceding chapters carefully and have taken a long, hard, honest look at the nature of your feelings and behaviors, you've seen that the patterns don't contain even a seed of the openness, affection, and potential for growth that characterize a truly intimate relationship. In fact, you've seen that the relationship itself is a phantom; the true connection was dissolved by divorce. What you're wrestling with—in your loneliness, jealousy, pity, guilt, or endless, fruitless battles with your ex—are unresolved emotional issues that date back to the marriage and before and in most cases have been greatly exacerbated by the divorce process and its aftermath. Seen in this light, the order and calm of the "business relationship" provides a welcome contrast to the chaos, confusion, and destructive emotions that characterize the continued bond to the ex in all its forms. There's no reason you can't substitute that model for whatever currently obtains in your dealings with your ex.

After years of trying to "fight it out" or "work it out" with her ex-husband, Leah, a patient, decided she'd had enough. She put it to her ex-husband point-blank: "There are only two topics I'll discuss with you: the children and money." She was through arguing with, confiding in, and trying to change her ex-husband. She was finished with crying, begging, playing on his guilt, and even groveling to get him to visit the children. With her divorce decree in hand—a little yellowed, since it had taken her some years to internalize this approach and put it into action—Leah hit on the ideal mode for discussing those matters that had to be handled. And she could sum it up in just two words: "strictly business."

When the executives of two corporations sit down to negotiate a deal, they bring to the conference table three essential ingredients:

1. The Demand for Respect. Unless both parties conduct themselves as potential winners who expect to be recognized and treated as such, there's no meeting. Why should there be? The results would be a foregone conclusion and the acknowledged winner obvious.

2. A Fiercely Guarded Sense of Privacy. Both parties understand that personal concerns—for example, marital status, sexual preference, personal finances, and so forth—have no place in the business arena and that any reference to such concerns is inappropriate and potentially destructive to the meeting's objective.

3. A Set of Company Rules that Define the Boundaries of the Negotiations. No experienced corporate representative enters into negotiations without studying the project in the context of the corporation's established house rules. The contenders know before they begin how far they are willing to go in achieving the goal under discussion and what points they will not concede under any circumstances. In a very real sense, these preset rules define the nature of the corporation and give it its particular character.

These three prerequisites make a business meeting work; without them any attempt to achieve efficiency and eventual consensus is likely to break down into explosive and emotion-driven argument. After all, almost all business negotiations are efforts to find a compromise solution between two contenders, each of whom is fiercely protecting his or her particular interests. Ring a bell? It should because this description neatly fits the unavoidable interactions that take place between ex-spouses—over children or finances, for example. And it's a short leap to apply these three prerequisites for successful business interactions to your dealings with your former husband.

R-E-S-P-E-C-T

Most women desire respect above all else, yet many wives, given the basic marital power imbalances we have examined, are unable to demand it. And husbands in such marriages often have their own reasons for withholding respect from their wives, often in order continually to reassert their own "superiority," particularly when they are not perfectly convinced of it themselves.

Within marriage, you needed respect—everybody needs respect from the people with whom they live. But the marriage is over now, and what you need is not respect for your accomplishments and personal goodness but *respect for your right to live your own life and for the rules you set up to make that happen*. Let me put it another way: You don't need *anything* from your ex-husband *except* respect for your rules. Even if he dislikes you, hates you, denigrates your value as a human being, it makes no difference. You no longer have to worry about the quality of your life together. The only thing you need to concern yourself with in your current relationship is, as in any business relationship, *efficiency*. And the efficiency of the relationship—that is, the ability to accomplish the necessary tasks, such as arranging a visitation schedule, securing the decreed support, and solving problems involving children—depends entirely on *his* respect for *your* rules.

PRIVACY: A SHORT, THOROUGH COURSE

Marriage is a shared experience, and with the end of the marriage comes the end of the sharing. This statement might seem self-evident, but for women trained from infancy to please and nurture men, the impulse may seem to have acquired a life of its own. Once the marriage is over, these women are faced with two problems: how to quell the impulse to share and how to replace it.

The answer to both problems is the same, and obvious as it sounds, it is an answer that many women with the Ex-Wife Syndrome, especially those connected by the "caring" emotions, have difficulty coming up with on their own:

All individuals have the right to privacy. In healthy marriages, both partners learn how to keep a part of themselves separate from each other, to keep private some personal desires, wishes, likes and dislikes, and fantasies as their own. In marriages based more on possessiveness than mutual respect, an attempt to maintain this separateness may seem downright threatening to the partner trying to do the "owning." Furthermore, some people mistakenly define intimacy as the complete knowledge of another person's thoughts, memories, and fantasies rather than as simply trust, and they consider such privacy to be a sign of the failure of the marriage. Finally, many women have just never had a chance to develop their sense of privacy by living on their own. All these circumstances, both internal and external, contribute to the difficulty divorced women often have in discerning and protecting their right to privacy.

Webster's defines it succinctly enough: "private: belonging to or concerning an individual person." Your personal life belongs to you. You are under no obligation, legal or otherwise, to share it with your ex-husband. If you have children, this does not mean you must never speak to their father. Quite the contrary—unless you claim and protect your privacy against invasions by your former husband, the joint decision-making process required by your biological connection will be hopelessly freighted by the profound emotional pain associated with the Ex-Wife Syndrome.

So take your cue from Leah, who insisted on sticking to "strictly business" with her ex: *everything in your life that does not involve the children or unresolved financial matters constitutes your private life.* Your private life is now *completely off limits* to your ex-husband, and you need to make the boundaries around it clear—both to yourself and to him—by setting your own "house rules," the only rules you'll play by whenever he's involved.

THE RULES

The First Rule

"Easier said than done," you might mutter, as you contemplate this new task. Even if you've begun to cultivate your sense of privacy, "laying down the law"—and enforcing it—can seem like an overwhelmingly complicated and daunting task.

Once you are able to set the *first* rule, you'll find that the rest follow more easily. Deciding on and enforcing that first rule require careful pacing: it has to happen when it *can* happen. What makes it possible is an inner certainty that cannot be forced but that will emerge gradually. Thus, a woman might decide that her first rule is "Meetings by appointment only," but she may need weeks or even months to ruminate, resolve all inner conflict, and allay any attendant anxiety sufficiently to voice the rule to her ex-husband. Remember that you can't fake certainty but must let it take hold as it will, after deep thought.

The secret is to focus on *one thing* your ex-husband does, not everything at once, that triggers the emotional response in you that strengthens the destructive connection.

Does he tell you about his girlfriend, triggering waves of jealousy? "No exchanges of information on social or sexual matters."

Does he touch your face when he says good-bye, bringing on a surge of love? "No physical touching whatsoever between ex-spouses."

Does everything you hear about him intensify your loneliness and reinforce your belief that he's the only man for you? "My ex and all friends and family members are hereby informed that all information regarding my ex-husband and any aspect of his life is absolutely unwelcome."

Does he pick fights over your parenting style, venting his temper in the name of concern for the children? "No yelling, hollering, or screaming. The moment a voice is raised, the offended party ends the meeting by leaving the premises or demanding that the offender leave."

Does he frighten you with physical threats? "The police will be called"—You will see with this rule how authentic your level of strength must be before you can set and enforce it—"The police will be called at the first suggestion of a physical threat."

Beth's ex-husband of four years, Jerry, called her almost every weekday morning to discuss the children. It was part of his daily routine: since the children were a source of friction between him and his new wife, he would wait to phone until he got to the office, and since he was a morning person, that meant 8:00 A.M.

Now, Beth's job as a convention organizer was very demanding and often involved late evenings at hectic convention sites. Frequently she didn't go into the office until 11:00 A.M., and on mornings after late nights she tried to sleep in. But no matter how often she asked him to call at another time, like clockwork Jerry would arrive at work in the morning and reach for the phone.

Jerry's calls were "informational," of course: "Did you get Johnny's bike fixed? Are you going to let Sue sleep out again this Friday before she finishes her report?" Despite the ostensibly practical nature of the calls, however, Jerry always managed to convey criticism of Beth's behavior. Thus, "Did you . . . ?" became "Haven't you done that yet?" and "Are you going to . . . ?" became "You don't mean to say you intend to . . . !?" Guilt would wash over Beth. "I haven't been keeping up with things," she would say to herself with a sinking heart. "After all, he's their father. The least I can do is carry out his wishes for his children since he's not with them to carry them out on his own."

Let's look at this connection by guilt through a zoom lens to see how it reaches into and affects Beth's life. On a typical morning, Beth lets Jerry rant until he quits on his own; then she heads for the shower, determined to make herself forget the call and think about something cheerful. But the phone call has altered her mood, and when she goes to work she's cranky and has a disagreement with her boss. She retreats to her office and feels the signals of depression—exhaustion, a dulling of her senses, a heaviness to her body—start to drag her down.

When we break down the morning's events into this sequence, it's easy to see that Jerry's phone call started a chain of events that led directly to depression. But Beth ascribes her misery to the encounter she has had with her boss, never tracing it to the fundamental connection that has her tied to Jerry as tightly as ever. And the wave of anxiety she feels that night before falling asleep —complete with hyperventilation, shakiness, and a sense of impending doom—she attributes to too much coffee, never realizing that each night she fears the next morning's phone call and the emotional havoc it will make of her day.

Life is hard enough without our having to suffer psychological distress of this type. Beth has a difficult and demanding job, and she's lonesome for male companionship. She's worried about her children's adjustment to the divorce and wonders if her son's falling grades have anything to do with it. She feels capable of addressing these problems in their turn and living with them as long as it takes to find solutions. But does she need an undercurrent of depression and anxiety working against her while she's attempting to solve the practical problems of everyday life? To free herself of this extra burden of psychological distress, Beth must face its sources—her still-vital connection with Jerry, dominated by her guilt at "taking his children away from him."

Once Beth sees the pattern, the obvious solution presents itself naturally. The next morning, Jerry wakes Beth up with his usual call. "Where were you last night?" he begins. "I called and Joey said you were out." Ordinarily, Beth would have felt guilty at leaving the children on their own, a practice Jerry strongly and vociferously disapproves of, but on this particular morning she feels a particular resistance to his question. As it happens she had gone out with a man after work the night before and had had an unusually good time. This momentary resistance is enough to break Beth's usual pattern of response, and she has a sudden insight: In a flash she realizes that *she doesn't have to answer Jerry!* After all, they're divorced; where she went is her business, not his. "I was out," she says. That's it.

Just saying that much feels *great*. And from there it's a small step to Beth's first house rule: *No more eight o'clock phone calls*. First, she buys herself an answering machine. Then she calls Jerry and tells him calmly, "I won't talk with you at eight in the morning. If you need to call, please do it after five. If I'm not home, leave a message and I will return your call."

Jerry hates the answering machine and refuses to leave messages, and often he conveniently forgets her rule. So Beth makes sure the machine is on before she goes to bed each night and lets it pick up his early-morning calls. The lack of access infuriates him, and the issue becomes a battleground. This situation isn't easy for Beth, and holding firm to her plan gives her a lot of anxiety. Listening to Jerry sputter into the machine at eight o'clock tightens her throat and weakens her resolve.

But anxiety is a given *whenever* you take a new step. Beth takes it in stride and resolves to tough it out. Determinedly, she leaves the room and shuts the door as soon as she hears the phone ring in the morning.

Whenever Jerry does reach Beth, he is so irritated by the inconvenience her rule puts him to that he's often in a fighting mood. The ensuing disagreements upset her so much she has to set another rule: *Whenever you upset me on the phone I'm going to hang up.*

Again, actually enforcing this new rule the first few times brings on awful attacks of anxiety and uncertainty. But by now Beth expects these reactions in herself and understands them as part of the process of disengagement and self-assertion. Slowly she develops a formula—at the first sign of that sinking feeling, she makes herself say, "This won't get us anywhere. I'm hanging up now." And that's that.

Like Beth, you'll discover that setting rules—defining your personal boundaries for all to see—is an important *psychological* as well as practical step. For the first time you're saying, "This far and no farther." The clearest psychological benefit is that by pointing out the boundaries you will identify them clearly for yourself and thereby give yourself a basis for a new decisiveness. From this decision flows a freedom from confusion and ambiguity that you may have longed for but never, in your dealings with your ex, experienced before.

Some sample house rules.

1.　No sexuality between ex-spouses.
2.　No gossiping—about who died, who's fighting, who was at dinner the other night, what's going on socially and sexually.
3.　No entering the house without ringing the bell.
4.　No entering the house if I'm not home.
5.　No visits—to me or the children—without an appointment.
6.　No "borrowing" of anything from the house without prior arrangement.
7.　No spontaneous meals; all meetings and meals by appointment only, and then only on neutral territory. Neither party cooks for the other.

Selecting that first rule, the one that will address the most pressing problems in your relationship with your ex, is, of course, a highly personal process. But seeing how some other women made their choices may help you make your own. Recall Celeste, for example, described in chapter three, who was stalled in her recovery from divorce by loneliness. Once she realized that returning to John during her bouts of loneliness only reinforced her unhealthy connection to him, she set her first rule accordingly—and this was a rule directed at her own behavior, not his: *No more phone calls to John, no matter how lonely I get.*

At first, sticking to that rule felt like going cold turkey in the attempt to break a chemical addiction. Celeste found herself making six or seven phone calls a night to friends and family members in order to stave off the temptation to call John. But she had set her rule and was determined to enforce it. She enlisted her best friend's help, explaining the situation and using her as a stand-in when she wanted to contact John. And she posted some notes on her refrigerator door and phone as reminders to herself: "Don't you dare call him!" She also wrote a letter to John informing him that for an extended period of time she would be unable to speak with him and requesting that he use the mail to communicate with her until further notice (she resisted the temptation to explain: she simply *stated*). Eventually, as the days passed, Celeste was able to turn her attention from her desire to call John to healthier ways of alleviating her loneliness. She began to push herself out of the house to "go through the motions" of socializing. Celeste discovered the truth in that old saw "Necessity is the mother of invention." Gradually John became for her merely somebody she used to know.

Linda, remember, suffered tremendous guilt at leaving Howard. Through intense self-exploration, she came to see that every encounter with him was sabotaging her efforts to start a new life. Her number-one rule became *No shared holidays—none!* This entailed making prearrangements so the children could celebrate major holidays and birthdays with each parent separately. Initially, Howard tried to play on Linda's guilt to wear down this rule, but her early efforts to enforce it gave her a delicious taste of freedom. Spared his destructive comments and behavior, her holidays were truly joyous celebrations. And the children, she saw, were no longer saddled with an artificial sense of "the old family" that might feed in them the hope of reconciliation. Linda's first rule was right on the mark, and the palpable benefits it yielded gave her the confidence to set others that would shape her new life as she wished to live it.

Finally, think back on Adele in chapter four, whose postdivorce relationship with her ex was filled with anger. During each encounter she had with Fred she endured pain, abuse, and disrespect. Armed with the insight that their volatile encounters perpetuated the dynamics of their marriage, Adele set her first rule: *Any raising of voices or disrespect on the part of either party signals the end of the conversation*. Fred ridiculed her for insisting on so "artificial" a rule, but the next time he called—to chew her out for allowing their son to have his ear pierced—she responded, "I told you, Fred, that any shouting or abuse meant the end of the conversation," and then she hung up. He called back, enraged, and she suggested he calm down and call the next day—and then hung up again. When the phone rang again, she ignored it and left the house. After a couple of days, Fred called back, this time much more controlled. After a few more phone calls that gave evidence of the effectiveness of her rule, Adele felt strong enough to set a second one: *No more meetings without a third party present*. It was a radical requirement but one that she knew was necessary to prevent their meetings from erupting into chaos. With careful thought and admirable resolve, Adele was on her way toward living life *her* way, with the ground rules clearly spelled out.

Limiting Access to the House

One house rule, while clearly a necessity in all cases, seems to be a particular stumbling block for women—limiting the ex-husband's access to the house, particularly if it's the house they shared during their marriage. Even though the house is part of her divorce settlement, years later her ex-husband is still carrying a key, dropping in spontaneously, stopping by even when she's not home to rummage around in the attic, and spending time there with his children to avoid conflict with his new wife. Through all the years of the marriage, his footsteps on the gravel, his hand on the knob, his tread on the stairs have all "seemed right somehow." Worse, "it seems wrong somehow" to deny him access to "his own house"—or, at the very least, "his children's house."

Wait a minute, I'd say at this point in a therapy session. "*His* own house?"

"Well, I mean, he bought it and everything. His children live there. I just don't feel right . . ."

"But if it's *his* house, does that mean he's just letting you stay there? If it's *his* house, where's yours?"

"Well, *legally* . . ." she begins to explain, but that's where I have to interrupt. *Legally* is exactly right. Legally the house is yours. Even if the settlement gave you *half* the house, it will also have given you "exclusive use," which means that by law your ex-husband can enter only at your discretion.

Maybe you remember playing hide-and-seek as a child. A certain tree would always be the safe zone, the place we called "home free." We'd run and run toward that tree, dodging all sorts of obstacles to reach it before "It" tagged us out. Let's call all the difficulties that can assail you "the outside world" and your house "home free." It's in the decree: through the medium of the judge, society at large has deemed you the rightful owner of the house. Now you must extend your sense of personal boundaries to encompass it.

Your house or apartment is your private domain, a refuge from the outside world—of which your ex-husband is now a part. This is the home you have created (perhaps re-created after the divorce) to give yourself and your children peace, calm, and a feeling of safety. Any time your ex-husband enters without your express permission, your privacy has been invaded. If you permit him free entry at his convenience, you are providing him with the opportunity to contaminate your personal space with those same behaviors from which you expected the divorce to free you.

For years, for example, Ruth let Daniel drop over whenever he could to help the children with their homework and tuck them into bed. He did this two or three nights a week, but never by prearrangement. Whenever he was in the house Ruth could feel the tension escalate. Even if she stayed in another room, she could hear him getting annoyed with the children over their homework. Or she would come upon him eyeing her personal papers in passing. And often, when he yelled at the kids, she would feel the need to intercede. Then she and Daniel would immediately square off, just as they had throughout their volatile marriage, and the children would take on *their* traditional roles. Sean and Kevin would become hyperactive in an attempt to divert their parents' attention from each other, and Annie would retreat to her room in gloomy silence.

Many was the night Ruth lay in bed after one of these episodes realizing with a sinking heart that divorce had forced her standard of living down, upset the children badly, and sent her into the work force . . . but it hadn't put an end to the endless arguing that had driven her to seek an end to the marriage in the first place. After all was said and done—four years later—they were still going at it as furiously as ever.

If Ruth had prohibited Daniel's free entry to the house, she would have made her house "home free"—free for her and for the children, who would have been secure in the knowledge that they always had a calm refuge. The inescapable solution was to set a rule prohibiting Daniel from entering except by prearrangement.

You can and should expect an angry reaction when you set such a rule in your own home. After all, men as well as women view the house as highly symbolic, and as long as his possession of the territory has not been challenged except by a flimsy *decree*, your ex-husband may continue to come and go as he wishes. To strengthen your resolve, remember that he belongs in your home no more than *you* belong in his new residence. Yours is yours; his is his. If he doesn't like it, suggest he complain to the judge.

The children too may react strongly. Young children in particular do not like change, and they may become frightened at the thought that their daddy might disappear from their lives if he is no longer allowed to visit them in your home. Have confidence in your resolve, reassure them as best you can, and quickly institute arrangements for the children to see their father on *his* turf.

I can hear a contingent of readers muttering more loudly than ever, "Easier said than done." No, I don't expect it will be easy. But claiming your own territory is an essential step, and if you find it nearly impossible to establish this rule (or any other rule) in conversation, consider falling back on that very useful business model: write a letter. This strategy is not only effective, but it establishes the businesslike tone that should be the ideal you are striving for in all your relations with your ex-husband. Here's a sample, written by one of my patients:

Steven:

The past five years have been a hellish experience for me in relation to you. Your erratic behavior and continual lack of respect for me have been abusive and have created one upsetting experience after another . . . [Your behavior at a recent family party] and the way you tried to cheat me and not stick to our agreed-upon terms were and are sickening.

At this time I have decided upon the following guidelines so as to decrease my contact with you.

1. From now on when you call this house, call on Janie's line. Obviously, if no one answers the kids aren't home.
2. I do not want to see you physically unless it is necessary—for example, at graduations or weddings.
3. Any discussion between me and you will be conducted between nine and five o'clock Monday through Friday. The discussion will be limited to the children and/or finances.
4. I am forced to tell you again that you are *not allowed* in this house. The only time you can enter is by personal invitation or during an emergency.

Up to this point the issue of receiving the maintenance check that supports your children has been a nonissue. But I will never again tolerate your not sending a check at all. The courts ordered that the check be issued on the first and that is when I expect it.

If you believe that you have found a new resource with which to manipulate me—namely, the check—I suggest you think very carefully about the logical extensions of your actions. I will not hesitate to use every means available to me to deal with this issue.

I am not in a position to tolerate your games any more. That is for your wife. I gave it up and I really don't want anything more to do with you.

Jacqueline

In a less complex world, a woman who resolved the inner conflicts that nourish and perpetuate the connection to her ex-husband might be able to walk away from him forever. Indeed, many women who have no children and who are satisfied with the distribution of property are in a position to do just that. Breaking the cord will not necessarily be any easier for them, but once free they can, and usually should, arrange their lives so they never have to see the former husbands again.

But women who have had children with their former husbands, and women still grappling with ongoing financial and other property matters, generally find themselves continually involved in unavoidable interactions with their ex. Picture the mother of three young children trying to avoid interacting with her ex when he arrives every Wednesday and Saturday to take the children out to the park. As her children grow, they come to various developmental and logistical crossroads that require serious deliberation and joint decision making. A woman attempting to seek legal redress from an ex-husband who refuses to make his court-ordered maintenance payments cannot reasonably expect not to see him, think about him, or harbor any feelings about him. For such women, staying free of the Ex-Wife Syndrome means anticipating and protecting against emotional reentanglement over a possible *lifetime* of unavoidable interactions.

Where there are children and the father remains involved, a lifetime of encounters is not just a possibility, it is a certainty. Although popular belief suggests that parental responsibilities end when the child reaches eighteen, the parents of a child remain *biologically* connected throughout the child's lifetime.

The challenge, then, is to move beyond the first step in breaking old patterns to take on a broader task: defusing and redefining the whole relationship completely and permanently. As you assess and reassess your current relationship, you will undoubtedly find yourself returning with new eyes to those points of contention that have plagued you for years—those unresolved issues that serve married couples all through a marriage and long after the divorce as well-worn battlegrounds for the endless, continually erupting power struggle between the sexes. This time, though, you bring to these battlefields a new and potent arsenal: the fierce and uncompromising demand for respect, a well-honed sense of privacy, and a developing skill for personal rule making. With these weapons, you will be able to build strategies designed to neutralize permanently your emotional involvement with your ex-husband on every front.

THE COMMUNICATION BATTLEGROUND

Nowhere is conflict so evident between the sexes as in the genders' differing styles of communication, and on no battlefront are power imbalances between spouses more explicitly expressed. A study conducted by Candace West at the University of California at Santa Cruz reveals that in conversation with women, men interrupt 96 percent of the time. Says West, "They just have a subconscious need to control intergender conversations," and interrupting to get their point across is a proven way to do it.

In light of that tendency, consider another research finding, this one by the American Association of Matrimonial Lawyers: "poor communication" is cited most often as the chief reason couples divorce. A coincidence? Not at all. Just as free-flowing communication can make a marriage work, thwarted communication—especially when deliberately thwarted by one party for the purpose of controlling the other—turns marriage for the thwarted partner into a bondage of frustration.

Whichever partner eventually instigates it, the divorce puts an end to such bondage—or should. There is no reason any longer to suffer such frustration in your attempts to communicate with your ex-husband.

When you must talk with your ex-husband, treat the encounter like a business meeting and prepare carefully for the conversation ahead of time. If he is an interrupter who knows how to overpower you verbally, beware that conversations are a danger area in which you need to protect yourself against his gaining the advantage.

1. Make an agenda and stick to it. Write the agenda down point by point if you have to, and don't be ashamed to refer to your notes.

2. Know beforehand that your ex-husband is likely to take note of your new communication strategies and do what he can to override them. He might ridicule, 'scoff,' get irritated, or even go into a rage over your insistence at sticking to your agenda—in fact, he'll use *any* of the strategies he used within the marriage to control communication, including stomping out of the room to end a conversation he can't control. A man who is used to being in control does not give up his advantage easily—so be prepared for a struggle.

3. This strategy is an extension of the previous one: when he struggles for control in his characteristic way—by interrupting you, ridiculing you, yelling at you, threatening you, trying to provoke your guilt, or whatever his methods might be—*end the conversation*. Make this a ground rule, and remind yourself of it before you begin. Have a clear, direct explanation prepared—"I will not go on if you keep interrupting me"—deliver it in as calm and firm a voice as you can muster, and get off the phone or leave the room. Period. Later, if you find that you did not accomplish your agenda in your abbreviated conversation, proceed to strategy number 5 (below).

4. *Never pass information to your ex-husband through the children.* This strategy is taboo for many reasons. It's indirect and inefficient, it unfairly involves the children in your relationship, and it complicates what should be an ever more *simplified* form of interrelating.

5. Use the postal system whenever possible to carry your messages—and for doctor bills (carefully itemized to show your ex-

husband's share), communications from the court involving the divorce, anything you can. The idea is to *depersonalize, neutralize,* and *simplify* your communication—with the ultimate intent of depersonalizing, neutralizing, and simplifying your relationship.

THE INFORMATION BATTLEGROUND

One battleground you may never have identified as such in all your years of marriage is the use of *information* as an instrument of power. But those who *know* can use what they know, and in marriage as in a less-than-ideal postdivorce relationship, information can be used quite effectively as a means of exerting control.

Consider Judy, divorced from Bryan for four years. In the summer of that fourth year, Judy went on vacation to Mexico with the man she had been seeing for more than two years. She and Bryan arranged for Bryan to stay in Judy's apartment to take care of their seven-year-old son, Darren.

On the fifth day of the vacation, at eleven o'clock at night, Judy got a call from Bryan in her hotel room: "Where the hell have you been? I've been calling all day and night. And where the bloody hell do you keep the thermometer in this place?" So began a conversation in which Bryan vented his irritation over the elusive thermometer (he could have gone out and bought one for $1.50), aroused Judy's concern about Darren's health (the child had a runny nose and, as it turned out, no fever), and—by his tone of voice as well as specific remarks ("Lord, Judy, the way you have things arranged around here, nothing is in the logical place; you still have absolutely no sense of order, of efficiency")—managed to criticize her way of life. He also, incidentally, succeeded in taking the romance and pleasure out of her evening.

So went another round in the power battle between Judy and Bryan, four years after the divorce and across a distance of three thousand miles. Inadvertently, Judy had given Bryan access not only to the apartment but to herself as well.

Here's how she could have arranged things differently:

1. For the week involved, three days of which overlapped with Darren's spring break, Bryan could have cared for Darren in his own apartment, even though this arrangement would have been less convenient for him. During their marriage, Judy's housekeeping had been a constant bone of contention, and his criticism of it had always devastated her. The information he gained by inhabiting her space restored his power to trigger her guilt and uncertainty about "the way things *should* be."

2. If Bryan refused to care for Darren in his house, she could have hired a baby-sitter. Under these circumstances she could have instructed her sitter not to give out her whereabouts to anyone except in an emergency, making sure to inform Bryan that the sitter had been so instructed.

Think carefully about what your ex-husband needs to know. He needs to know everything about the children, but unless your children are preverbal, you can and should depend on them to do their own talking. Beyond that, and any financial or property matters that arise as a result of the divorce settlement (which should be taken care of by mail as a matter of course), does your ex need to know where you go, what you do, whom you see every day? Does he need entrée to your home, where he can deliver his opinion on how you live? Does he need to meet your boyfriends or know anything about your private social life? Does he need to know that you're concerned about your weight and considering joining a weight-loss program? Does he need to know about your troubles on the job?

The answer to all these questions is adamantly *no*. Given the difficulty of the psychological work you are doing plus the ordinary challenges of day-to-day living, in at least some of these areas you are bound to be less than fully secure. Allowing your ex-husband information on any of these very personal subjects not only fuels your connection but gives him additional means to influence you emotionally. Why stack the deck against yourself? Your priority, along with cutting the cord, is finding ways to support, not undermine, yourself.

Remember, too, that information flows two ways. It's as important to staunch the flow from him to you as to staunch that from you to him. By now you know that all emotions that have connected you to him for so long—*too* long—die hard. Breaking their grip on you takes more than a single decision; it takes a plan of concrete steps designed to reinforce and preserve the realization that from now on the relationship between you two must be "strictly business":

1. Since information feeds the emotional connection, cut off the flow and starve it. Ask your family and friends not to discuss your ex-husband with you anymore. As in a business relationship, what has passed between you and him and what continues to pass between you is of no concern to others. If your family and friends have no right to offer unsolicited advice on your business dealings, why should they have input into your relationship with your ex-husband? Ask them politely but firmly to bow out. Experience shows that although they may not voluntarily hold their tongues—during the divorce proceedings, they may have grown accustomed to offering their opinions and advice freely—they will respect your clearly stated request that they withhold all information and opinions regarding your ex-husband.

2. Never get to know or develop a friendship with your ex-husband's new wife or girlfriends. The impulse to do this is common (one of my patients made herself "invaluable" to her ex-husband and his wife as a baby-sitter!), and the result is always the same: if your overtures are rebuffed you will suffer pain, and if they are accepted your emotional connection will be perpetuated.

3. By extension, do not ask anyone about these "new women" or let your ex-husband speak to you about them.

4. Teach your children not to report to you about your ex-husband's life except where their well-being is affected. In this, be direct: "I'm not interested in Dad's new house or Dad's new dog. I'm only interested in how *you* feel when you are at Dad's place—do you feel comfortable and safe?"

One final warning regarding the power of information: break any old reliance you might have developed during the marriage on your ex-husband's "expertise" in certain areas. He may indeed have more knowledge than you about some things, and turning to him for information and advice might well be very convenient. But your work now is to turn away from, not toward, him and to reduce the power he has over you, not hand him more. Here's an important house rule to add to the list: *never* ask your ex-husband for advice or answers to questions. If he's an ear, nose, and throat doctor and you have an earache, find another ENT. If he's an accountant and you need help with your taxes, go to the library and read a tax guide or find another accountant. Use the rule even in minor situations: if you can't find Johnny's bicycle pump and you think your ex might know where it is, don't lay yourself open to accusations of carelessness by asking him about it. Buy another bicycle pump or, better yet, have Johnny track the old pump down at Dad's place himself.

THE FINANCIAL BATTLEGROUND

Money enables us to realize our hopes and plans. Without it, those hopes turn to ashes and we are left with a sense of our own impotence, or powerlessness. In the conventional marriage and even in many two-income families, as I've noted, the husband controls both the income and outflow of most of the money. In extreme cases the wife has an "allowance." But even where the control of money in a marriage has been equal and the monetary decisions have been made jointly, after divorce the financial arena tends to become the main battleground. And where a woman has the Ex-Wife Syndrome, her ex-husband's control of money almost always inhibits her recovery.

Recall Lenore Weitzman's shocking statistics: in the first year after divorce, on average, a man's standard of living rises by 42 percent, a woman's drops by 73 percent. Given such circumstances, it's not hard to see how and why women can be manipulated by that support check. Moreover, where children are involved, women find themselves having to deal with their ex-husbands about financial matters above and beyond child support and maintenance. Carol needs skating lessons or Robby's school is organizing a class trip. Extras like these crop up throughout the child-rearing years. If the woman has custody of the children, she is constantly having to ask her ex-husband for money, thus laying the groundwork for financial warfare.

Who should pay for Jill's new prom dress? It's really a question of figures. If the incomes are equal, each party pays 50 percent. But if he's up 42 percent while she's down 73, the contributions should differ proportionally.

Let's use another example, the consequences of which are a little clearer. Paul and Corinne have joint custody of little Petie, who is three and a half and enrolled in a full-time preschool program. Paul has an increasingly successful cabinet-making business that he built up from a home operation into a small factory. Corinne is a struggling free-lance editor trying to establish herself with publishers so she can spend more time with Petie and eventually cut his preschool hours by 25 percent. Both parents think the school is perfect for Petie and worth the high tuition. Given the joint custody arrangement, there is no support and maintenance agreement between them; each is to absorb half the child-rearing costs.

The trouble is, Corinne can't handle the tuition payments. The agreement is that she pay the school every other month, but when the time comes she's still awaiting payment on invoices she's sent out to clients or she hasn't finished a job so she can't bill yet. Though it galls her, every two months she has to ask Paul for the money, knowing that the school will respond to late payment by dropping Petie from the program.

The first couple of times, Paul is magnanimous about paying the tuition—at least, he feels he is. He makes the extra payments in full and states clearly that he considers these outlays to be loans. He asks Corinne to make up a schedule of repayment that will work for her and tells her he's willing to wait up to a year for repayment. He considers himself to be very reasonable on the matter, but by the third time he's furious, and by the fifth he's disgusted. They had an agreement, he tells her, and she's not holding up her end of the bargain. She's supposed to be in business, but she's so disorganized, he tells her, that her billing system is a mess. She should be invoicing her clients by the month, sending out second notices early, etc., etc. He's been all through the early years of making a business work, and he's come out with a solid reputation and the trust of many clients, so he feels qualified to criticize her when her requests for money "prove" that she hasn't taken his valuable, time-tested advice.

But Corinne just isn't earning enough money. She's at the beginning of her free-lance career, and in a good month her billing amounts to about a third of what Paul takes home. Though she's agreed to pay for half, she simply can't do it. This is a practical problem requiring a practical solution. If no one pays the tuition, Petie must leave the school. But Paul wants Petie in the school, and he has the money to keep him there. If Paul doesn't think of the solution himself, Corinne needs to propose to him that *he* shoulder the larger share of tuition based on the discrepancy in their financial resources. And she doesn't have to invite him to dinner to pose the solution. It would be far more appropriate, and far less dangerous, for her to write a letter—which will also give her an opportunity to display the clarity of her thinking, contrary to his assumptions.

There's no guarantee that on paper this proposal won't raise Paul's ire as much as it would face-to-face. The point is, Corinne won't be around to take the flak. Let Paul fret and fume on his own time and his own turf. Since the solution is sensible, if the letter is composed carefully he may well come around to agreeing on the solution. If he doesn't, the *practical* consequences of their inequitable arrangements, and not an argument, will ensue. After all, if Corinne can't pay she can't pay. Thus, if Paul doesn't pay, Petie leaves the school. It's as simple as that.

Once again the point is to choose the alternative that is the *least emotionally charged*. The objective of cultivating a businesslike approach is to neutralize the charge as much as you can in your dealings with your ex. And the most certain strategy for neutralizing is to avoid face-to-face or telephone contact in which he can use the power strategies he knows from experience will work.

Here are a few guidelines for coping with matters on the financial battleground in an impeccably businesslike manner:

1. Whenever possible, *stay away and write it down*!

2. *Never beg*. Begging inevitably diminishes both your self-esteem and his respect for you. At best it will get you money only some of the time, and it will damage your mental health.

3. *Never cry*. Crying is a plot to evoke his pity. You can control your tears if you are absolutely determined to do so. The negative effects of crying in the course of financial negotiations are the same as those of begging—crying crodes both your self-esteem and his respect for you. Even if you know crying will work, *don't cry*. Your sense of yourself is as much at stake as the money. Look at it this way: you and your children would be better off without a new washing machine this year than with a downtrodden head of household plagued by self-loathing.

4. If you can't avoid a face-to-face or phone presentation, rehearse! When you need to ask for money, develop a logical plan—again, a business proposal. There are books to teach you how to do this if you want to get technical, but all you really need to do is write the proposition down and, in a forthright, orderly way, present the reasons that would justify his expenditure. Show what's needed, why it's fair that he pay, why you can't, and the consequences of going without.

Then, before you deliver the proposal—rehearse, rehearse, rehearse. Read the proposal aloud; then memorize it. Try to anticipate his objections and write down responses to all of them too.

Presenting a carefully composed business plan could raise your percentage of successes to about 70 percent. But the real boon won't be measurable. You'll escape the battered self-esteem, the blows to your pride, the impulse to grovel and apologize, the realization that you're acting like a pitiful child, and above all the devastating effects of self-hatred.

5. Even if you follow these rules, 30 percent of the time you won't get what you need. Again, take a clue from business. Prepare for rejection and have a contingency plan ready. His refusal to pay may well be a temporary, symbolic *no*. He may, with reflection on the consequences detailed in your proposal, come back with a yes or a counteroffer. But he also may not.

At this point you have a critical choice to make, one with far greater ramifications than the money matter at hand. You can either become enraged at his stinginess and fall into old ways of relating that show you're still "married" despite the divorce, *or* you can diffuse your anger and invest your energy in developing a new strategy. Even though you *know* he can well afford to pay for the prom dress or the tuition or the karate lessons, be prepared to make a concession—but one that's realistic for you. Perhaps you could offer to contribute twenty dollars. It might not make much practical difference to him, but it would certainly reflect both the reality of your situation and your willingness to do what you can.

After their divorce Ted absolutely refused Jane's request that he pay the $3,000 cost of sending their daughter, Natalie, to the camp she had attended since she was a little girl. Ted was a wealthy man and during the marriage had never given the money a single thought. Now, however, Jane and Natalie were living in a two-bedroom apartment and Ted was footing the bill for his new step-son's braces. His rationale seemed to be that everything had changed, and that went for camp as well.

Jane had disconnected pretty smoothly. Her head was clear and her priorities straight. When Ted refused to pay (taking the opportunity to dramatize the extent to which the divorce had changed his way of life), Jane sent a note informing him that though the camp cost $3,000 the deposit was $250. "How would it be if I paid the deposit?" she offered in her note. "It's not much, but it *is* deductible from the total cost." His display over, Ted acceded, and they dealt with the rest of the matter by mail.

Let's take a moment to look at the larger financial picture. We're talking about basic sustenance and fair play, not retaliation or petty wants and needs. The sort of maneuvering described above becomes necessary because most support settlements are unfair and many are unenforced. Judith Wallerstein describes the overall situation:

In general, men earning $30,000 a year are ordered to pay about 10 percent of their gross income for child support. Of the millions of women who are entitled to child support, fewer than half receive payments as ordered, about one-third are paid a fraction of what they have been promised, and one-fourth of the women get nothing. Wealthier men do not have a better record of child support. Several men in our study [in a wealthy suburban community] unilaterally cut child support when their ex-wives began to earn good salaries or married well-to-do husbands. Others reduced child support when they themselves remarried, especially if they acquired stepchildren or had more children with the second wife. Not one father in our study voluntarily raised child support because his ex-wife was physically or psychologically not well.

There are many battles to be fought to right these inequities, and many of them will be settled not between individual adversaries but in the political arena. There, if lawmakers so will it, noncompliers will eventually face consequences for failing to share fairly in their children's support. For the purposes of this book, however, it is important to see that the financial power a man automatically holds over a woman as a result of this basic inequality puts the woman at risk of never breaking free. If you are committed to the process of separating from your ex-husband and resolving your internal conflicts, it is imperative that you understand the size of the risk. Everyone is frightened of poverty, and, today the possibilities of plummeting into poverty following divorce are great. But if you let your fear of poverty inhibit your efforts to break free, you will be enslaved to your ex-husband for life—no doubt struggling financially all the while.

Read this as a call to courage: commit yourself to finding a way to become financially as well as psychologically independent. Realize that if you achieve the former, the second will almost certainly follow, or will at least be in sight. There are many important reasons for a woman to work—to gain personal gratification, to elevate her self-esteem, to gain contact with the outside world—but nothing is so important as having your own money and the freedom to go about your business, rendering all the careful strategizing described above obsolete.

Many women, of course, do leave a marriage with their own money. If and when you carry your own income with you, here's a universal rule of thumb to apply to your financial dealings: *never, unless your divorce decree makes it mandatory, let your ex-husband know how much money you have or what you are doing with it.* If you have occasion to need financial advice, ask a friend or hire a consultant. Protect your privacy by cutting off at the source your ex-husband's information power over you. As we all learned at our mother's knees, privacy extends very much to the pocketbook (my mother's purse represented twelve square inches of privacy, her *only* privacy, so she never let anyone look inside it). Now it's time to learn that privacy extends to your bank book too.

THREATS ON THE BATTLEGROUND

Given the built-in inequities of most divorce settlements, ex-husbands have a ready weapon not available to most women: the common, everyday, garden-variety *threat*. Ex-husbands usually have the financial and often the physical advantage, and as too many women know too well they are not always shy about threatening to use these powers. Threats are a simple and effective strategy, and divorced women connected to their ex-husbands by fear generally have a hard time seeing a way around them. As long as these women are vulnerable to their ex-husbands' threats, they have very little chance of breaking free.

Let's look at the threats ex-husbands commonly use:

"If you don't (do what I want you to do—for instance, get Charlie to call my wife 'Mom') . . .
"I'll see to it that Charlie knows what kind of woman you really are."
"I'll take Charlie away for the summer."

"You won't see another penny from me."
"I'll never talk to you again."
"I'll hurt you."
"I'll wreck your life."
"I'll kill you."
"I'll kill myself, and my death will be on your head."
"I'll go to court and get full custody of Charlie."

My experience in my practice and interviews tells me that *90 percent of such threats are empty*, designed solely to scare, manipulate, and control.

The last threat on the list—taking away custody—is the one used most frequently because it packs the most power of all, even more than the threat of physical attack. Nothing is more frightening to a mother than the possibility that she might lose her children. But few men actually try to carry out this threat. Moreover, in my fourteen years as a psychotherapist dealing with women I have never personally seen or even heard of a single case in which a woman lost her children in this way—even when the ex-husband went to court.

Most single men are unwilling to rearrange their lives to accommodate their children on a full-time basis, and married men have new wives and often stepchildren, which complicates matters. But when a man threatens to take the children, a woman rarely imagines he will back down in the face of reality, so a detailed look at the situation is worth discussing.

Beyond the question of whether the man is truly equipped to deal with his children full-time lie the legal difficulties of his obtaining custody. Though joint custody is relatively common in some areas, transferring custody from a mother to a father is virtually unheard of. Doing so requires that the father unseat the "tender years doctrine" that is firmly in place throughout the court system. This is the assertion, reinforced by the psychological community, that young children need their mothers during their years of development. This doctrine has been challenged here and there, but it has been intact for years and remains so at this time.

The father's only alternative in the face of the tender years doctrine would be to prove the mother mentally incompetent and emotionally unfit to have custody. Hearing this alarms many women,
especially those suffering the anxiety and depression characteristic
of the Ex-Wife Syndrome, because their self-concepts are poor and
their sense of self-worth is at an all-time low. But such "proof" is
hard to come by: the judge would need to be convinced that the
mother had deserted the children, was certifiably mentally ill, had
shown herself to have truly despicable morals, or was seriously
chemically dependent—all conditions rendering her dysfunctional
as a parent. Even if you are a victim of the Ex-Wife Syndrome,
with its attendant unhappiness and symptoms of psychological distress, that does not mean you are less than fully capable of functioning as an effective and responsible parent.

The other threats on the list can be disposed of with a casual "so
what?" or a quiet reference to the appropriate authority. You won't
ever talk to me again? All the better, since the point is to minimize
contact. You'll wreck my life? The proper authorities will be interested in seeing how you do that.

But what of "I'll hurt you" or "I'll kill you"? Your response to
such threats must be prompt and definite, and you must be prepared
to follow through. Advise your ex-husband that you will call the
police or have a judge slap a restraining order on him. Then *do* it—
take every step necessary to ensure your safety. Some local police
stations will do a free security check on your house or apartment;
change your locks and have your home made as secure as it can
be. But don't stop there, and don't rely solely on the police to
intervene. Police departments in general are reluctant to intervene
in family disputes, where they are often the casualties of violent
tempers. Go a step further by contacting your local battered wom-
en's center to learn about safe houses and other options in your
area and to get the support you need from people who know what
you're talking about. You might even consider taking a self-defense
course. You may not wind up with a black belt in karate, but you
will certainly find like-minded women in such a course, intent on
making themselves feel at ease in the physical world. While im-

proving your watchfulness and teaching you to use your strength, such courses can build your confidence as well.

Of course, it's not easy to face down fear. It takes courage to stand up to even an empty threat. When your ex threatens to withhold the support check as a means of getting his way or when he threatens to hurt you, the immediate consequences for yourself and your family might seem far more dire than the long-term emotional consequences of knuckling under. But if the threats come often enough, and especially if he follows through on them, the woman struggling to disconnect and to heal will recognize the pattern and, in her commitment to change and growth, find the courage and resolve to break it.

Consider the case of Carolanne and Frank. He would consistently threaten to withhold support as a way of maintaining control over his former wife. Each time he touched on the possibility of withholding, Carolanne became terrified and agreed to his demands. One day, though, she'd had enough, and when he enraged her by objecting to her way of handling a problem with their daughter's teacher, ending his diatribe with "You're lucky I'm still writing those checks at all, the way you act," she took the step. Instead of swallowing her rage, she whirled on her heel and, in a new, deep, controlled voice, asserted herself clearly: "Look, stop browbeating me. It's not luck, it's the *law*—you *have* to pay that support. I won't have you threatening me with turning off the money."

Sure enough, at the end of the month, no check arrived. Carolanne surprised herself with the degree of coolness she displayed. She didn't get hysterical, she didn't—as she might have done a month before—pick up the phone and beg for the check. Instead she called her lawyer, who quickly drafted a letter demanding payment and citing the consequences of failure to pay—a subpoena to appear in court and a possible contempt-of-court ruling resulting in a jail term. That was all it took. The lawyer express-mailed the letter, Frank express-mailed the check, and Carolanne had the satisfaction of having taken swift, effective action on her own behalf.

The criminal justice system is making little progress in tracking down and controlling fathers who fail to make their support payments, but the court system today is taking increasingly swifter, tougher action on men brought to them for noncompliance. Therefore, it's up to individual women to initiate legal action. If you belong to a divorced women's support group, you might suggest that it join the effort to lobby for more stringent enforcement, along the model of Mothers Against Drunk Driving (MADD), the highly effective lobby that has led the crackdown on drunk driving.

I grant that it's not easy for most women to contemplate the idea of throwing the father of their children in jail. But the alternative to using this action is caving in to the threat. Often your *own* empty threat about initiating legal proceedings can be enough to get you your check. But if you are having a truly terrible time of it, you can and must follow through. An arrest warrant delivered to your ex-husband's place of work by the sheriff can be a highly effective motivator and a productive extractor of cash since a man served such a warrant must pay the amount in full or go to jail. True, jail is a possibility, but if the warrant isn't effective, a night in the county jail may well be. These are tough measures, but they are sometimes the *only* measures open to women. In following through on them, a woman moves out of the role of victim and into the role of self-advocate.

I do not throw around the advice "call a lawyer" lightly. As a general rule, lawyers cost money. But in a crisis of this type, when you need help in extracting from your ex-husband what is legally yours, there are resources open to you even if you have no money at all. Check your phone book under "legal assistance" or "legal aid."

When you consistently run up against the problem of nonpayment, you could decide to arrange for the support check to be issued through a third party—namely, the court or the state. In this arrangement, the father pays the court or state, and if he's late, *that* entity goes after him and does it quickly. So if you have a conventional arrangement that is not working out, I urge you to look into changing it to a third-party system, again with the help of an attorney.

These means of extracting payment should give you the confidence to face down any threats your ex-husband may make to withhold support. One important fact worth knowing—and using if necessary—is that if you decide at any point to go back to court to have support or maintenance payments adjusted, the judge won't look kindly at a father who has a history of nonpayment or late payment on his record. The court recognizes such behavior as a form of abuse.

So if you have long been connected to your ex-husband by fear, and if he has had a history of stopping you cold on the battlefield with threats of withholding money, you don't need to struggle to be a "good girl." There are very good reasons for him *not* to follow through on a threat to withhold the support required of him by the judge. If you are not sure of those exact terms, dig your divorce decree out of your drawer and *read it*. Many women, in the effort to forget the tumultuous and painful time of the divorce itself, stash the decree away and never look at it again. But you may find out when you read your document that you have rights detailed in it that you didn't know you had. Many divorce decrees, for example, contain a contingency clause that allows you to go back into court to ask for more money when your ex-husband's income increases.

MINIMIZING ANXIETY AND DEPRESSION

The process of disengaging from your ex-husband and setting new terms for your unavoidable dealings with him is gradual. Along with the real progress you are making, you can expect many peaks and valleys, as in any period of change. And in the valleys you are certain to meet those two unwanted companions, anxiety and depression, that inevitably come with the territory.

There's no way around these symptoms, but there are ways to minimize them. There are many books on the subject, but here are a few first-aid strategies that should become routine.

For Depression

- *Exercise regularly*. In general, psychotherapists have long been remiss in failing to acknowledge the tremendous value of physical exercise in counteracting depression. Recent research has proved that exercise actually produces chemicals that reduce depression. Choose your form of exercise to match your state of health and physical abilities. If you are in good health, jogging, swimming, or aerobics will help you the most in combating depression. If age or health is a limiting factor, though, try brisk walking. Such physical activities will not only help you with depression but will contribute to your overall health and put you in touch with other people.

- *Rigorously limit your dietary intake of sugars, other carbohydrates, and caffeine, and bulk up your protein intake*. Eating large amounts of sugar creates a short-term increase in the blood-sugar level, which you might experience as a temporary burst of energy. After the burst, however, you'll experience a dramatic decline in blood sugar, which can contribute substantially to a feeling of depression. To avoid such chemically induced mood swings, eliminate that morning sweet roll or doughnut and forget about candy and chocolate for a while. Also, put some effort into curbing other carbohydrate intake since a high-carbohydrate diet can intensify fluctuations in your blood-sugar level throughout the day. Toast and orange juice (both high-carbohydrate foods) will start your day by putting you on the same roller coaster a sugary doughnut will. To achieve what control you can over your emotional state, combine your carbohydrates with foods that are high in protein such as eggs, cheese, meats, and nuts. Pay attention to your cholesterol intake, which proteins tend to boost, and try to balance the decrease in sugars and carbohydrates with an increase in protein since your system breaks down protein fastest when you are under stress.

  Caffeine stimulates both the central nervous system and the liver. The result of liver stimulation is a surge of glucose in the bloodstream, followed, in about an hour and a half, by a steep drop in blood sugar that can contribute to depression. Do yourself a favor and strictly limit your caffeine intake.

- *Strictly limit alcohol, and avoid drugs.* Many people are unaware that alcohol is a depressant. It might make you feel good for a brief period, but the high will *inevitably* be followed by a low, even more extreme than the one with which you started. Other drugs will anesthetize you emotionally for a time and/or confuse you. Since the watchword in this book is "face facts," the last thing you need to contend with in fighting off depression is a chemically induced distortion of reality.

- *Monitor your depression carefully.* This book is not intended as an advertisement or even an argument for psychotherapy, but if you find that your depression doesn't lift or that it is regularly accompanied by thoughts of suicide, I strongly advise you to seek the guidance and support of a qualified therapist. Where suicide is not a risk and you are committed to working on your own, however, it is critical that you monitor your actions vigilantly during periods of depression and stop yourself from reaching out to your ex-husband to repair your feelings. Reach outward, yes—but to anyone but him. Take any chance you can to spend time with other women like yourself. Consider joining a divorced women's support group, if there is one available. Just being in touch with women who have been through the disconnection process will give you not only strength but a sense of direction.

For Anxiety

As there are steps to defeat depression, there are things you can do to allay or reduce the temporary anxiety that is natural to the disconnection process. I highly recommend first aid in the form of physical exercise, meditation, relaxation exercises, and biofeedback, to name only a few proven anxiety-reducing strategies.

One absolute necessity as you move forward through the process is to talk honestly with a trusted friend. Nothing strokes fear like solitude; nothing allays it like putting your fears into words.

Though psychotherapy is by no means a requirement for disconnecting successfully, if you have no one you can speak with honestly, it's worth considering seeking out a therapist. There is great therapeutic value in hearing yourself talk.

Beware, however. Guard against anyone who, however well meaning, encourages you to maintain your connection to your ex-husband. Assess your friend's (or therapist's) reactions as you reassessed your attorney's approach to your divorce. Listen for warnings: "Honey, don't rock the boat—he might cut you off." Listen for discouragements: "Why would you alienate him at this point? You're so alone as it is." Listen for moral judgments that undermine your sense of privacy and boundaries: "I don't see how you can lock him out. After all, they're *his* children too." You will have worked hard to find productive, self-respecting responses to these comments, however well meaning. The last thing you need is to backslide into uncertainty.

One more word about seeking out friends. You may have discovered, to your surprise and disappointment, that when you looked for support from your old friends, those to whom you felt closest during your marriage, no one was there. Divorce is famous for frightening even lifelong friends away, and the new consciousness you've begun to acquire may seem not only alien but downright dangerous to your married friends. You're changing now, moving into a different world, and you and your best friend may find yourself with little to say over coffee.

Furthermore, as a single woman, to some friends you may have become—well, somebody to keep an eye on. It can come as a shock to notice suddenly that your best friend is finding excuses for not inviting you over for Sunday brunch. Once the crisis has passed and you're standing on your own two feet, you may catch a wary glint in your old friend's smile.

For all these reasons, seeking out a therapist or a divorced woman's support group may be a wholesome option. Make full use of trustworthy friends to help you through, and be prepared to weather some difficulties even with them as you make this critical transition. But at this point the priority is to secure yourself a safe place to talk so you can hear what you have to say without fear of contradiction, criticism, or nostalgia for the bygone life.

Still, even with supportive people all around you, moments of anxiety during disconnection are inevitable. You're going to feel fear every time you take a new step. Let's look at what will happen when such a moment of fear overtakes you.

Suppose your ex-husband has a habit of dropping in on you at your workplace—to try to get you to agree to a change in the visitation schedule, to talk about money, and so on. You've resolved to put an end to this. You know his temper and sense he might throw a tantrum, as he's done every time you've set a new rule. Sure enough, he flies into a rage. What happens? You get scared, that's all. You experience the feeling. You don't fall apart, you don't faint, you don't have a heart attack, you don't even hyperventilate. He *is* shocked and angry, but you have a new response to his anger that you didn't have in marriage: you can walk away, and you do. Perhaps your heart speeds up, your limbs shake, your breath comes more quickly, you sweat and feel a bit sick. But despite his yelling, his pounding of his fist in his hand, even despite his threats—from which you are legally protected—he never upsets your workday again by walking into your office unexpectedly.

That victory didn't come cheap. You paid for it with some sleepless nights and half an hour or so of shaky limbs and voice. But your new freedom is a bargain at the price. You've begun to see concrete results, to emerge from limbo into the wide world of possibilities.

6

MYTHS, FANTASIES, AND WISHES

Chris and Susan were married for eight years and have been divorced for four. After her divorce, Susan had suffered a period of intense and sometimes despairing loneliness, but she had slowly worked at facing the facts of her condition and breaking the connection with Chris. She devised and enforced a set of rules designed to simplify and reduce their contact, and eventually she sold their old house and moved closer to the university where she was studying computer programming. Two years ago she got a job in a health administration agency and worked out a schedule with her boss that meshed with her children's school hours. Intuitively, Susan sensed the value of minimizing her interactions with Chris, and limited her contact with him to exchanges of the children at the door of her home, so she wouldn't have to see him at all. She made sure their visitation schedule worked smoothly and strictly enforced the terms of the court-ordered child support. In short, Susan had gone a long way toward breaking the bond with Chris and living life on her own terms.

One evening, Chris calls Susan. He'd like to have a serious talk, he tells her. Could they set up a date? Susan looks at her calendar, and they agree on a time and place.

They meet in a coffee shop. "Look, Susan," Chris tells her almost at once, "Madelyn and I are planning to get married."

To her surprise, Susan feels her stomach lurch. "Well, congratulations," she tells him, working hard to control her breathing. She's humiliated to realize that her voice is shaking.

"Will you tell the kids—you know, kind of pave the way for me?"

Susan gets control of herself: "I think this is something you need to discuss with them directly. After all, you're talking about presenting them with a stepmother. This isn't something I should do for you, Chris." She's relieved that she's managed to come up with a cogent response to his request but worried that she's not going to be able to keep it up. Her voice won't stop trembling: she's afraid he'll notice her turmoil. Abruptly, she pushes herself back from the table, offers Chris her hand, and walks briskly out of the restaurant.

At home, Susan spends the evening wandering around the house aimlessly, as if she's in shock. What's going on? she asks herself. So he's getting married. So what? What's the big surprise? After all her good work, Susan is dismayed and alarmed to discover that somewhere below her consciousness she always expected Chris to come back to her. This expectation was born of a fantasy, the fantasy was born of a wish, and the wish was born of a myth—a common misconception—about how human behavior works. In reality, there was never any chance that Chris would come back; he was long gone from the marriage even before he initiated the divorce. To protect her freedom and preserve her new life, Susan found she still had work to do.

If you've begun to put into practice the advice of the preceding chapter, by now you've probably started to see and feel dramatic changes in your day-to-day life, both emotionally and practically. You've probably also gotten a feel for the interaction between insight and action in the recovery process: once you are able to recognize persistent, unproductive, or self-destructive patterns of feeling and behavior, you are able to see what actions are necessary to change them. Those actions in turn reinforce your new sense of self and make further insights—and actions—possible.

There's a wonderful symmetry to this process, and it shouldn't discourage you when I tell you that now, when health and wholeness seem within your reach, it's especially crucial that you turn your gaze inward to seek out—and dismantle—the remaining *internal* stumbling blocks to full recovery.

These internal obstacles represent the last stronghold of the obsolete bond of the past. They take three forms, all of which might seem benign on the surface but are in fact destructive enough to undermine all the good work you've accomplished:

1. *myths*, or common misconceptions reinforced by society
2. *fantasies*, which are unrealistic scenarios embellished by the imagination
3. *wishes*, or outright desires

Though the three take different forms and have distinct psychological origins, they all have the same destructive effect: they *distort reality* and thereby interfere with the recovering woman's crucial effort to see and respond to things as they currently are.

1. *"If I am understanding, fair, and rational with my ex-husband, he will be the same with me."*

This is the most common—and stubborn—of the internal distortions women cling to, even after repeated evidence to the contrary. Unfortunately, women who entertain this belief are nurturing flawed expectations, which will consistently backfire in the course of everyday life.

The reason I can state this so confidently is quite basic: in the relations between ex-spouses, the social rules we ordinarily rely on are turned topsy-turvy. The postdivorce world is Alice's Wonderland, but few acknowledge or act on this fact.

To understand the topsy-turvy state of social rules after divorce, we must look again at the contrast between your pre- and post-divorce relationship. In marriage, trust is fundamental. In fact, a basic function of the legal marriage contract is to cement the inherent mutual promise "I trust you will not leave, hurt, or betray me." But after divorce, the legal affirmation of trust has been withdrawn. Most men seem to understand this change, but women are often under the delusion that mutual trust still exists.

For example, Ted asks Gloria to pick up the children from his house and take them to soccer practice. She doesn't want to but trusts that if she's nice to him he'll do something nice for her. Turnabout is fair play, after all.

A week or so later, Gloria's wallet is stolen, and with it her gasoline credit card. Part of her divorce settlement stipulated that Ted would pay for her gas, on the grounds that she would be doing a tremendous amount of car pooling and that her prospects for a high-paying job were poor. She tells Ted about the theft and he agrees to send away for another card. But, five weeks later she still hasn't received it. When she presses him on the matter, he tells her, "Oh, yes, it came in the mail three weeks ago. I just haven't gotten around to sending it is all." For Gloria, a clerk-typist with four children, the card is a major resource; for Ted sending it is an inconvenience, just one more detail to be handled at the office.

In their marriage, Ted and Gloria would have helped each other out with such matters even while they were arguing. But the divorce wipes out the old rules, and expecting fair play from your ex-husband makes as much sense as expecting him still to love, honor, and cherish you.

Cultivating a healthy sense of caution in dealing with an ex-husband comes hard to those women who continue to assume that mutual trust still obtains. After all, for most of us, men and women alike, the sense of fair play is not simply a matter of following the rules but a moral imperative. And indeed, many successful post-divorce interactions are consistently marked by mutual courtesy and common consideration. But with the Ex-Wife Syndrome, we are dealing with dynamics that bind women to men whom they are trying to quit permanently. Too often, these women nurture the expectations, in the face of all evidence to the contrary, that if they "do the right thing" they will be treated fairly.

Indeed, it is realistic to expect quite the opposite. Experience tells us that for a man who plays out both his marriage *and* his divorce "one step up," disrespect and diminishment are the most likely results. On a psychological level, such a strategy serves to reinforce his version of what happened and thus to protect him from the truth. Were such a man to agree to the rules of fair play, he might have to admit to and experience the pain of failing in marriage. He might even have to consider the possibility that he made a mistake in entering the marriage or in seeking the divorce. In short, where a power imbalance in the marriage put the man in control, he will have compelling self-protective reasons for *not* treating the woman fairly after the divorce since fair play is rooted in the truth and the truth, as we know, can hurt.

In the interest of facing facts, then, let me restate this hard but necessary one: to cope with the divorce and/or maintain some vestige of control, a man who was angry and abusive in his marriage will probably *never* "come around" after the divorce and begin to deal fairly with his former wife—no matter how well she treats him.

If you still hope he will, if you still treat him with impeccable fairness in the hope that he will someday see the light and help you to break free and move on, *give it up*.

1. Remind yourself that the marriage is over and that the rules of marriage no longer apply.

2. Remind yourself that not only are your ex-husband's opinions of you and your life irrelevant to you now, but they could be dangerously distorted. Cut off the flow of information about your life that might elicit his opinions.

3. Remind yourself that your main job is building your self-esteem and that looking to him for help in that area is not only misguided but dangerous. Women with the Ex-Wife Syndrome keep going back to their ex-husbands as the godlike source of their self-regard. Again and again when they return—"If I'm nice to him surely he'll . . ."—they find themselves put down or let down. So

stop being nice to him, *stop* doing for him. You need only count the favors he's done you in return to see that common courtesy is not operative here.

4. Again, rely on the business model. Don't assume; *stipulate*. Gloria would have been much better off had she made it plain, in a note or an efficient phone call, that in return for her favor in taking the kids to practice, she was expecting the credit card to be sent to her as quickly as possible. Successful business contracts rest on clear language and contingency plans to head off anticipated trouble; successful postdivorce interactions between ex-spouses are no different.

SELF-DISCLOSURE

A special word is necessary here on the common impulse among women to self-disclose. In the "normal" world, if I tell you something private about myself, something that I wouldn't tell everybody, the silent if subconscious understanding is that you will respond in kind by disclosing a truth about yourself. In this way, we come to know each other and draw closer together into what we call an intimate relationship. This exchange of information, which psychologists call *self-disclosure*, is the major tool human beings use, knowingly or not, to forge intimacy among themselves.

But the relationship between ex-spouses is unlike any other, and the formulas we're used to simply don't apply. Like Alice, you have stepped into a topsy-turvy world where familiar guidelines and models are of little use. If and when you are stricken with momentary panic at not knowing how to behave, remember that the normal process of socialization does not prepare you—or indeed any woman—for the world of divorce.

So here's an essential rule to steer by: *do not self-disclose to your ex-husband—ever*. Self-disclosure creates intimacy, and intimacy is the opposite of what you are trying to achieve. That in itself is a good reason to follow this basic rule. But there is another, more self-protective reason for playing it close to the vest. Intimate self-disclosure should be based on the trust you have in your listener—and trust means that the person in question intends you no harm and wishes you well. But you can no longer trust that your ex-husband is concerned about you and your well-being. In the divorce experience, there are too many factors that set you at cross-purposes. This means that, far from engendering intimacy, by self-disclosing you may well be handing over ammunition that could be used against you in a future conflict. Don't kid yourself. Keep your secrets safe, and reserve your trust for your friends.

If you answer yes to most or all of these questions, you may be assuming a level of mutual trust with your ex-husband that isn't there.

1. When you do a favor for your ex-husband, do you expect the same in return?
2. When he disappoints you, do you find yourself making excuses for him?
3. Do you find yourself hurt and angry when he has behaved unfairly but trusting him anew once he becomes "reasonable" again?
4. Do you still have a strong need to believe you can trust him?

2. *"We can still be friends."*

Many, many divorced women make this statement to me, in the form of either a wish or an assertion. But trying to be friends with your ex is a great way to sabotage the critical work of disengagement. Just as the woman expecting or hoping for fair play maintains and even nurtures the bond by setting up expectations that can only be disappointed, so the woman who seeks to be friends with her ex-husband promotes the sort of interactions that can only feed the Ex-Wife Syndrome.

Unfortunately, the "we-can-still-be-friends" fantasy is frequently reinforced by society, which holds up the "amicable divorce" as the ideal, if only "for the sake of the children." Occasionally one runs across magazine articles about merry two-family holiday gatherings where ex-spouses and their new spouses socialize happily. These articles are generally studded with breathless observations about the good fortune of the friendly foursome's children.

The mental health profession, too, sometimes points to the amicable divorce as the goal. In *Living and Loving After Divorce*, for example, Catherine Napolitine describes her own relationship with her ex-husband:

> *And he still flirts with me . . . He also tantalizes me about his life. He'll mention where he had dinner with his "lady friend." He'll let me know he's tired because he came in from a party at six-thirty .. Recently he gave Nicky [their son] some silky bikini underwear he didn't want anymore. I felt he was subtly letting me know that he was now wearing sexy bikini pants and not his married boxer shorts anymore!*
> *I think that all of this is relatively harmless . . .*

One fact alone, highlighted and substantiated by research, is enough to alert us to the perils of harboring such a relationship with your ex. In her ongoing study of ninety-eight divorced couples, researcher Constance Ahrons found that 12 percent, or one pair in eight, could be categorized as "perfect pals." These couples reported that they "enjoyed each other's company and tended to stay involved in each other's lives, phoning to share exciting news, for example. They were also very child-centered and tried to put their children's interests ahead of their own anger and frustration. Many had joint custody and"—here comes the significant fact for our purposes—"*none were remarried or living with someone*" [italics mine].

Ahron attributes the fact that her perfect pals remained single to their child-centeredness, but my experience suggests that interest in the children's welfare is a constant among *most* divorced adults with children, regardless of how they interact. I would hazard to predict that the reason none of these subjects married or formed significant sexual relationships following divorce was *because* they hadn't completely severed the marriage bond.

In the context of the Ex-Wife Syndrome, it becomes clear that idealizing friendship between ex-spouses is dangerous. For many people, indeed, such friendship is clearly impossible; the former spouses can't stay in the same room with each other without a conflict brewing. For others, where the divorce went smoothly, or "amicably," friendship is possible, but its potential threat to a woman's growing autonomy seems too great.

WHEN YOU CANNOT BE FRIENDS

To see why friendship is not possible for some divorced couples, consider the components of a friendship:

mutual respect
trust
free-flowing communication
honesty
a mutual enjoyment of being together

It is clear when you see them listed that the ingredients of a successful friendship are the very qualities necessary for a successful marriage. With such a foundation, a marriage can weather any crisis. Without it, scratch the surface of a surviving marriage and you will find one in deep trouble. And if it didn't work as a marriage, there is no basis for a friendship, no soil in which warmth and mutual trust can suddenly take hold. Continuing to hope or expect that it will flies in the face of reality and provides a breeding ground for disappointment and frustration. Still, as I have made clear, if you have children they will link you to your ex-husband for life, and you will have to come up with a style of relating that works.

To be free of the Ex-Wife Syndrome and the thousands of disappointments that attend a relationship burdened with unmet expectations, the business model is the only viable option. Business associates do not need to feel affection for each other to accomplish their goals and execute their agreed-upon duties, and neither do you, as ex-spouses. All business people need to be is *civil*, and clear about the work at hand. And that's all you need too. Expecting, wishing for, or dreaming about more impedes disconnection and delays the season of freedom.

WHEN YOU SHOULDN'T BE FRIENDS

The case for not remaining friends is clear-cut when ex-spouses have difficulty remaining civil, let alone friendly, during necessary interactions. But when the marriage and subsequent divorce experience weren't abusive, and where an air of mutual cordiality or warmth survives, many women feel a strong temptation to nurture a friendship with their ex, attempting to salvage the best of the relationship—a little companionship, a little sympathetic support, a few laughs—while they let the rest of it go.

Be warned: a carefully nurtured friendship like this can mask a damaging bond to your ex-husband the way a painkiller can mask a serious illness. Remember that your primary job now is to find a way to relate to your ex-husband that permits your autonomy to flourish. Any other goal grows suspect, given the risks.

"Oh, risks!" patients have scoffed. "We're civilized beings, and we're merely attempting to act like civilized beings. There's never been anything wrong with being friends." But there has—when it puts you at risk of sustaining a destructive connection. Here, specifically, are the dangers inherent in cultivating a friendly relationship with your ex:

1. You become highly vulnerable to hurt—much more so than with a normal friend. When he says to you, "Let's be friends," ask yourself: is it possible to erase ten or twenty years of intimacy and replace them with a newly forged relationship free of your shared history? The answer is always no, and part of the baggage you carry together is a profound knowledge of how to hurt each other. After years of marriage, your new "friend" has in his possession a full battery of the weapons that can devastate you emotionally. Cultivating the friendship puts you back on the firing line.

2. By entering friendship you enter another realm in which you

can be manipulated by guilt. Whereas before you were open to accusations that you were being a bad wife, now you open yourself to accusations that you are being a bad friend. Given your history and your decision to exit the scene, why render yourself vulnerable to emotional manipulation all over again?

3. If the wished-for friendship doesn't work out—for the above reasons or because, for example, his new wife won't put up with it—the experience of loss is inevitable. By now you know that healing from a loss is no light matter. Does it make sense to lose him as a husband and *then* risk losing him as a friend?

The healthy alternative is to express your civility in a businesslike way: use a friendly voice, but minimize the chitchat and limit your relationship to externals, rigorously excluding the sharing of intimacies, secrets, and personal feelings from your interchanges. The result will be the neutralizing of that emotional charge that is the source of pain in women who are still connected emotionally.

Some women, inevitably, will decide that this approach is too restrictive and will go as far as they can to cultivate and maintain some form of friendship with their ex-husbands. If you are one of them, at least keep watch for the danger signals that may crop up over time:

1. *You begin to feel obligated*—that is, you begin to feel you *should* do him certain favors, the favors friends do for each other, whenever he asks.

2. *You feel taken advantage of.* The boundaries you've set start to give way and, for instance, he begins spending too much time at the house, taking things back to his place without discussing them with you, changing the visiting schedule, and so on.

3. *You become jealous.* He begins to get serious with another woman and you feel left out, for example. Remember, this is the man you divorced.

4. *You find yourself newly drawn to him.* Encouraged by your friendship, you start to congratulate yourself on how well it's going and to fantasize about how much closer you could be.

5. *You are constantly stirred up emotionally.* Frequent feelings of anger, jealousy, loneliness, excitement are signs that your new "friend" is really getting to you.

6. *You're bored by other men*—because you're being "loyal" to your former husband and new friend.

All these danger signs have one thing in common—they are the signals that the emotional connection is deepening and drawing you to your ex-husband more and more tightly. I'm not a doomsayer, but it's part of my job to scrupulously point out risks. Hoping for and seeking out a friendship with your former husband are risky situations. If you flirt with them, keep a wary eye on yourself or someday down the line you'll be facing the hard work of disconnecting all over again.

If you answer yes to most or all of these questions, you may be hoping for a friendship that could limit your freedom.

1.   Do you continue to confide in your ex-husband, and does he confide in you?
2.   Are you ever hurt, angered, or disappointed by information he shares with you about his life?
3.   Is he judgmental or critical (in the name of caring) of your behavior?
4.   Does your "friendship" with your ex-husband interfere with or irritate new men in your life?
5.   After seeing or speaking to him, do you often feel sad?

3.   *"He understands the support arrangement the way I do—as a portion of my bona fide income."*

Marlene's daughter, Vicki, was graduating from junior high, and Marlene bought graduation pictures from the school photographer. Donald, Marlene's former husband, called to demand angrily, "Where are my pictures?" "You have to order them," said Marlene, "just the way I did. You have to order them from the company." Donald exploded. "And just where do you think the money came from that paid for 'your' pictures?" Marlene hung up, furious and shaking. In a flash she saw the pattern. Whenever Donald came over he took food from the refrigerator as if he were in his own home. Suddenly she knew that he felt the food was *his*, the pictures were *his*. He believed everything she bought was *his*!

The money you receive from your former husband may be called child support, maintenance, or alimony. Whatever it is called, when it comes to you it is yours. The check is made out to you, not to the children, and the court issues no guidelines as to how it should be spent. Obviously, you will use the money to maintain the children and your household, but you have the legal discretion to dispose of it in any way you see fit, without reporting your spending habits to anyone.

Nevertheless, many men perceive the situation differently, seeing the money or the things you buy with it as belonging to the children—and, by extension, to them. Some men acknowledge this feeling outright, but others who do not still harbor it. So if your ex-husband seems unreasonably angry with you and you're not sure why, look at his attitude about his support payments. Could he be viewing you as spending "his" money unwisely? Might he resent the fact that "his" money is contributing to your well-being while feeding and clothing his children? This is the kind of riddle you can't solve until you have stripped yourself of your own fantasies and wishes. It isn't enough to hope his attitudes about the support payments converge with yours. Understanding that his attitudes may differ from yours and, further, that any resentment he has about payment is immaterial as long as he pays on time, will free you from a nagging sense that you might have "done something wrong."

If you answer yes to these questions, you could be harboring a myth about how your ex-husband views your financial arrangements.

1.   Do your children believe that Dad pays for everything?
2.   Does he tell the children he pays for everything?

3. Does he get angry when he finds out you purchased something for yourself or you go on vacation?
4. If he is allowed to enter your house, does he help himself to anything he wants (food, washing machine, for instance) without asking permission?
5. Does he question you about how you spend money?

4. *"If I'm really in a jam, no matter how much he hates me, how terribly he treats me, or how thoroughly remarried he is, he'll be there for me— financially, emotionally, and any other way I need him."*

Many, many women stay connected to their ex-husbands on the basis of this single myth alone. For them, the cord back to him is still the lifeline, and it's still pumping life's blood into the relationship. Even when the man is hurtful, cruel, apathetic, or completely uninterested, a woman connected in this way will maintain the relationship because she subconsciously believes her survival depends on him. This myth is particularly prevalent in women who were raised to think of themselves as helpless and to conceive of a husband as a surrogate father.

Irene, one of my interviewees, has maintained a connection with her ex-husband for sixteen years for exactly this reason. Although their children are grown and have families of their own, Irene calls George once or twice a month to keep him updated on her life. This is a matter of habit with her, a habit she hasn't once considered breaking since the divorce. In our interview, I asked her to recount the instances in which George had come through for her in a crisis. Her response indicated that she has handled many of her life crises very well on her own. When George reacted at all, his intervention either proved useless or made matters worse. When Vicki, their teenage daughter, ran away and left a note, Irene called George and said, "What should I do?" even though she *knew* very well what she should do. The buried reason for her call was to solicit his emotional support. Instead, he berated her: "I *knew* this would happen," he yelled. "You've always been so strict with her, she was bound to bolt. Now, *where is she?*" Afterward, Irene collected her thoughts and called on Vicki's friends until she located her daughter, but all the time her hands and voice were shaking with unexpressed anger at George and fear of his wrath.

In our talk, it became clear that the phone call had made a difficult situation much worse, and several other incidents she recounted fit the same pattern. In my entire sample, in fact, very few women were able to report that their ex-husbands came through for them even intermittently in crises. Most of the men were completely involved in their new lives and would have been absolutely amazed to learn that the women who had divorced them continued to view them as primary emergency resources.

The healthy alternative is to learn to orient yourself away from reliance and toward the practical development of your own resources. Here are some suggestions: look for a job; build a backup system of child care to reduce your vulnerability to life's unexpected lightning bolts; make a realistic assessment of how your family could help you in ways you would feel comfortable accepting; invest in career counseling; investigate psychotherapy; join a divorce group. I'm aware that developing your resources in this way can be a lifework, but this is the lifework you have already undertaken, since life as a mature, self-reliant adult requires a constant search for relevant materials and skills.

Use your answers to these questions to help disclose any hidden dependency on your ex's readiness to "come through."

1. When you have a problem, is your first instinct to call your ex-husband?
2. How many times has he actually come through for you?
3. When he *has* helped you, has he exacted a sexual, emotional, or other kind of price?
4. Does your sense of security rely on your belief in his "coming through"?
5. Do you believe that he is the *only one* in your life who can help you if you are in a jam?

5. *"I can still have a relationship with his family."*

Joanne lost her mother at age five, and when she married Bryon, she and Bryon's mother formed the kind of mother-daughter bond

Joanne had always missed. After the divorce, the two women remained close—in fact, their relationship didn't change very much at all.

I've seen a few situations in which women remain close to their sisters-in-law or mothers-in-law after the divorce. But successfully sustaining such closeness depends upon a special set of circumstances, in which the woman-to-woman relationship has developed independently of the marriage, usually in response to deep psychological needs on the part of one or both women.

If you have such a special relationship with members of your ex-husband's family, I'm not suggesting you give it up. But you must be cautious and extremely observant. You must lay down the same ground rules here about passing on information and giving advice that you've made with your own family members. Well meaning as your mother-in-law or sister-in-law may be in telling you about your ex's new car, new wife, or new baby, such information is poison if you're attempting to neutralize the emotional charge between you. You know what your needs are, and you must be the one to lay down the law.

There are good reasons why such separate and special relationships with ex-in-laws are rare. The old adage "blood is thicker than water" has real meaning; for example, when disputes arise, mothers are more likely to believe sons than daughters-in-law, and sisters tend to believe brothers. What a woman needs in a contentious situation is *allies*, and her ex-husband's family is about as unlikely a source as you can name.

Some women pursue friendships with their ex-husband's family hoping that this will please the man and elicit better treatment. That is a total myth. Remember, we're in the postdivorce world now. Whereas your closeness with his family might have endeared you to him within your marriage, after the divorce it might well irritate or even enrage him—not to mention his new spouse or girlfriend. If you're using closeness to his family as a strategy, forget it and concentrate on strategies for disengaging and moving on.

Use these questions to help determine whether you are using your ex's family as a road to closeness with him.

1. Do you feel you are supposed to retain a relationship with your ex-in-laws?
2. Do you believe that your ex-husband will "behave" if you have a relationship with his family?
3. Do you believe he will like you more if you maintain that relationship?
4. Do you believe his family can be objective about the divorce and postdivorce situation?
5. Are you afraid his family will dislike you?

6. *"I need a man to take control of my life (i.e., "I can't take care of myself.")*

If this myth is true for you, remind yourself that though the male-female power imbalance is built into our culture, each woman must right it on her own. Even if you were socially conditioned to believe you needed male guidance, even if this erroneous belief was built into the very architecture of your marriage, as a single woman with a life to live and decisions to make, you can no longer afford to believe this dangerous, self-defeating myth. Not only will a woman who believes this continue to rely on her ex-husband, but she is likely to allow other men—her father, brother, even her son—to take control of her life after divorce. Suddenly she will have regressed even *further* back than marriage—into her childhood, when any male was granted more intelligence and authority than she.

True, in taking control of your life you may make mistakes. But who doesn't? Men certainly do, though they are raised to be reticent about admitting it. The fact is, corny as it sounds, mistakes are the greatest teachers, for they require rectifying, and in searching for solutions we grow.

Use these questions to help determine whether you believe deep down you need a man to take control of your life.

1. Do you continue to let your ex-husband make decisions that affect your life?

2. Do you consistently turn to other men in your life (father, brothers, new men) when you have problems?
3. Do you have little confidence in women in general?
4. Do you treat your own decisions as stopgap measures, not the final word in solving your problems?
5. Do you dismiss your female friends' suggestions as untrustworthy or "too emotional"?

7. *"I can be friends with his new wife."*

With a shining face and a big smile, Grace told me about "the strangest thing that happened." She had gone to a wedding she had dreaded for many months, knowing she would see her ex-husband with his new wife there. Grace had never met the wife and had never wanted to, but . . . "You know what, Sandra? I really liked her. We had a kind of gossip session about Jack and ended up laughing hysterically about what he looks like when he wakes up in the morning. I don't think I've *ever* gotten to laugh like that with anybody about Jack. She's really a doll and, you know, she needs a friend almost worse than I do, being married to that bum!"

All my internal alarms went off, and Grace could see the answer in my eyes before I said it (of course, she knew it herself all along): currying favor with your ex-husband's wife or girlfriend is a form of cultivating the connection with your husband.

Forget it. Friendship under these conditions is impossible, and even to attempt it is self-destructive. Behind a woman's urge to be friends with her ex-husband's wife is the unconscious goal of developing a new role for herself in her ex-husband's family unit. She's making herself what I call a "shadow wife," who hovers in the background of the marriage, making herself present in an ethereal kind of way. It's a definite role but one that leads nowhere; its function consists of standing passively behind the new wife and peering over her shoulder. The only active part about it is that it keeps the woman actively involved in the ex-husband's life—and that, of course, is exactly what she must stop herself from doing if she is to complete the divorce and move on.

One of my clients managed to make herself mentor to her ex-husband's young, glamorous, but highly inexperienced wife. My client had convinced herself that offering her wisdom to the younger woman was a valuable, even generous service. I asked her what on earth *she* could be getting from the association. Why, affirmation, she told me—affirmation of the wisdom that she'd gained from her greater experience. And what did they talk about? To what did the wisdom pertain? A self-mocking smile came over her face. Why, Herb, of course. Wasn't she, after all, an expert on Herb? Indeed, the lofty sessions in which mother-figure passed her wisdom to daughter-figure were really indulgent gossip sessions about Herb. With every gabfest, my client was binding herself more tightly to her ex-husband's life. Had she not wised up and broken off with the new wife, she may have ended up like the woman who routinely found herself baby-sitting for her ex-husband's (and new wife's) child.

Use these questions to help determine whether you've been using the new wife as a road to your ex-husband.

1. Do you feel embarrassed when you tell people about your relationship with your ex-husband's new wife?
2. Do you ever feel jealous of her in any way?
3. Do you spend large amounts of time discussing your ex with her?
4. If you spend time with her, do you really like her or do you just like hearing about him?
5. Do you compare yourself to her?

8. *"It will all be better when he remarries."*

Since her divorce Ruth has had nothing but trouble from her ex-husband. They simply cannot exchange the kids or handle routine interactions without arguing and wiping each other out emotionally. But rather than face the fact that the worst conditions of the marriage have persisted unchanged beyond divorce, Ruth believes that if she can just stick it out until Randall's forthcoming marriage, *her* life will improve dramatically, automatically.

But far from solving her problems, Randall's marriage creates a new, undreamed-of level of conflict. His new wife appears irritated, even threatened, by Ruth's presence in Randall's life, and her resentment shows in her dealings with Ruth's children. Moreover, Ruth discovers that Randall's new financial obligations make him even more intractable about money matters.

Waiting for remarriage to somehow miraculously cure your woes is a corollary to that common fantasy discussed earlier—"After my divorce, all my problems will be over"—and equally untrue. Remember the relief, the celebration, at the formalization of the divorce? Remember the slow fading of relief in the face of dawning reality? As you now well know, getting divorced is only the first step, and your ex's remarrying won't magically whisk you through the disconnection process. The real work is to practice the strategies discussed in this book, tailor them to fit your situation, and *do it now*. If you wait for some outside force to break your connection—either the decree itself or his marriage, the birth of his next child, even his *death*—you're waiting too long. This is not a dress rehearsal; it's your only life.

Use these questions to determine whether you're expecting your ex-husband's marriage to solve your problems.

1. Do you believe that when your ex remarries he will no longer attempt to control or upset you?
2. Do you believe that his new wife will be sympathetic toward your situation?
3. Do you feel that he will be happier when he remarries and therefore nicer to you and the children?
4. Do you believe he will be more generous when he remarries?
5. Do you believe he will still be there for you when he remarries and that all the troubling aspects of your interactions will drop away?

9. *"When I remarry it will all be okay."*

This fantasy is a variation on the preceding one, but in fact, in some cases remarriage can dramatically alleviate the Ex-Wife Syndrome. There is a tendency, after all, for ex-husbands to back off when another man is solidly in the picture, and a woman can enjoy the benefits of this side effect of remarriage without in any way exploiting her new husband. If the new marriage is a healthy one, the new husband's loyalty and the sense of unity with his wife will result in an experience of family—from which the ex will be wholly excluded.

A cloud floats over this pretty picture though if the woman tries to conceal the particulars of a troubling relationship with her ex-husband from the new one or from a close boyfriend. Concealing facts in a marriage is always a bad idea, but when a woman is struggling to break a destructive connection, keeping the struggle secret can cloud the new relationship and deprive the woman of the blessed relief of sharing the facts fully. If you are involved with a man with whom you hope to have a future, I strongly recommend educating him about the Ex-Wife Syndrome and apprising him of the details of your problem. In the disconnection process, you're fighting for your very freedom to live and love. Cutting the new man out of so central an effort is to compromise the closeness between you—once more, for the sake of your ex. This is not to say that you should enlist the new man to fight your battles; rather, you let him know they exist.

Use these questions to help determine whether you are relying on your new marriage to end the old connection instead of working on the health of the new and the dismantling of the old.

1. Do you believe your ex will automatically have a healthy respect for your marriage and new husband?
2. Do you believe he will finally stop trying to control you when you remarry?
3. Do you believe he will finally stop "playing games" with you because there will be a new husband on the scene?
4. Do you believe when you remarry you should keep your new husband out of the situation between you and your ex?

5. Do you feel that you need to remarry in order to resolve your problems with your ex?

10. *"I'm a failure because I'm divorced," or "There must be something wrong with me."*

Many a divorced woman sees herself as a flop because she was raised with the idea that marriage was her lifework. This feeling is generally reinforced by her parents, whose old-fashioned view of marriage she probably adopted whole. And it can be doubly reinforced by her ex-husband if he sees in her tendency to blame herself a means of getting off easy.

Such a woman is frozen in her view of herself—she looks in the mirror and failure is all she sees. When I treat a recovering woman who still has this view, it's my job to help break up the ice by suggesting another version of reality, one that is not only healing but is also *true* in most cases. Women tend to forget that getting a divorce takes a tremendous amount of courage. Any woman considering divorce is looking at brutally difficult financial, emotional, parenting, social, and psychological issues. No one argues with this, but the question is *why?* Why take on these trials and enormous risks? What's the payoff?

The answer, if you need to be reminded—and women plagued by a sense of failure do—is *to pursue the right to happiness.* Rather than resign herself to a miserable but familiar marriage, the woman who divorces has decided to face the unknown and begin to seek ways of leading a more fulfilling and satisfying life.

But what of the woman who had no say in the divorce, whose husband left her, perhaps for another woman? Consider smart, funny, fast-talking Rebecca. Twelve years ago, she rose up from the remains of her marriage, which ended when her husband, Sam, left her for another woman, to breathe life into the cottage industry they had together—handcrafting leather handbags. In three years, her company had a strong international trade in one-of-a-kind leather goods. Rebecca is well read, well connected, and well loved by friends and family. But she calls herself a failure in love, and not once since her divorce has she even looked at another man. "I

couldn't make Sam happy," she told me. "I couldn't do whatever
it is people do to make marriage work. And if I couldn't do it with
him, how am I going to do it with somebody else? I'm not going
through *that* again," she says, referring to the trauma of being
abandoned. "I just don't have 'it,' that's all."

Most women are experts in finding a way to shoulder all the
blame for difficulties in "love." It should be clear by now that,
although both parties contribute to the collapse of most marriages
to one degree or another, women blame themselves completely
because they were raised to feel solely responsible for the well-
being of the relationship. So Rebecca has a definite theory about
why her husband left her: it was *all* her fault.

Very often, however, a man's reasons for leaving have nothing
to do with his wife as a person at all. A lot of men leave for their
own reasons—midlife crises, a mad love affair, a longing for more
experience of the world. If you are a self-blamer, it's important that
you lift your head and look around in order to acknowledge the
complexity of the world. If a man is having a problem with his
self-esteem that he thinks only a twenty-two-year-old woman can
fix, face facts! If you're forty, you can't be twenty-two. You can
be wonderful, nurturing, interesting, smart, funny, beautiful, sexy,
intriguing . . . but you can't be twenty-two, and there's no point
in blaming yourself for it.

Take Fred, who feels overwhelmed by the responsibilities of
married life, as do many men who seek divorce. The children are
past babyhood now, and real nuts-and-bolts parenting has replaced
baby care, which he enjoyed. And the details of running a household—they're endless! The lawn, the plumbing, the *financing*! He
feels unable to keep up; he's tearing his hair out.

"I'm not happy," he says to Alice. "We don't have a relationship
anymore—in fact, we haven't in years. The sex hasn't been good
for longer than that, and the house is dirty, we order out too much,
and you don't understand me at all. I've tried and tried, I really
have. I even went to that marriage encounter thing with you that
weekend. I've grown, you haven't. You care more about the children than you do about me . . ."

In short, "You should have done better, bye-bye."

And Alice buys it.

Suddenly *she's* mowing the lawn, taking the kids to the doctor, having the roof fixed, and so on.

Only *she* has no way out.

For Fred, divorce is a divestiture. Once it's accomplished, he has only to write a check once a month; that's the extent of his obligation to Alice and the children. Otherwise, he's free to pursue the simplest life he can devise for himself. No longer is he mowing the lawn, taking the kids to the doctor, sorting through stacks of invoices with Alice on those awful bill-paying nights. He's free!

I don't have to tell you that this story is a very common one. What I may have to point out, however, is that when a divorce comes about in this way, it does not reflect on the woman's skill as a nurturer, lover, woman, or wife. If Fred is so emotionally weak that he chooses to duck out of the less exciting aspects of adult life, how does that reflect on Alice? The answer is, *not at all*. Alice may have had her own complaints, and she may have contributed to the marital problems. But when a man throws up his hands and runs out, it in no way follows that the woman has failed.

If you feel you're a failure just because you have divorced, remind yourself that ideally marriage is a two-party contract. You can draw a man to marriage but you cannot make him share—especially when by walking out he can materially improve his life to a truly staggering degree. Furthermore, you can recognize your *own* mistakes without consigning yourself to a lifelong sense of failure. Forgiveness begins at home—with yourself.

Use these questions to help you determine whether you equate divorce with failure—*your* failure.

1. Do you believe that in general women are responsible for their divorces to a greater degree than men are?
2. Do you believe you should have been able to endure your marriage longer, that you bailed out too soon?
3. Do you believe that everyone who counts in your life is disappointed in you because you are divorced?

4. Do you feel that everyone new you meet sees you as a failure because you are divorced?

5. Were you raised to believe that "good women" *never* get divorced?

As you let go of the deep, residual myths, fantasies, and wishes that have been crowding your inner landscape—those we've examined and others, you will discover yourself—you'll be amazed at how spacious and inviting the external world begins to seem. There's a whole universe out there, and you'll find that you can see what it offers more clearly as the symptoms of the Ex-Wife Syndrome recede.

For a divorced woman with no children, stepping out into the social and sexual arenas becomes the next concern, and I address this in chapter eight. But for a divorced woman who is also a mother, once she has begun to heal herself no single problem looms so large and perplexing as how to ensure a good life for her children in the aftermath of divorce. Therefore, in the next chapter I turn to the complex, often daunting challenge of single parenting.

7

THE NEW MATRIARCH

Since the early seventies, when divorce rates began to skyrocket, we as a society have tended to treat divorce as a temporary phenomenon, something we expected would eventually settle down and go away. We seemed to believe that adjustments would be made, attitudes would alter, and marriage as an institution would adapt so that the divorce figures would flatten out. We are slowly coming to realize, however, that the figures aren't going to change dramatically and, moreover, that the female-headed family is an alternate life-style that's here to stay.

With our acceptance of this situation, a new task becomes imperative: we must examine child-rearing as it occurs in this alternative life-style and come up with guidelines for bringing up our children effectively. In this book, the word *effectively* connotes, among other qualities, self-reliance, self-confidence, and autonomy on the mother's part.

Many divorced women who head their own households are still parenting on the two-parent model. Intellectually they know there's no father on the scene, but emotionally they're still mothering *as if* Dad were there. In the traditional marriage, a mother's discipline might take the form of freezing the frame when a problem arises and "waiting for your father to come home." If any stance were custom-designed to perpetuate the Ex-Wife Syndrome in the divorced woman, this is it.

Divorced women who continue to parent in this style thwart themselves doubly: by keeping their ex-husbands constantly in their awareness and by undermining their sense of competence as parents. As a result, they feel disadvantaged, even victimized, by their altered domestic circumstances, and those feelings reinforce the Ex-Wife Syndrome.

Let's take an inventory of the circumstances again, keeping in mind that divorce is here to stay. At this writing, as summed up by Judith Wallerstein, statistics tell us that "one in two recent marriages can be expected to end in divorce. Children born in the mid-1980s stand a 38 percent chance of experiencing their parents' divorce before they reach age eighteen." Divorce is no longer an aberration, it's a norm. You and your family are not weird or different; you're part of the mainstream. Look around you. Female heads of household are everywhere.

But here's the corollary: the parenting role you now play is significantly different from the one you played as a mother in a two-parent family—different and much greater. You are no longer just a mother; you are a *matriarch*.

In a two-parent family, *matriarch* and *patriarch* are ugly, challenging words. When there is a patriarch, there can be no matriarch, and vice versa; the terms don't suggest a fair division of power.

But within your one-parent family, you are the primary possessor of the power to control—and the full bearer of responsibility for—your family's fate. Here the term *matriarch* is appropriate because it embraces this notion of power. In fact, it embraces the principles discussed individually in this book: your claim to your own home and privacy, your right to set the household rules, your goal to minimize and neutralize your interactions with your ex-husband to enhance your own autonomy, and your authority in decision making as the family's sole responsible adult.

The father, if he is interested, can make suggestions about major decisions affecting the children, but it falls to you to decide if those suggestions fit into the pattern of your household. *Yours is the final word*. In this short sentence lies the source of your strength—the source of potential strength for every divorced mother running her own household and ready to assume the role and responsibility of the new matriarch.

Let's look at an example of how this new matriarchy works. Johnny asks his mother, Rachel, if he can miss school tomorrow because his friend's parents have invited him to the Cubs game. She tells him she'll think it over. On his next visit with his father, Dan, Johnny asks the same question. Dan calls Rachel. "You know, I'm really against John's missing school. He's just not doing well enough." But Rachel knows her son's doing fine at school, that he's showing a real concern about getting his assignments completed and that he hasn't missed much this year. And she's aware that she knows these facts better than Dan ever could, for she monitors Johnny's homework, talks with him about his classwork, speaks with his teacher, and participates in his class as a reading coach once a week, whereas Dan's sole source of information is the semester report card. So Rachel makes her decision based on the information at her fingertips: she permits Johnny to miss school.

To reinforce her role as a decisive, self-reliant parent, Rachel has made it a policy not to discuss day-to-day household problems with Johnny's father. Such deference to his opinion would only diminish her self-respect and perpetuate the Ex-Wife Syndrome, were she prone to it. Further, the self-respect she exhibits in making a confident, independent decision causes Johnny to respect her and to look to her as the source of power and responsibility in the household. Without the children's respect, the divorced mother will never achieve status as the new matriarch. And unless she demonstrates her capacity to decide rather than to defer to her ex-husband, she will not have the children's respect.

THE MANTLE OF POWER

Initially, some divorced women fantasize about playing out a dreamy kind of summer-camp democracy in which everyone has an equal voice. But children need direction, and to give direction mothers must be careful to retain their power as head of household. I am not talking about running a military camp; I'm advocating fair-minded, reliable parenting by a woman who trusts her own judgment.

A common inclination among divorced mothers to make their children their "best friends," with whom they discuss their personal problems and to whom they even turn for advice, puts too heavy a burden on the children while depriving them of what they need most—a mother willing to shoulder responsibility for her family and even to risk making mistakes in her effort to ensure its well-being. Sure, the children can have input into the way the household is run, but always remember that you are the adult in charge and they, after all, are children.

THE PERILS OF PERFECTION

Some women respond to the challenge of single parenting by over-compensating for what they see as their losses—losses their children must innocently suffer with them. Meet Anne, who was referred to me but put off calling for nearly a year because she "simply didn't have the time for therapy." It was true, she didn't. Anne got up every day at four-thirty to clean the five-bedroom house that had become hers in the divorce settlement. She also did a couple of loads of wash and often fixed a casserole before waking her two sons, readying them for school, and then jumping in the car to drop them off on the way to work. She was a crack legal secretary who had made herself indispensable not only to the attorney she was assigned to but to all the lawyers on her floor, and she rarely said no when they begged her to take on a rush job. At noon she squeezed in a quick workout at the gym and gulped down a yogurt and an apple. After work she sat with each son as he practiced his musical instrument—one piano, one clarinet—made dinner, and then sat down to do homework with the boys, never letting them turn in an assignment until she had made sure it was perfect. By ten o'clock, Anne was so overtired she couldn't fall asleep so she settled down in front of the television, but never without a pile of the mending she needed to do to keep her wardrobe in shape.

When Anne finally came in for therapy, it was hard to tell which benefited her most, the therapy itself or the delicious luxury of an hour a week spent just sitting in a chair and talking quietly about herself. She had been positively driven by the urge to compensate for the many ways in which her divorce had disrupted her family, and, losing all sense of proportion, she determined to be the best-dressed, prettiest, thinnest, fittest, most competent, most hard-working mom with the greatest, most demanding job and the cleanest house and car. Her underlying need was to prove to herself and the world that she was not only fine but better than fine—completely perfect.

On the face of it, this dreadful urge seemed positive to Anne. Subconsciously, as a typical overcompensator, she was out to prove to herself, her children, and anyone else who looked that she was strong and unaffected by the experience of divorce. But her obsessive dieting, exercising, grooming, mothering, and housekeeping—in short, her urgent concern with *appearances*—were clues to her overwhelming (if unconscious) sense of loss, which was draining her strength daily. When Anne came to me she was addicted to sleeping pills and on the verge of collapse.

Facing facts includes focusing on what's important. *Now* is important, not *then*. Solving problems is important, not wondering how much better things would have been *if* this and *if* that. Most of all, making your house "home free" for yourself and your children is important. And the last thing "home free" means is House Beautiful. The first thing it means is safe and secure—a haven from the outside world.

You can only answer the question of how to make your home the place you feel it should be by turning inward. Tune out the voices of others, and try to concentrate on what feels right and comfortable to *you*. Ask yourself, with pencil in hand if it helps: What colors do you like, what kind of furniture, when is it most comfortable and practical to have meals, what kinds of foods should you stock, what should be the rules on curfews, what should be the policy on bedtimes? The answers lie nowhere but inside you and your children, though you might trigger a flow of ideas by turning to books and magazines. Finally, try to accept the fact that it's okay to make a mistake. If you make a mistake in your own home, look for another solution. The objective is to build enough flexibility into your household rules and policies to make them easy to change.

The new matriarch needn't see herself as having to be the best mother and woman ever, but she should see herself as a source of protection to her children. Children fear abandonment above all, for they know they are not yet equipped to make it in the world on their own. In particular, children whose fathers have withdrawn or whose fathers confuse them by expressing ambivalence need reassurance from their mother's actions and words that she will always be there to care for them.

It should be clear to you by this point that it is precisely the ability to protect the children and offer them security that is sapped by the Ex-Wife Syndrome. The strength of a woman who is nurturing an unhealthy connection with a man who has begun a new life without her is diverted from herself and her children. If you've begun to grapple with the issues covered in the preceding chapters, you've undoubtedly already come a long way toward the new matriarchy as you've cast behind your old bonds.

SIGNIFICANT OTHERS IN YOUR FAMILY'S WORLD

While you must see yourself as the guardian of your children's security, you need not be the only significant person in their world. This may sound pretty basic, but far too many women—some out of pride, some out of an urge to overcompensate—are reluctant to accept help from their friends and extended families, no matter how sincere the offers. These might include offers of baby-sitting, of advice, of a strong male presence in the form of a brother or father, and of financial help.

Why refuse all help out of hand? Why not acknowledge that your situation is hard—not insurmountable, but difficult? There's a very simple rule of thumb for weighing the help families offer: if the help comes with "strings attached" in tacit exchange for the right to tell you how to raise the kids or live your life, refuse it. If the help is offered freely and if it could make a difficult situation easier for you, embrace it.

Failing to call on your family out of a fear that you will be seen as an incapable parent not only deprives you of support and aid but it deprives your children of a diversity of relationships. Entering into the extended family doesn't mean you're weak and needy. Rather, it means you're looking for other significant relationships so you and your offspring won't become isolated.

Your role as matriarch may feel like a fearsome responsibility; indeed, it is. But a wonderful thing about being a single householder is that you are not in competition for the power, authority, loyalty, and affection that are often up for grabs in a dual-parent family. Remember, setting your own rules means doing things *your* way. So the next time you're tempted to share the load or defer to your ex-husband's decision, pile your kids in the car and go see a movie— one you know he'd hate.

JOINT CUSTODY AND THE MATRIARCH

Across the country, divorced parents are increasingly agreeing to joint custody—the fifty-fifty sharing of parental time and responsibility. Generally, in a joint custody arrangement the child shifts residences on a prearranged, equal-time schedule.

If you are involved in a joint custody arrangement, you can assume the matriarchal posture when the children are with you. But if, in the end, you conclude that it is impossible to be your children's rock with the mandated judgment to share custody, consider writing a letter to your ex-husband that details your concerns. Focus on the difficulties the children are experiencing (do not men-

tion your own difficulties)—for example, "Debby is terribly unhappy because her friends have stopped calling her altogether
since they never know where she will be"; "Mark has said several
times, 'I get scared in the middle of the night because I forget
where I am' "; "the children are miserable about how much we
argue, and the only solution I can see is to minimize our interactions." Then propose that you meet to make some changes in the
arrangements—in the scheduling, in the pickup and delivery system, in the way vacations and weekends are handled—without
going back to court.

If you meet a brick wall, however, and still conclude that the
situation is untenable, you have the option of going back to court
to try to alter the arrangements. If you meet another dead end,
there is only one option open, but it is an option of considerable
force: embrace the role of matriarch, be a model of decisiveness
and self-reliance to your children whenever they are with you, and
you will have the satisfaction of knowing that at least on a part-
time basis they will be learning what you have to teach them and
benefiting from what you give.

The concept of the new matriarch is a health- and power-giving
one, and it provides a workable model for single parenting with
pride and competence. But there is no getting around the fact that
divorce can traumatize children, as it can traumatize everyone involved. A central function of the single mother's role is to monitor
her children constantly for any difficulties they might be having in
adjusting to their new status as "kids of divorce."

It is outside the scope of this book to serve as a primer on children's psychological adjustment to divorce or as a troubleshooter
on developmental problems related to divorce. There are many fine
books on these subjects, and if you are having difficulties with your
children and need professional guidance, you could find no more
fruitful beginning than turning to one of them. (See the list at the
end of this chapter for suggestions.) This book focuses on your role
in your children's adjustment to their altered life circumstances and
their restructured relationship with their father. Like you, your

children have to learn new patterns of relating to their father that reflect the postdivorce arrangements. Helping them cope with the difficulties that inevitably arise *while protecting your own hard-won emotional well-being* is a central part of your new role.

MONITORING THE FATHER-CHILD RELATIONSHIP

It's no easy task to monitor and assess the children's relationship with a man no longer on the scene—the information that comes through can be very sketchy and contradictory. Yet if you are in recovery from the Ex-Wife Syndrome, the last thing you can afford to do is increase your contact with their father in order to pump him for information. From that quarter, then, you may not get much beyond hints and obscure (and sometimes deceitful) clues about the true nature of the father-child relationships.

For this reason, you'll need to depend heavily on your observations of the children and their own reports in order to piece together a true picture of what's going on. Watch their moods and behavior carefully after they return from visits or have conversations with him, and think hard about their comments. What does it mean when a seventeen-year-old son says, "I really feel sorry for dad. He just doesn't have it" or when an eleven-year-old daughter slams down the phone and whispers, "Dad really makes me sick"? A mother needs to be alert to situations developing between father and child that require her intervention, and she must be ready to take action.

Remember, however, that any interchange about the children between divorced parents is a potential minefield. In no other context is the need to stay centered and in control more critical, and in no other context is the effort more difficult. Here are some specific guidelines:

1. Avoid face-to-face meetings.
2. Take the initiative to set up a phone appointment so you're not caught off guard and unprepared.

3. Write down the points you want to cover.
4. Arm yourself with information you want to get across, and keep your notes close by.
5. Work as hard as you can at keeping the emotional charge out of your voice and out of the discussion. The tone is to be one of business, devoid of personal feelings. If things get hot, hang up.
6. Stay strictly to the issues. Don't allow yourself or him to go off onto tangents. "I've called because Johnny's doing poorly in math and needs a tutor. We'll need to come to some financial arrangement on it."
7. Back up your discussion with as much outside information as you can, such as teachers' reports and counselors' opinions. Use this information to strengthen your position.
8. Focus on the child and on his or her preferences and expressed desires.
9. If your ex becomes irrational or overwhelms you, end the meeting and get off the phone. Tell him you'll call him again at a specific time, and let him know you expect him to be more civil then.
10. If the meeting doesn't work out, write a letter.

Most divorced mothers don't need a book to encourage them to watch their children closely. If anything, they tend to be hyper-vigilant for signs of emotional damage—at the expense of losing sight of the children's individual identities and stages of development. It is true that divorce is traumatic for everybody, and it is true, as I will discuss, that long-term problems are a risk. But not every child-rearing problem—not every broken rule, fresh remark, or temper tantrum—has its roots in divorce. It's important to remember *who your children are* as you assess their psychological response to the changes in their lives.

One happily married friend of mine has an amazingly energetic child—"a pistol," she calls him—an irrepressible six-year-old with a stubborn will of his own. When I hear her recount his adventures in trying to get his own way, I can easily imagine what she would be saying about Andrew if she were divorced: "He's so *willful*, Sandra. He needs so much attention since the divorce, and since Rob stopped visiting regularly he throws fits any time I say no." At school, a teacher or administrator might intone, "Oh, we see this acting out so often in the kids of divorce." All too often, teachers and principals leap on divorce as a convenient explanation for unconstrained behavior. The fact remains, however, that my friend's child is a delightful but willful, hard-to-handle kid; he always has been, and he probably will be until he finds some positive channels for his boundless energy and determination. Before you blame the divorce for harming your children, remind yourself of their individual personalities and their indomitable urge to be themselves.

This caveat applies to parents of children of all ages, but parents of teenagers require a special reminder about the truly radical nature of adolescence itself. Listen to one of the founders of modern child psychology, Anna Freud:

> *Adolescents are excessively egoistic, regarding themselves as the center of the universe and the sole object of interest, and yet at no time in later life are they capable of so much self-sacrifice and devotion. They form the most passionate love-relations, only to break them off as abruptly as they begin them. On the one hand they throw themselves enthusiastically into the life of the community and, on the other, they have an overpowering longing for solitude. They oscillate between blind submission to some self-chosen leader and defiant rebellion against any and every authority. They are selfish and materially-minded and at the same time full of lofty idealism. They are ascetic but will suddenly plunge into instinctual indulgence of the most primitive character. At times their behavior to other people is rough and inconsiderate, yet they themselves are extremely touchy. Their moods veer between light-hearted optimism and the blackest pessimism. Sometimes they will work with indefatigable enthusiasm and at other times they are sluggish and apathetic.*

Now, I could preface this quote with "This is the typical pathology that results from parental divorce on teenagers," and many readers would believe me. But remember, Freud is describing *normal* adolescent behavior. Who needs divorce as an excuse? Adolescence is wild enough on its own.

Nevertheless, divorce is no light matter, and protecting the children against long-term damage is a central and crucial concern. Children, like adults, go into an unavoidable crisis following divorce. They must adjust not only to the loss of the old life but (usually) to the loss of their father's daily presence and often to a new residence and a change (usually a drop) in material status. They must also adapt to a new *social* status—as a child of divorced parents.

The initial crisis takes about a year to play itself out. During that time, behavioral problems often show themselves, taking different forms depending on the child's developmental stage, the emotional environment at home, and the child's particular personality. As it does with adults, time itself helps children heal from loss and traumatic change. This is not to say that serious adjustment and long-term developmental problems cannot occur. Research confirms that two factors often account for these significant problems in the children of divorce:

1. unresolved conflict between the parents
2. desertion by the noncustodial parent, usually the father

The second factor is a delicate matter requiring extremely sensitive handling, which we will get to later on. But the first is by far the more common and the most relevant to this book. Let me state it another way: *long-term damage to the children of divorce stems primarily from the parents' inability to psychologically and emotionally end the marriage.* Sound familiar? It should. The fact is, if you suffer from the Ex-Wife Syndrome, it doesn't just hurt you—it hurts your children as well.

Conflict between ex-spouses interferes with the parenting function, and the parenting function is the only job they share once the marriage is over. The resolution of conflict—the cessation of the fighting, the pain giving, the game playing—can permit a businesslike approach to the problems of parenthood that arise inevitably over the lifetime of the child.

TELLING THE CHILDREN THE TRUTH

Marsha's husband, Randy, lied to her all the time about everything—his affairs, his finances, his plans for the future. He hated responsibility and seemed to consider marriage something like reform school—a trap he couldn't escape. Like a rebellious child, he was always making petty attempts to get away with what he could. Throughout the marriage, Marsha covered for him in front of their two children, especially about their financial difficulties. It was important to her that they think well of their dad.

After the divorce, Randy continued to pull all kinds of hurtful stunts, including finding endless reasons to withhold support payments. He manipulated the children by getting them to feel sorry for him and lied to them to get their sympathy. They saw him as a poor soul whom Marsha had driven out of the family. He hinted that she restricted his access to them, but actually Marsha spent many a night on the phone after the children were asleep tearfully begging Randy to spend more time with them. His retort was always the same: *she* was turning the kids against *him*.

Through it all, Marsha cleaned up Randy's image for the kids' benefit. He couldn't make it this time, but he'd surely make it up to them. He wasn't able to help them out this month, but he'd had a tough time and she knew he would help next month. He didn't call them when he promised, but his work was *so* unpredictable and he was working *so* hard, he must have been called away.

To borrow an apt phrase, Marsha was dancing as fast as she could. She moved in on every disappointment, every broken promise, and transformed it into an unavoidable accident right away. Predictably enough, she wound up taking all the heat. The kids blamed her for "driving our dad out," for the family's financial difficulties, and for their father's terrible visiting record. But the real deprivation they were suffering was a lack of the facts.

Many if not most mothers feel that the postdivorce family situation is so precarious, so unpredictable, and often so terrifying (not least of all to themselves) that attempting to give their children the full picture of the situation and what's led up to it will only frighten them, no matter what their ages are. This protective strategy is a common one. Elisabeth Kübler-Ross tells how parents often use it to protect a child from the full impact of a death in the family, and in her valuable book *On Children and Death* she shows what damage these well-meaning parents do. In effect, they steal from the child the chance to go through a healthy mourning period and come out on the other side. But with divorce as with any loss of a loved one, there's no getting around the initial pain. A child who is not guided through the pain is left to deal with it alone, forever. Kübler-Ross cites many stories of adults for whom this has been true—left to recover as best they could from the loss of a parent or sibling, they never recovered at all.

There are many reasons, well supported by research, to tell children the truth in an age-appropriate way as they are growing up:

1. Children are better at dealing with truth than with dishonesty and lies. Dishonesty in parents conflicts with reality and interferes with the development of the child's healthy sense of logic, which in turn will impede his or her development of judgment and decision-making powers.

2. A child who eventually finds out he or she has been lied to loses trust in the deceitful parent and, by extension, in all adults.

3. The child who does not learn a healthy respect for the truth early in life may never learn to decode reality accurately.

4. In the context of divorce, the woman who manufactures an explanation for the family's changes binds *herself* to her lie, thus

subverting any efforts she might make to face facts squarely and take effective action to end the marriage cleanly and permanently.

I could give you many, many more reasons, on moral and psychological grounds, for telling children the truth. During and after the crisis of divorce, however, leaving the children to interpret the facts as they might or offering them contrived explanations that conflict with reality puts them at particular risk. When children do not receive guidance and clear explanations from adults, they typically develop fables to make sense of what's happened to them. Adults do this too, as Sigmund Freud explains in *Totem and Taboo*:

> *There is an intellectual function in us which demands unity, connection, and intelligibility from any material, whether of perception or thought, that comes within its grasp; and if, as a result of special circumstance, it is unable to establish a true connection, it does not hesitate to fabricate a false one.*

Further, as Jean Piaget makes clear, up to the ages of seven or eight, children's thought patterns have little consistency and their tolerance for contradiction can lead to what might seem to adults to be outrageously nonsensical explanations for mysterious real-life events. Until this age, he writes, "children make no effort to stick to one opinion on any given subject." Not only can children construct exotic explanations, but they can construct and successively believe in more than one, in fact many, contradictory, exotic explanations—all of which may well be completely unknown to their parents.

So, mothers who try to protect their children from the true circumstances surrounding a divorce and their new life together actually give the children the opportunity to project all kinds of frightening and distorted fantasies to explain their world. For example, when a parent leaves or dies, the spontaneous fear that occurs to children of most ages is, "What if I lose the other parent? Then I'll be all alone." Even if your child doesn't articulate this fear, he or she might be in a constant state of anxiety from it after the breakup of your marriage.

As Margaret Mead suggests, this fear does not fall into the category of exotic fantasy but is really quite reasonable, the result of the disappearance in our culture of the extended family: "We have constructed a family system which depends upon fidelity, lifelong monogamy, and the survival of both parents," she writes. "But we have never made adequate social provision for the security and identity of the children if that marriage is broken, as it so often was in the past by death or desertion, and as it so often is in the present by death or divorce . . . 'What will happen to me if anything goes wrong, if Mommy dies, if Daddy dies, if Daddy leaves Mommy, or Mommy leaves Daddy?' are questions no American child can escape."

Marjorie, a patient of mine, had a little daughter, Angela, five, who in a matter of weeks went from happy sociability to a withdrawn sullenness. Soon Angela began waking with nightmares, and Marjorie couldn't figure out why. When this pattern continued, Marjorie took her to a child therapist who, with the help of a sand table and other play therapy techniques, discovered that the mother of one of Angela's classmates had died. Angela was so terrified that her own mother would die she was afraid even to say it. Learning the truth enabled Marjorie to reassure Angela that her mother was in good health and intended to take very good care of herself, and the girl gradually gave up her fears. But Angela may have harbored her painful secret for a very long time had Marjorie not taken action.

If you sense that your child might be harboring frightening fantasies or distorted explanations of his or her changed world, you can try a number of techniques before resorting to psychotherapy. Like all the suggestions in this chapter, these techniques are geared to match the child's cognitive and developmental levels. Although truth is truth, the *form* truth telling takes with a four- or five-year-old will obviously differ from that for a fifteen- or sixteen-year-old.

For Preschool Children (up to age five). Child psychologists often invite very young patients to indulge in doll play and then listen carefully to the stories they tell. You can do the same with your child, providing a mommy, daddy, and child doll and asking the child to tell you stories. You can help focus the child's play on a subject that concerns you by setting up the scenario—and then pulling back to let the child take over without coaching. Thus, you might sit down with the child and the dolls and say, "Daddy's dropping Joey off after taking him to play at the park. What does little Joey say? What does he feel?" If the child tells a story of how Daddy pulls away from the curb and drives straight into a scary black cave filled with monsters, you have a clue that he or she might need some accurate information and reassurance about where Daddy goes now that he no longer comes in the house but drives away and disappears.

The aim is not to play amateur psychologist but to elicit information about your child's inner world, particularly gaps in knowledge or misunderstandings about the current situation. You may not be able to alleviate all your child's anxieties (and may indeed decide to engage professional help for that purpose), but the truth itself is usually reassuring and calming in the face of such fantasies. In response to the cave story, you might answer, "Boy, I'm sure glad *your* dad has his own apartment to go to where he'll be safe and comfortable whenever he leaves here." You can then elaborate on that theme to make sure the child understands that the father doesn't simply disappear into the great unknown but has a life of his own centered around his own safe place. Even if he or she has visited the father in his own home, a child this young needs help in conceptualizing the new arrangement and may not identify the father's apartment, seen sporadically, as a safe home to which the father returns.

For Children Ages Six To Twelve. With children this age it is possible to be much more explicit about the value of understanding things as they are. You can explain what fantasies are—secret wishes or thoughts and imaginings about the way things are—and ask them to share some with you that have to do with Mommy, Daddy, our house, our lives, why we got divorced. As with adults, self-disclosure elicits self-disclosure so beginning with a fantasy of your own might ensure a more free-flowing response. You might say, for example, "I hope I'll marry again someday to a new man" or "Sometimes being a single mom is really rough because I have to make decisions on things I don't know too much about." Or— getting right down to it—"Sometimes I have the feeling you don't really like me." Kids are more likely to run with leads like this than they are to respond wholeheartedly to a vague "Tell me what you're thinking."

For Adolescents (Ages Thirteen Through Eighteen). Don't expect as much enthusiastic interchange with teenagers as you do with younger children. Adolescents are very private people, which makes it rough to bring any distortions to the surface. Self-disclosure can still be helpful, though by breaking down the automatic defenses teenagers erect against prying parents. At least it can trigger discussion of some sort, and it could turn up something that needs attention. For instance, you might offer your own fantasy related to the financial situation resulting from the divorce:

"I sure would like to get a fabulous job so I can make a lot of money and not have to ask your dad for any."

Now, listen hard. "I bet," says the teenager, "I bet you wish you were still married to Dad so things would be easier for you."

Jump on this opportunity to clarify the point. "Sometimes it's hard, and I'm having a rough time, honey, but I have no desire to be married to your father anymore. We were divorced because the marriage wasn't working, and it was exactly the right thing to do."

Children can handle the truth delivered in an age-appropriate manner. This doesn't mean you must tell your children every intimate detail, every secret, every coming and going of your private life. Rather, it means explaining everything and anything that impinges on them and that could confuse them about how well loved and safe they are. And it means delivering such truths *more than once*—delivering them repeatedly throughout their lives in a style adapted to their particular level of understanding. Children need to know and deserve to know about the divorce, their father, the household finances, the living arrangements, the court decisions, and all future plans as they become clear. If they don't learn the truth about these matters, they'll make up their own versions, and then you'll be battling *their* myths, fantasies, and wishes as well as your own!

THE TRUTH ABOUT THE DIVORCE ITSELF

Young children of preschool through school age rarely ask for a full explanation of why their parents divorced. Adolescents might ask, but they don't often stick around to hear the whole story and may cut you off with that familiar, "Okay, okay, I get the picture." But neither the failure to ask nor seeming lack of interest should be taken at face value. They don't ask and don't want to find out for the simple reason that they are afraid *they themselves* are the reason behind the divorce.

This is a perfect example of the destructive potential of "leaving well enough alone." A child's suspicion that he or she is to blame for the divorce and all the high emotion that surrounds it can fester for years and do untold damage to the self-esteem, self-image, and self-acceptance of that child.

If you have left your children with an unclear picture of why you and your former husband divorced, you have perpetuated a less-than-true explanation. A blithe "Oh, your daddy and I just stopped loving each other" or "We wanted to find out what it was like to live apart" are too vague to serve as satisfactory explanations and keep you bound to a half-truth as well.

I urge you, then, both for the good of the children and for your own sake in breaking the connection, to complete this piece of unfinished business if you have not yet done so. Even if years have passed since your divorce, if you have never explained the reasons for it truthfully to your children, you are blocking your own progress and putting them at the mercy of their own possibly self-destructive fantasies.

How, mothers will ask, are you supposed to tell your six-year-old son, for instance, that your ex-husband was unfaithful or that he beat you up? How do you tell a teenager that her father was not the kind of man she believed him to be throughout her childhood?

Whatever the age of the child, the key is to give up the habit of *protecting* the father while maintaining the urge to protect the children.

With the preschool child, you might begin by saying, "In your class at nursery school, think of all the little boys and girls you've been with. Some are real nice, and you like playing with them. But some are mean and you don't ever want to play with them because they might make you feel bad. Maybe they're nice to some of the kids, but they always act mean to you. Well, that's how it was with your dad and me. He was mean to me, and I didn't like it. So I decided we weren't going to live together anymore because I didn't want to live with somebody who hurt my feelings all the time. But you know that daddy's not mean to everybody. And he has a place of his own where he can be with you because he loves you and wants to be with you as much as he can. We figured out a way to live so that Daddy and I didn't live together anymore but that both of us could spend time with you."

With a child aged six to twelve, you can be even more explicit: "You know how you've felt with some kids you really like but who start to pick on you after a while and then to hurt you and you stop liking them? That's what happened here. I was very unhappy because your dad stopped liking anything I did, and he criticized me all the time. I decided I didn't want to live with your dad anymore because I didn't want to feel hurt and sad. We made arrangements to live apart in a way that we could both spend time with you. Your dad loves you and will always be around for you. You'll just spend time with him at his house now."

With the adolescent, straightforward, unembellished truth telling is called for: "Dad and I were very young when we got married, and we didn't know a lot about each other. As time went by, though, your dad started to criticize me all the time and to spend more time with his friends than he did with me. I could see that he didn't really want to be with me at all and that all the time we did spend together was going to be hurtful to me. All our conversations ended in an argument, there was no real love between us, and our sex life had been nonexistent for a long time—and love and sex are necessary in a marriage. I finally decided there was no point in living together anymore. In a court of law our lawyers helped us work out the living arrangements we have now so that you and I will be together here and you can be with your dad at his place."

A mother who must explain a father's obvious lack of interest in them to her children is faced with a more difficult situation. She must be very sensitive to the fact that along with prolonged, unresolved parental conflict, parental desertion can have severe consequences for the child developmentally and emotionally, a subject I will discuss in detail later in this chapter. She must be careful to balance the need for honesty and clarity with the need to protect the child against a sense of abandonment or responsibility for the father's absence. It's a delicate problem, and, sadly, a common one, but with some thought and an awareness of the issues it is possible to be both protective and honest.

With preschool children, the mother can use the example of the nursery school classroom again to help the child conceptualize through comparison. "You know how some children in school are wild and some are calm, how some laugh and are happy and some, maybe one or two, are quiet and seem sad? Daddy is like those sad little children in your class. He has a hard time being happy, and he doesn't want to make you sad by seeing you when he feels bad. The trouble is he feels bad most of the time. He loves you and wants to make you happy, but he has a lot of trouble figuring out how to be a happy person."

With a child aged six to twelve, you can explain, "Dad is sad all the time lately. He looks at everything and feels sad. You know how you feel when you look out at the rain and can't play outside that day? He feels that way all the time and doesn't want to see you because he doesn't want to make you feel sad. But his sadness has nothing to do with you. It has to do with the fact that he doesn't know how to make himself happy. He loves you very much and thinks the best thing he can do for you is to stay away when he's sad."

With the adolescent, you can say, "I need to explain something about your father. You need to know it so you don't blame yourself if he doesn't come around much or if he's unhappy when you're with him. Your father is a depressed person—this doesn't mean that he just has bad moods; it means that he's sad all the time without understanding why and without being able to change it. Everyone who loves him tries to make him happy but it doesn't work. He needs help, and maybe someday he'll get it. Until then don't expect him to spend much time with you. He loves you but feels that it's best for you if he stays away. It's his decision, you and I can't change it, but we can try to understand and live with it."

Of course your own situation is unique, and these responses may not entirely fit it, but trust me—*every* situation can be rendered accurately and age-appropriately:

"I decided it was important for me to get a job that I cared about, but your dad didn't want me to do it."

"I was very unhappy living with your father because I loved another man and felt I belonged with him."

"Your father was very unhappy living with me because he loved another woman and felt he belonged with her."

"I changed since I got married and discovered that your father's goals in life were different from my own."

"Your dad started getting angry and hurting me, and I decided we had to live apart so he wouldn't hurt me anymore."

In every case, with every candid explanation, you will have to face the consequences of the truth, and this might not be easy. You might stir up your children's anger, confusion, resentment, and protectiveness of their father. But when that happens at least you'll have an authentic argument on your hands, not a morass of deceit and playacting, as Marsha did in trying to justify Randy's behavior.

On a more positive note, each conversation on the subject will give you the opportunity to reassure your children on two basic points: they will always be loved, and they will always be taken care of. All of us, not just children, need a sense of security about the future, and no one can be reassured too frequently about it. You'll notice that the preceding sample explanations always make reference to the child's living and visiting arrangements. This lets the child know that these matters were central issues right from the beginning—that you weren't making a single move without planning for his or her security.

One final note on how to tell the truth about why you divorced: if finding the words takes creativity, keeping rancor out of them takes self-control. When I urge you to tell the truth, my emphasis is on conveying the facts, *not* on heaving the emotional baggage you've been carrying onto your children's shoulders. This is no place to vent your fury at Daddy—do that in a letter to him. Stay with the facts, and keep control of yourself. In a truth-telling session, the point is to *clarify*, not burden the children with feeling. I advise my patients to choose the timing of the sessions very carefully and to keep the purpose of the sessions—clarification—uppermost in their minds. Sure, it's difficult, but what's easy about divorce?

Here are some additional guidelines for holding truth-telling sessions with your children:

1. Try to keep the emotional charge out of your voice—traces of anger and pain will confuse children of any age. Unless your voice remains neutral, the children will be more apt to respond to your upset feelings than to the message you are attempting to convey.

2. Don't bring up anecdotes about the father that have nothing to do with the children. Remind yourself that once you begin to talk on this subject there's a strong temptation to start justifying your position by citing evidence against him. The goal is explanation, not vindication.

3. Make every attempt to keep your feelings about your ex to yourself.

4. Give the children the opportunity to ask questions. Don't lecture, and pause deliberately for their input. Those hard-to-elicit fantasies are liable to emerge here.

5. You know your children's tolerance for this sort of session.

Remind yourself of their attention spans, and time the conversation accordingly.

THE TRUTH ABOUT CUSTODY

No matter how much care you have taken to reassure your children from the very start that the divorce meant not simply separating from Daddy but also working out arrangements for keeping them safe, secure, and in touch with him on his own turf, sooner or later—whether your children are four, eight, fifteen, or seventeen years old—you're probably going to hear those famous and shattering words:

"I want to go live with my dad."

Usually, the words trigger a blast of hatred and rage toward the ex-husband, intense emotions you've worked hard to be free of. "Why is he doing this to me?" you wail to yourself. "Why is he still, *still* trying to wreck my life?"

When you hear these words, don't panic, and don't let your fantasies about what *could* be going on distort reality. Instead, remind yourself that most children of divorce learn how to use the custody issue to manipulate their mothers—just as children in an intact marriage find other ways to use the parents' pattern of relating to get their own way.

Stand firm and let the child know that the technique isn't going to work. "I love you," you might say, "and you're not going anywhere. The arrangements are permanent, period."

There is a double advantage to taking this unequivocal stance. It is always possible that below the level of manipulation another, deeper dynamic is at work: the child says, "I hate you, I want to go live with my dad" *not* because it's true but precisely because it's *not* true. The remark itself is a test of the child's security. When you respond as above, the message comes back loud and clear: "I can kick and scream and make myself obnoxious, and Mommy's still going to keep me safe at home." By responding directly with the truth you are taking the opportunity to reinforce the child's sense of security by clarifying the situation once more. But, if you react with rage and panic, you throw away that opportunity and leave the child confused and ill at ease.

In my experience, this straightforward technique usually takes care of the problem. In a few cases, though, the father might really be pressing the child to come live with him. If the issue recurs a lot—not periodically but consistently—ask the child directly what the father has said about the matter. If, in fact, the father has raised the possibility with the child or invited the child outright to live with him, get out that trusty old typewriter and direct a little truth *his* way:

> Dear Burt,
> After reviewing all the particulars in the case, a judge deemed our custody arrangements permanent and in the best interests of our child. The only way the arrangements could change is if I were to voluntarily agree to change them—and there is no possibility of that.
>
> Please make no more mention of a change in the arrangement to Jackie. You are confusing and upsetting him with your innuendos, and he often comes back from visits to your house in a state of agitation. His emotional health depends upon his sense of security and continuity, and your references to "coming to live with me sometime" are undermining these essentials.
>
> I know that, like me, you want what's best for Jackie. I trust that once you receive this letter and understand the adverse effects of your remarks you will end all references to altering the living and visiting arrangements.
>
> Amanda

This approach works well in most cases, but there is an exception that bears special mention: when a teenage boy is not only continually expressing the desire to live with his father but is also completely incorrigible—disrespectful, always in trouble, making his mother's life utterly miserable—it may make sense to consider altering the custody arrangement. I'm not saying that *every* mother having trouble with a teenage son ought to consider giving custody to the father. But where the situation is extreme and everyone is suffering, something must be done. Perhaps the boy does need and will respond to the presence of a male role model at home, and if this is so, switching custody can be a productive option. The catch, of course, is that the father must agree. If he does not, what might have been a good solution becomes a dead end, and the question is unlikely to arise again.

THE TRUTH ABOUT MOM AND DAD NOW

You are the head of your household, and your own house rules apply. You have set your rules with both your children's and your own best interests in mind, and for you privacy and a sense of "home free" are essential. But most children will complain about a rule that bars their father from the house, and in arguing about this you may discover that despite your efforts to explain your divorce to your children, they still don't understand your relationship—or the lack thereof—with your ex-husband. This may be less a function of their ages than of a lack of clarity on your own part stemming from the Ex-Wife Syndrome. Here's where a straight reiteration of the facts comes in, for all your sakes, no matter how often it is necessary:

"Your father doesn't live here anymore. He has his own house now. We aren't married anymore, and part of not being married means that he has his house and I have mine. The place for you to be with him is at *his* house."

Unless your children understand these facts very clearly, they might entertain fantasies of reconciliation, especially in the months following divorce. Any confusion on your part about who heads the household and the father's place *outside* it can feed such fantasies.

Consider Ted, who at sixteen heard his divorced parents talking on the phone every day and assumed they would eventually make up and get back together. When their interactions started to drop off, Ted "coincidentally" started to cut classes—and clumsily, so he was sure to be found out. This spurred a flurry of concerned phone calls between his parents, as he knew it would. His attempt to induce communication between them was conscious, or at least partially so. Another example is the very young child who "feels too sick to go to school" although he or she is clearly healthy; this child may be subconsciously working to keep his or her parents talking in the hope that they will reconcile.

It is imperative that you actively monitor for this sort of misunderstanding. As often as you feel it is necessary, tell the children explicitly that you and their father will *never* be married again. They must see that not only are you not married anymore but you aren't any sort of a unit together, not even friends. Because children easily misinterpret adult interactions, it's important to be very direct:

"The relationship is over, and we're not in love. We really can't be friends because we don't share the things that make friends like to spend time together. We don't have fun, laugh, talk, or want to go places together. So I will have a relationship with you, and Dad will have a relationship with you. And the only time Dad and I will have a relationship together is when we need to talk about you. We both love you and care for you—the *only* thing your dad and I share now is *you.*"

The point here is to convey the idea that each parent's love for the children will endure forever, even though the connection between the two parents is permanently broken. The children need to understand that any form of connection between the two can't be good for anyone and that the answer will always be *no* to pleas of "Can't we all go out to dinner, just this once?" or "Can't we have Christmas together?" Your answer has to be as clear as you can make it: "Daddy and I will both be there for graduations, weddings, and recitals—things that concern *you*—and our separate relationships with you will *never* be broken, but anything involving the old-time roles is gone forever, and expecting it can only bring you pain."

THE TRUTH ABOUT THE FUTURE

It's important to have the visiting schedule—who's spending time with whom when—clearly defined. This is a potential rat's nest of confusion that can produce just the kind of long-drawn-out inter- actions with your ex you're attempting to avoid. Here's a chance to serve both your own and your children's interests by writing everything down. In fact, give the children their own calendars, and let them keep track of their own visiting schedules. Try to foster in them a sense that the visitation arrangement spelled out there is an aspect of their own lives, not simply a stricture you are imposing on them. Clarity on this will add to their sense of security and prevent them from feeling caught in the middle. And you will experience the advantage, which you can consciously nurture, of the children scheduling their own visits with their father, thus requiring ever less input from you in the matter.

THE TRUTH ABOUT MONEY

Kathleen was divorced from a very wealthy man. The settlement for the support of her three children was particularly stingy, and she had to get a clerical job before she could seek the training that would have given her more options. She had proposed to both her ex-husband and the judge that provisions be made for her training, but she was roundly defeated. Still, whenever the children complain to their father about being "latchkey" children and missing their mother's full-time attention, he responds, "I don't know why she insists on working. I give her enough money." This is the same man who, whenever Kathleen succeeds in badgering him into buy- ing the children something they truly need, deducts the amount he spends from her next support check!

So guess who's taking the flak, not only from her ex but from her children as well? A recent study has confirmed that even small children "transfer part of their feelings toward the departed father to the mother and direct more . . . aggressive pressures toward the mother." Kathleen, then, finds herself coping with the drop in her family's living standard, a low-paying job, single parenthood, and her children's concomitant sympathy for their father and resentment of her.

Fortunately, Kathleen has some control over the last two conditions: she can and must tell the children the truth.

Children have the right to know exactly why their life-style has changed and why they can no longer have all the things they used to have and that other kids have. Otherwise they may feel they're being punished—and if they are living with the idea that they caused the divorce in the first place, this second delusion only confirms the first. So you see it is not enough to apologize to the children if there's been a drop in living standard, to stroke their hair and tell them how sorry you are. For their own and your own psychological well-being, they must be told what's really going on: it's not because they are bad, it's not because of the divorce, it's not because their mother is mean and selfish that they have less than they did; it's because their father doesn't give them enough money.

When children reach the age of nine or ten, it's important that you encourage them to begin to approach their father themselves for the things they need, and they will have a head start in doing this if their mother has been modeling assertiveness and clarity of purpose. Children are often frightened to ask a mostly absent father for anything, but they are less afraid if they have seen their mother behave in a straightforward manner. But they also need her to encourage and reassure them that they are doing the right thing and even to rehearse them in their specific requests. If the father refuses the request, then at least their anger will be focused appropriately—not on her but on him.

Let's walk through an example. Billy, age eleven, discovers that his baseball glove has been stolen from his school locker. He's on the majors in Little League and needs a new glove or he can't play. In the past, his mother, Alison, might either have said, "No, I can't afford it," never explaining why, or have immediately phoned Glenn and begged for the forty dollars—and Glenn would have refused. But this time Alison explains why there's no money for the glove—it's close to the end of the month and she's had to pay a deposit for summer camp, which she needs as child care while she works at her full-time job. "I think you should ask your dad," she tells Billy, reassuring him that she thinks this is a perfectly reasonable request. But Billy is still nervous, so she helps him rehearse.

"First, honey, just let him know what happened."

"Okay: 'Dad, my mitt was stolen from my locker last week.'"

"He might get mad; let him know as calmly as possible that it wasn't your fault."

"'Kids go around and unlock the lockers. I don't know how. They just do it.'"

"He might tell you the last mitt was just too expensive. It was your responsibility, and you blew it so he shouldn't have to put out another forty bucks. Remind him that you won't be able to play without a mitt."

"Okay, here's what I'd say. 'Dad, you wanted me to play baseball, you come to my games, and you played yourself when you were young, so you know what happens if you don't have a mitt. I'll be benched until I get one. They won't let me play.'"

Maybe Glenn will still refuse to buy another mitt, but at least Bill will be closer to knowing exactly what's what.

In a few cases, the opposite situation prevails: the father plays Santa Claus, overindulging the children by meeting their every request. This not only makes the life Mom provides seem paltry and difficult, but it encourages a materialism that may clash with her household values. Lilah, for instance, can barely pay the phone and electric bills. But ex-husband Paul has bought his two teenage sons, who live with Lilah, compact disc players and the latest electronic accessories. In this way, Paul competes with Lilah for the boys' affections and wins out every time. At sixteen and seventeen, the boys are obnoxious and insulting, and their mother has little power to enforce her own house rules because Paul has bought the boys off.

This is a terrible situation to be in. What's the solution, especially when things have gone this far?

What Lilah must *never* do is try to argue Paul out of spoiling the boys. He's conducting a seduction for the affection of his sons, and she is his rival. Therefore, no amount of arguing is going to sway him, and *any* amount will result in a tighter bond between Paul and the boys.

The only course open to Lilah is to write Paul a letter articulating her observations: the children are becoming spoiled, and their value system has been ruined by his indulgences. She can thus have her say without losing her head.

Next, while she cannot take away Paul's gifts to the boys, she can restrict their usage. The boys live under her roof, after all, and are subject to her rules. She must make this a clear and consistent fundamental principle of their lives together; how effective it will be is another matter. If they blatantly disobey her, she can enforce her rules by taking away possessions or privileges. She might start by restricting their access to the car, but she may have to move to the most drastic measure of all—simply to stop doing for them, period. She must stop waking them up for school, stop nudging them along, stop cooking for them, stop cleaning for them, stop doing their laundry and their favors. And with it all she must cut off the cash flow to their pockets. It won't be pleasant, but it may be effective.

All the while, *Lilah must tell the boys the truth*: "What your father is doing is overindulging, and I do not approve—not because I don't like to see you have nice things but because you are becoming confused about what's important in life."

The probable upshot of this three-pronged approach? The boys will consider Lilah more of a drag than ever.

But children think their parents are drags *whenever* they say "no." That's just part of being a child, and it happens in two-parent families too. Yet children are amazing in this: they rarely stop loving their parents, even when they hate them. Children *need* their parents. Their love is an expression of their vulnerability and dependency, and therefore, even under the most trying circumstances, they continue to love them.

The truth at least provides a basis for argument—a two-sided argument in which the mother as well as the children are able to voice their positions. Such dialogue may come to nothing but a stalemate, and Lilah may even consider rethinking her custody arrangements, but she will be dealing face to face with the two who share her home, not with an absent father intent on sabotage.

THE TRUTH ABOUT FATHERS

Let's begin this difficult subject by facing the facts:

> *In a nationally representative sample of children in the United States between ages eleven and sixteen, Frank Furstenberg and his colleagues found that most children of divorce have had no contact with their noncustodial fathers within the past year. Only one child in six (16 percent) saw his or her father at least once a week. Another 16 percent saw their fathers at least once a month, and 15 percent saw them at least once a year.* The remaining 52 percent of the children had had no contact with their fathers whatsoever in the past year . . .
>
> *They also report that the process of the father's estrangement from the child typically begins soon after the marriage breaks up. The rate of frequent contact appears to drop off sharply after about twelve months. The proportion of fathers who have had no contact with their children for at least a year rose to 64 percent among individuals whose marriages had broken up ten or more years ago.*

So writes Lenore Weitzman in her landmark book, *The Divorce Revolution*.

Of course, your children's father may be a caring man who has found a way to maintain a responsible and loving relationship with his children. He shapes his relationship to match the children's needs and experiences fulfillment in doing so. He understands that the children need to know he values them—as Wallerstein puts it, that he "wants and accepts them." In addition, he enjoys his children and views his participation in their lives as a pleasure, not just another pressing responsibility.

But statistics demonstrate how rare such a father is in the post-divorce world. In my experience, problem fathers make up a large percentage of the whole. Here are three kinds of problem fathers, each of whom contributes to the emotional maladjustment of his children. And any woman divorced from such a man is at risk, circumstantially, of developing the Ex-Wife Syndrome.

Most obviously problematic is the absentee father, who is not actively involved in the children's lives at all. While any time this man may spend with his children is not necessarily destructive, his absence from their lives and all it implies about how much he values them puts the children at risk psychologically. Frequently, a woman divorced from such a man perpetuates a dangerous bond with him by constantly begging, bribing, wheedling, hoping that he will show some sort of interest, however fleeting, in the kids.

The involved father who is immature and needy is usually prone to drawing his children into his own difficulties rather than meeting their psychological and material needs and reinforcing their self-esteem. The woman divorced from such a man may feel compelled to guide, bribe, or otherwise direct him into acting right by the children, thereby reinforcing her unhealthy connection with him.

An *over*involved father may subvert house rules and work against the mother, causing serious difficulties within the home. In such a case the woman may find herself in constant, highly charged contact with the father in order to try to block his assault on her relationship with the children.

You know by now that the antidote in every case is simply telling the truth. But although I urge you to tell the truth whenever possible, I do *not* encourage you to suggest to your children that their father does not love them. To imply this, even if you think it's true, is to risk doing serious psychological damage to your child.

There are many ways of accounting for a man's lack of attentiveness to his children—immaturity, painful childhood experiences, a lack of knowledge or understanding, self-protectiveness, a sense of shame, guilt, or embarrassment—without *ever* hinting that he does not love them. It's important to offer *some* truthful explanation because otherwise your children may draw their own conclusions: "he doesn't love me; it's all my fault" or "my mother's driven him away and won't let him be with me the way he wants to be." Still, in attempting to explain his absence, focus on the circumstance that makes the man unable to act on his love: he's depressed, or always late, or an alcoholic, or a perennial cheapskate—never, *ever* "your father doesn't love you."

Facing and accepting the fact that the father is as he is can become a healing therapy for child as well as mother. Together they can explore the reasons for his absence, and come to understand that he'd be the same even if the two hadn't divorced. Divorce doesn't alter fathering; it just throws it into bold relief. Mother and children take up the unavoidable challenge by facing up to what they were dealt with and seeking a way around it.

DENYING FATHERS ACCESS

Wherever possible, children need access to their fathers. Even immature, irresponsible, careless, and insensitive fathers can be a source of security and love and a last bastion against the sense of abandonment children suffer when their fathers desert.

There are a few instances, however, in which a woman has not only the right but the responsibility to deny the father access to the child:

1.   when the father deliberately withholds support
2.   when the father is sexually abusive
3.   when the father is physically abusive

I am aware that behind these phrases lie thousands of painful real-life tragedies. When abuse is the problem, the need to protect the children is clear-cut. But if you don't see the necessity of denying access when support is withheld, read on.

In the standard postdivorce situation, the man has financial power while the woman has the power inherent in her control of the children. The *only* justification for her exercising that power is to respond to abuse or to the man's withholding of a court-ordered support check.

When the father deliberately withholds money (that is, when he is capable of paying but does not), he is expressing lack of interest in the child's welfare. At the next scheduled visit, Annie says, "Why can't I go with Daddy?" Her mother, having resolved to tell the truth, says, "Because Daddy didn't send the money to buy the food you need."

Annie knows what the check means to the survival of the household. And if she doesn't, she should—she should know when her father participates in her support and when he does not. Child support is the child's lifeline, to be used at the mother's discretion. Look what happens when a child understands that.

Annie's father calls and says, "Gee, Annie, I really missed seeing you this week. Mommy wouldn't let me see you."

When his slipups were a secret, Annie would blame her mother. But now Annie asks, "Well, how come you didn't send our check?"

Suddenly the facts are out, with these positive consequences:

1. Annie's father has to answer for his actions.
2. Annie's mother can stop protecting him and break the connection formed by her collusion in the fantasy that he's participating wholeheartedly in Annie's life.
3. And—no small thing—Annie's father pays up . . . and continues to pay. Whereas he's unashamed to reveal his true self to his former wife, he's quick to reform under Annie's eyes.

Once again, telling the whole and simple truth becomes a win-win situation.

THE ADULT CHILD OF DIVORCE

One used to hear much talk of couples "waiting until the children are grown" before they divorced. As divorce becomes more commonplace, that attitude is eroding, but it is still not unusual to meet people who were adults before their parents divorced.

For adult offspring, just as for children, the results of deceit and whitewashing are confusion, resentment, and emotional chaos. If the divorce resulted from a partner's infidelity, for example, the parents may be loath to make their secret "public" to their children. But adults, like children, seek patterns of meaning, and frequently adult children see their parents' unexplained divorce as evidence that "it's in the genes." From this misinformation, combined with the psychological phenomenon of identification, they often conclude that they too are likely to divorce. The parents owe it to their children to relieve them of this self-defeating myth.

If you have been withholding the truth from your adult children, even for many years, it is only fair to them—and critical to their psychological adjustment—that you tell them the truth now. You can expect them to feel deceived, angry, and even betrayed. They may even inform you furiously that your failure to tell them sooner has made their own lives a lie. Acknowledging the seriousness of the distortion and offering your children the truth—the specific truth—will certainly make it easier for them to forgive you, and in time it will enable them to see that yours was a particular case, a one-of-a-kind set of circumstances that in no way implies a "genetic propensity" toward divorce.

As ever, the psychological first aid you perform on your children's behalf will serve you well in your own psychological adjustment. It is not too much to hope that in telling the truth, even after years of deceit, you will be liberating yourself from a still charged and unhealthy relationship with your ex-husband. Nevertheless, you must be careful to gird yourself for the flow of feelings your disclosure may trigger. Do not let your concern for your children or any disapproval they show erode your confidence in your past decisions. Even if you now regret the course of action you took with your children, this in no way implies that you lacked love or concern for them. Nor does it call the divorce itself into question. Remember, you have always had a right to happiness and you braved a grueling, confusing, often brutal experience to achieve it. It is no wonder that you made some mistakes, and your right to fulfillment remains.

Truth's best. This may be a cliché, but it's no less than the key to the emotional health of the family in the postdivorce household. I hope that this open-eyed stance in the world has become second nature by now. Nowhere will it serve you better than in the social and sexual arenas, which you may be about to enter for the first time in a long time. "Look to your own house first," my mother used to say. That done, in the next chapter we step outside the door.

SUGGESTED READING

Bustanoby, André. *Being a Single Parent*. New York: Ballantine, 1985.

Gardner, Richard. *The Boys and the Girls Book About Divorce*. New York: Bantam, 1970.

Salk, Lee. *What Every Child Would Like Parents to Know About Divorce*. New York: Harper & Row, 1978.

———. *An A to Z Guide to Raising Your Child*. New York: New American Library, 1983.

Teyber, Edward. *Helping Your Children with Divorce*. New York: Simon and Schuster, 1985.

Troyer, Warner. *Divorced Kids*. New York: Harcourt Brace Jovanovich, 1979.

Wallerstein, Judith, and Blakeslee, Sandra. *Second Chances*. New York: Ticknor & Fields, 1989.

8

REENTERING
THE SOCIAL—AND
SEXUAL—ARENA

Denise had been married for fifteen years and was divorced for five months. Whenever she pictured her future, she saw herself as remarried, but she found the prospect of entering the dating world and dealing with sexuality downright frightening. It wasn't just the idea of learning the ropes that scared her; she worried too about whether she could enter the game enthusiastically. Denise had completely lost her desire—she hadn't felt sexual for a very long time, not since well before her difficult marriage actually ended. "I don't just feel fat and old—though I *do* feel those things," she told me. "It's that I'm numb, completely numb, where all those sexual stirrings, fantasies, and passing thoughts used to be."

Still, Denise's friends were always urging her to go out, and finally she went. Nervously she prepared for the date—a blind date and her first date in sixteen years—reminding herself that she had no intention of going to bed with this man.

The evening went well. Phil was attractive and entertaining, and they had a terrific dinner together. On the way home, he pulled the car over and drew her to him. Denise had been surprised and delighted by how much fun she'd had, but she suddenly became aware of a feeling she had forgotten for sixteen years: I'd better go along with this if I want to see this guy again.

She felt absolutely neutral about the sexual exchange until Phil took her hand and placed it on his crotch. Then she became outraged and furiously demanded that he take her home. On the drive back and at the door she felt more confused and disturbed than she had in a long time. Was she being a fool? Had she revealed that she was completely out of it, over the hill and a prude as well? Things had changed drastically since her former single days. Maybe if she didn't come across she would never stand a chance of marrying again. Denise's uncertainty kept her up that night and for several nights afterward. When Phil called again to ask her out, she turned him down.

ENTERING THE SINGLE WORLD

When you were married, the social/sexual rules between your husband and yourself, however unsatisfactory they might have been, were clear. You knew what you could bring up in conversation, and what not. You knew how far you could go with a joke, and you had your own ways of responding to your husband's jokes. You knew when he wanted to make love and how to let him know when you did. In fact, if your marriage lasted for a while and was typical, every aspect of its social/sexual atmosphere was familiar.

Many, many divorced women find that when they begin to contemplate the wider social world, their ex-husband's views of them come back with a vengeance to haunt them. "I'm too fat," says Denise. "I'm too mannish," says Bernice. "I'm too pensive," says Wendy. "I'm too horny," says Gretchen. Each of these remarks reflects a self-image that an ex-husband imposed.

Difficult as they are, dating and other social contacts can help you challenge these demons by giving you the opportunity to meet men who like you and respond to you *as you are*. You may discover that the characteristics your ex-husband hated about you are among your best, most attractive qualities.

Perhaps your ex-husband constantly criticized you for what he called your "aggressiveness." You may have reached a stalemate on that conflict early on and remained at loggerheads for the duration of your marriage. Imagine your pleasure when a man with whom you've been carrying on a heated political debate at a party breaks off the conversation to tell you how he admires your ability to hold your own.

Just as you learned to do in re-creating your household, the aim here is to assess your needs and make gradual choices, leaving behind the old patterns of interacting that you learned in marriage so that you end up with a social life customized to fit *you*.

This goal, of course, is the ideal. The practical how-tos of meeting men and taking the first plunge are matters of temperament and geography, but a good rule of thumb is to begin with the general and move toward the particular. That is, join a group or participate in a nondate function with people who are clearly interested in socializing—take an organized wilderness hike, for example, or go to a party given by someone you know or by a reputable singles group. Specific social techniques and strategies are outside the scope of this book, but if you need encouragement and ideas take a look at the books listed at the end of this chapter. Here my job is to warn you against certain pitfalls that are of particular danger to women recovering from the Ex-Wife Syndrome.

1. *Be careful not to set your expectations unrealistically high.* You may be determined to avoid men who remind you of your ex-husband, but it's possible that in swearing him off you've set your sights on a man too perfect to exist. Try not to indulge in obsessive comparisons that might keep your ex-husband's image alive, and try to see each man as an individual and trust your reactions to *him*.

2. *Be careful not to begin competing with your ex in the dating scene.* Many women jump into the social world long before they're ready, spurred on by news of their exes' social exploits. "If he can do it, I can do it," they think—an unhealthy point of view that can send a woman frantically running from singles bars to birthday bashes to a mad round of holiday parties. If she doesn't jump on every

opportunity to run out and meet people, she often feels guilty for letting chances slip by, and she is ultimately defeated by a sense of failure if her ex seems to be having a better time than she is. She rarely enjoys herself at all because instead of going out for fun and to enjoy the company of other people, this woman is allowing her ex to find his way back onto center stage once more.

3. *Keep a sense of proportion and monitor yourself for franticness in your social life—a danger signal indicating an obsessive need to prove yourself.* A feeling that you *must* date, that you *must* have a man in your life, is a sign that you are still in the grips of the myth discussed in chapter six—that to have value as a "complete" human being, a woman must have a man. In encouraging you to step out into the social world, I am urging you toward enriching your experience of life by interacting with other people. I am *not* suggesting that dating and ultimately romantic or sexual involvement is a measure of your life's value.

Should a sense of frantic pressure drive you toward "meeting men," I urge you to treat it as a signal that you are suffering the kind of low self-esteem characteristic of the Ex-Wife Syndrome. The antidote is to give yourself a break from your schedule and try to turn your attention inward once again. Remind yourself of what you've been through, and try to treat yourself to an "emotional vacation," in which you look for ways to calm and take care of yourself. Focus on the strategies discussed in earlier chapters for fostering self-health, self-reliance, and pride in the person you are. Social interaction can be sheer punishment if you are suffering from a continual uncertainty about how you measure up.

FROM SOCIAL TO SEXUAL

Like perhaps nothing else, moving about the social world with increasing skill and freedom can reinforce your growing self-image as an autonomous, mature single woman. At the same time, perhaps nothing else on the planet can inspire confusion, self-doubt, and even the impulse to bolt more quickly than a social interaction that suddenly becomes a sexual encounter. For many women who are working to put their view of themselves as ex-wives behind them, crossing the bridge into postdivorce sexuality requires a new perspective on sexuality in general. In my experience, this is one of those must-dos that is easier said than done.

Society has a very high interest in sexuality, and there are many books on sexuality in general and sexuality in marriage, but postdivorce sexuality has received almost no serious attention. Perhaps the assumption is that previously married people have enough sexual experience to traverse the field without guidance, that in a sense they are sexual experts with no need to know what others do. Wrong! As you probably know, the last place to learn confidence and sexual techniques is in a rocky marriage headed for divorce. And the last people who need to remain isolated and without relevant information are those who are reentering the sexual realm, where much may have changed since the last time they were there.

Let's begin with a few facts:

1. According to researcher Paul Gebhard, a person who has had premarital or extramarital sex is more likely to have postmarital sex.
2. Gebhard also determined that the percentage of women who have orgasms in *every* act of intercourse is higher among widows and divorced women than among married women.
3. Researcher Morton Hunt has ascertained that nearly all divorced men and about four fifths of divorced women have postmarital intercourse.

This isn't much, so the rest of the information in this chapter comes directly from my patients and interviewees.

DIVORCE VERSUS DESIRE

Directly following divorce, many women find that their impulse toward intimacy is blocked by anger, rage, and pain, and, like Denise, they often voice the concern that they are "dead" sexually and will never feel attracted to anyone again. "I don't even look at men anymore," Diana, a young patient, told me. "I don't even fantasize. Sometimes I realize with a shock that I've gone for maybe two months without having had a single sexual thought, and when I do think about having sex, it strikes me as ridiculous, like acrobats performing a circus trick. And in another second I'm furious at my ex-husband because not only did he take away my marriage, my house, my life as I knew it, but he took away my sexuality too."

You've undoubtedly heard that the most important sex organ is the brain. The predicament Denise and Diana find themselves in demonstrates the intimate connection between brain and libido. When we're swamped by the intense negative emotions character-istic of the divorce experience, we close up to protect ourselves from more emotional pummeling. In our vulnerability, our very psyches protect us against more incoming feeling than we can take.

Many women with the Ex-Wife Syndrome remain stalled in this self-protective cul de sac indefinitely. But as women recover from the Ex-Wife Syndrome, they feel their libidos gradually revive. If you have been suffering from "sexual numbness" since your divorce, rest assured that the condition is not only normal but actively protective. As the acute pain and bitterness left over from the divorce recede and you stop feeling "married" to your ex-husband, feeling and fantasy will return.

Once you begin to feel desire in little ways, to notice sexual thoughts and feelings, if you have no new sexual partner you may feel a particular kind of longing. It is not loneliness, which implies missing company and social stimulation, nor is it only lust; it is a specific yearning for that most intimate form of social contact: touch to the naked body.

As adults, we don't lose our enjoyment of being hugged, kissed, and lovingly rocked nor do we outgrow the need for these pleasures. And in our healthiest state the grown-up versions are really no different in meaning from what they were to us in our childhood— to be kissed, hugged, and held is to be made to feel safe and loved.

PLAYING BY THE NEW RULES

Private yearnings are one thing; satisfying them in the real world, with real, live partners, is quite another. Like Denise, you may hope for a new relationship but feel a whole spectrum of anxiety-producing questions arise as you contemplate the prospect of satisfying the craving for intimacy that is natural and healthy to all adult human beings. You might look in the mirror and ask yourself, Am I appealing enough? Am I free enough to express myself sexually? Am I, perhaps, too old-fashioned to know how to act?

Many women, particularly those married before 1969 or those whose ex-husbands were their sole sex partner, tell me in therapy that as they watched the sexual mores change in the seventies and eighties, they came to feel distanced from and envious of the single women they saw enjoying new sexual freedom. Most felt during marriage that if the chance arose they would never be able to bridge the gap between the ways of interrelating sexually they learned as girls and the ways that had come to prevail in the single world. Now, inside their heads the same old tapes recorded by mothers and grandmothers years ago are still playing: sex outside marriage is wrong, bad, dirty, and the ruination of a good woman. Even women familiar with—and envious of—society's "new rules" as expressed in the movies and on TV can find that these messages inhibit them from taking the opportunities they see younger women taking and enjoying with impunity.

I'm not shy in therapy, and when a divorced client expresses regret for missing out on sexual freedoms, I feel myself tempted to grin. I let a short silence go by, and then I say, as innocently as possible, "So what's stopping you?"

We look at each other in silence for a while and then I go on.

"You don't have to worry about preserving your virginity anymore.

"You don't have to worry about him not respecting you if he knows you've gone 'all the way.'

"You don't have to worry about your mother or girlfriends thinking you're a terrible person if you have a sexual relationship.

"Listen, you're a grown-up. Everybody knows you're not a virgin. Everybody knows you're sexually experienced. Here's your chance, a golden opportunity to try what you feel you missed out on during marriage. Furthermore, nobody has to know what you're doing but yourself and your partner. And *because* you're mature and sexually experienced, your capacity for enjoying sex is probably greater than ever. Not only does research suggest that sexual satisfaction deepens with experience, but you're now out of a deteriorating marriage that undoubtedly interfered with your sexual pleasure."

Then I lean back and say, "So I repeat. What's stopping you?"

The answer, for some women, is the Ex-Wife Syndrome. A woman with the syndrome may be bound to her ex-husband not by a strong sexual desire or a sense of longing but by *his* antiquated notions of women and sexuality, notions that reinforce the message of those internal tapes.

While the emotional baggage carried by women who came of age in the forties, fifties, and early sixties has to do with the old "sex is dirty" myth, men's baggage often contains the old and terribly destructive madonna/whore complex. This is the idea that (1) good women are mothers, and (2) bad women love sex, but (3) these qualities are never found in the same woman. In this myth, motherhood is sullied by sexual responsiveness, and sexual responsiveness is eradicated by motherhood. Many men still believe in this duality and trap their wives into this orientation. It's an easy step from idealizing "the mother of my children" within the marriage to viewing a woman as a tramp once she is free to see other men.

It's important that you recognize this attitude for what it is—the result of early and misguided socialization regarding sexuality. But remember too that your former husband's old-fashioned attitudes no longer have to affect you. You may have played by his rules when you were married to him—you may even have seen yourself as he saw you—but you have worked hard to set your own rules for your life and to see yourself as you are, not as he wishes or believes you to be. Thus, you can begin to see a returning desire for sexual intimacy for what it is—a normal expression of your social nature as a mature adult human being.

MORE MYTHS

Of course, if shrugging off the old, destructive baggage—his and yours—and adopting healthy self-concepts were simply a matter of walking out the door, I wouldn't be writing this book and hundreds of thousands of women wouldn't be suffering the consequences of emotionally incomplete divorces. The fact is, after divorce most women need to do battle with and defeat one by one the myths about sex they internalized long ago—just as they had to root out their internal myths, wishes, and fantasies about their ex-husbands in order to end their marriages.

Here are myths my patients most frequently express as they struggle to achieve a new perspective on sexuality and the role it is to play in their postdivorce lives.

1. *"I'm too unattractive to appeal to a man. I'll only be hurt if I open myself up to a sexual encounter."*

As I mentioned in chapter four, sad as it is, most American women, old and young alike, are dissatisfied with their bodies. Afraid of male scrutiny, many divorced women scrupulously avoid potential sexual contact. Often their fears have been compounded by their ex-husbands' criticisms of their bodies—even though these criticisms may have been less an honest appraisal than a means of staying in control and/or keeping the women faithful.

It's very difficult to retain self-confidence and self-acceptance under this kind of onslaught. But those who do have the chance to learn that they *are* physically attractive to other men. Many men see the appendix scar, the breasts drawn low by nursing, the cesarean scar, even the mastectomy for what they are: signs of life, even badges of honor, and certainly not barriers to loving.

Many, many women in my practice and interview sample recounted experiences that matched those of my patient, Lenore, who looked into the mirror on a day some time after her divorce was over and managed to take a neutral inventory without her ex-husband's old sound track buzzing in her ears: "I looked and looked, and I thought, 'Hmm, I'm no femme fatale, but I've still got some

okay points. I've always liked my lips. And I've still got good legs.'
So I started to think maybe I could forget about things Jim had
said to me all along about the way I looked, that maybe he was
even doing a number on me with his critical routine." On the
strength of that suspicion, Lenore decided to accept a date from a
man about whom she had a good feeling. They hit it off. Over
time, as self-disclosure led to intimacy in conversation, as intimacy
in conversation led to a mutual impulse toward physical intimacy,
Lenore had to confront the old demons of low self-esteem and low
self-image again and again, but with the positive reinforcement she
was receiving in the present, they finally receded, like annoying
insects, into the swampy past.

2. *"My kids are just too young. I wouldn't know how to handle a sexual
relationship in front of them, and anyway I'm afraid of endangering my
custody of them."*

This myth too grows out of an outdated sense of propriety, from
a time when sexuality was hidden and children were supposed not
to "know." We've come a long way since sexuality was secret in
our culture, and not only are children today capable of understanding that their mothers, as adult women, are sexual beings, but we
also know now that providing frank and balanced information on
sex is imperative for their own sexual health as adults.

So, for them and for you, I urge you to open a dialogue with
your children and, in an age-appropriate manner, explain sex in
terms of natural and normal needs—needs related to affection and
intimacy, not shame and embarrassment. When there is a new man
on the scene, for preschool children, you can certainly use analogies
to their own desire for hugs and kisses and the nice feelings that
flow from them. School-age children can begin to see that sex is
an adult need and that it's as natural to Mom as to any other grown-
up. With teenagers, of course, the dialogue might be hard to open
if it hasn't been initiated before, but the language is there, as is the
feeling of desire—not easy for prepubescent children to understand—and so is the potential for a fruitful interchange.

Many women are stopped cold by the idea of allowing the man they are currently involved with to sleep overnight into the house. But if there's been an ongoing dialogue about the normality of sexuality, children can adapt with surprising ease to this evidence of their mother's sexuality. Potential problems can arise with the ex-husband, however. Before you invite your lover to spend the night, *check with a divorce attorney to make sure you won't be endangering the terms of the decree.*

3. *"With all the sexually transmitted disease floating around, I wouldn't dream of becoming sexually active now. It's just too risky."*

The fear of sexually transmitted disease is well-founded today, but there is a way—and one way only—to protect against all STDs, including the fatal AIDS: *always make sure the man uses a condom during sexual intercourse.* No amount of questioning a potential sex partner will ensure your safety. If you want to be sexually active but fear sexually transmitted diseases, take matters into your own hands: carry your own condoms, and never trust a man who refuses to use one.

4. *"I'm afraid I won't know what to do to please him or myself, and I don't want to make a fool of myself."*

It may help you to be reminded that the concern with performance is universal and is undoubtedly afflicting him too. Remember that men are trained from boyhood to look as if they know what they're doing, but especially regarding sexual matters, their outward confidence is often covering a desperate need to "do well."

Even more basic is the knowledge that sexual desire is its own teacher. If you have never made love to a man other than your former husband, you may not achieve heights of ecstasy the first time, but you can trust that if you are sincerely drawn to the man in question you'll "know what to do." Desire is really the voice of nature, and nature will take its course.

5. *"I know there's more to sex than what I had with my husband, but I don't want to learn what I need to know in front of another man."*

Once you have dealt with the internal myths that have been holding you back and have determined that you want to become sexually active, here are some actions you can take to groom yourself for satisfying and mature sex in your new, postdivorce life:

- *Read some books on sexuality.* Information on the reproductive systems and the human sexual response cycle in both men and women is a necessity for experiencing the fullest possible pleasure—and it's all there in the library! Start with the wonderful, comprehensive *The New Our Bodies, Ourselves* (make sure you read the latest edition), perhaps read *Masters and Johnson Explained* by Nat Lehrman on the ground-breaking research done in the early 1970s on human sexual response, pick up Lonnie Barbach's *For Yourself*, a marvelously empathetic introduction to women's sexual pleasure, and for heaven's sake read erotica (*not* pornography, which is distinguished by using and often hurting women and children) to get a sense of what thrills you that you may not have thought of yourself. Now's the time to do a quick, catch-up course. I guarantee that the reading will not be dull.
- *Learn how to please yourself sexually, and practice by masturbating.* If you have never masturbated and allowed yourself to fantasize sexually, now's the time. Although this form of sexual activity is healthy and pleasurable for everybody, it's particularly valuable for women who have had only one sexual partner and who are nervous about interacting sexually with other men. It's a way of rehearsing, getting familiar and comfortable with a range of sexual activities and the idea of having a new sexual partner. If you learn to turn *yourself* on, you're already halfway there and sexual encounters with men won't seem as daunting. And of course there's the bonus of relieving the sexual frustration and tension that build up in the course of daily life.

    Buy yourself a gift of lingerie. You might have been a flannel-pajama mama for a long time with a marriage-long habit of stocking up on plain cotton underpants. Why not give yourself a treat for yourself alone? You'll find it fun to change your image in your own eyes.

- *Give thought to your current gynecologist.* It's very important now that you be comfortable with your gynecologist—comfortable enough to discuss issues relating to your new sexual activity. For many women, the gynecologist is almost a family institution; they continue to go to the one their mothers first took them to as girls, the same one they saw all through marriage and the childbearing years. That's fine if you're comfortable with your doctor, but if he (or she) seems patronizing or difficult to speak candidly with, or has old-fashioned ideas about sexuality, consider a change. The last thing you need while trying out your new wings is someone suggesting that you clip them. And now more than ever you need a doctor with whom you can comfortably discuss birth control methods, sexually transmitted diseases, and physiological conditions that might affect your sexual activities.

- *Take action about birth control.* Far too many divorced women who are in their midthirties or older (and sometimes, amazingly, younger) believe, or choose to believe, that their fertility is on the decline and that intermittent sex therefore cannot lead to pregnancy. I've seen a lot of women who hold this attitude brought up short by the facts of life. And even where pregnancy isn't the result, missed or late periods can cause terrible anxiety in a woman who has been careless about birth control. Here's a source of anxiety that you can completely eradicate. Just do it.

- *Be informed about AIDS.* There is no question that AIDS is a reality every sexually active person must confront. Unlike all other sexually transmitted diseases, so far AIDS is untreatable and fatal. However, an abundance of misinformation is frightening many people unnecessarily. The greatest number of AIDS sufferers, and it is a huge preponderance, are gay men, IV drug users, and the children of IV drug users. Despite dire predictions to the contrary, sexually active non-IV-drug-using heterosexuals continue to make up the smallest group of sufferers. This doesn't imply that it's smart to play the odds. Transmission requires precise physical conditions, and those conditions can be controlled—by condoms.

- *Spend some time developing your own guidelines.* As I've noted, not much has been written on sexuality in the postdivorce period, and I can only hope that professionals as well as divorced women read this chapter with a new interest in the subject. But when it comes to establishing personal guidelines for your sexual behavior—deciding whether to have sex at all and how much, how soon to do what, what exactly to do and with whom to do it— no book can guide you, as you well know. You must look where you've gotten used to looking—to your own feelings of comfort.

As you have certainly learned in other areas of postdivorce adjustment, an inner feeling of uneasiness is a warning signal. Ignoring such a feeling can lead to a morass of self-deception and eventually self-dislike. But there's a simple test for evaluating your behavior in any sexual encounter: when you wake up on the morning after, look in the mirror and ask yourself how you feel. If the answer is "not so good," perhaps you've made a wrong turn or allowed yourself to break your own rules. But if the answer is "Great!" you're on to something.

My patient Patricia, for instance, was thirty-eight years old when she divorced after a fifteen-year marriage. She and her former husband had had a very active sex life, but Patricia had never experienced an orgasm with him. She had a long adjustment period after the divorce but finally began to realize that the men who called to ask her out had a genuine interest in her. After going out on a friendly basis with one fellow for about three months, Patricia had her first postdivorce sexual experience—and her first orgasm. What a revelation! She did the next-morning test and saw herself glowing with pleasure and satisfaction. "I looked at myself in the mirror and whispered, 'Go for it!' I felt like I was starting not just a new chapter in my life but a whole new book!"

THE FULL POTENTIAL OF SEX

Mature, mutually pleasurable sexuality really *is* all the books say it can be: a significant aspect of being a healthy, mature human being. Sexuality is not just an aside, not just a bit of frosting on the cake. And its healthfulness is not restricted to marriage. As a matter of fact, in many, many marriages, neither partner *ever* experiences the full pleasure and healthfulness of sex.

Having researched sexual behavior extensively for my last book, *The Kahn Report on Sexual Preferences*, which is about what people *really* want in bed, I can assert that the distance between what they want and what they report doing is often depressingly great, both within and outside marriage. The reason is simple: *people simply don't tell each other what pleases them sexually*. This is nearly as true within marriage, even long-term marriage, as it is among singles of all ages. One explanation for this is the inherent power imbalance between the sexes in our society and the resulting distrust. Another is the stubbornness of those distorted early messages.

But as a divorced woman reentering the sexual arena, you are in a unique position. You bring to a potential relationship years of sexual experience, even if they were less than ideal. You have the freedom to choose to have sex only with men you trust. And you can bring to your new sexual interactions the recognition of the fundamental importance of sexual dialogue. *The free flow of information* is the key to satisfying sex. Simply by knowing and acknowledging this fact you gain access to a "secret" that many fail to learn.

It will help you overcome any natural shyness to realize that most men know nothing about the female sexual response cycle. Why don't they know how to bring a woman to orgasm? Because Mom didn't teach them, prostitutes didn't teach them, and most of the women they dated learned early that men worried so much about whether "it was good for you" that telling them what they wanted to hear was a sure way to keep them happy. As a mature woman with acknowledged sexual experience and a renewed understanding of personal self-fulfillment, you have the opportunity to break through the ignorance barrier and teach as well as learn what it's all about.

WHEN THINGS GO WRONG

In our culture, anybody over the age of twenty-five knows that an active sexual life has its own pitfalls—traps every bit as difficult to escape as the Ex-Wife Syndrome. All these traps have one thing in common: one falls into them by using sexuality not as a rich and pleasurable means of expressing affection but for some other, unacknowledged reason. This reason usually has more to do with one's own unmet needs than feelings of caring for another.

If you become sexually active and then look in the mirror and *fail* the morning-after test, you're up against the need for some serious problem solving. Whenever having sex raises bad feelings in you about yourself, you're having it for the wrong reasons and are in a situation you have to get out of.

Here are some common misuses of sex:

- *Mistaking sex for intimacy.* Debbie loves love—she feels she's got to have it. The only problem is, ever since her divorce she's been falling in love with men who are obviously wrong for her. She's seen married men, men with whom she has nothing in common, and a string of men who have made it clear that emotional involvement is not what they are after. Eventually, there's a confrontation of some sort and "it's over," but Debbie moves on to the next man without a pause, jumping in with both feet.

    Debbie uses the electric excitement of sex to distract her from reality and, ironically, to protect herself against becoming too close to any man. Her marriage and divorce left her self-esteem in tatters; rather than face the possibility of more punishment, she distracts herself with the high drama of quick-fix sex. It works for a while—a time or two she looks in the mirror afterward and smiles, "Wow!" But after two or three rousing sexual encounters with a man who, if the truth be told, she isn't even interested in knowing, a terrible restlessness fills her, followed by waves of self-doubt and finally self-loathing at her own promiscuity. If she stops to evaluate the situation honestly, the first blast of excitement has faded and the sex itself has become about as exciting as a bank transaction. As soon as she faces this fact, Debbie bails out. She picks a fight, makes a dramatic exit, and heads for the guy in the wings.

- *Using sex to hold on to a man.* Marsha came out of her marriage feeling like a failure—she had done all she could to fill her wifely role, but Michael left her anyway. For eight months she's been involved with Mark, a commercial realtor so cool and calculating he frightens her. But scaring her more is the prospect of facing the world with no man at all—to her this would prove she has no value as a woman. Mark has a voracious appetite for sex, and he seems completely satisfied with Marsha as a sexual partner. Throughout the relationship, Marsha has felt no increase in warmth or closeness, but she has made herself completely available to Mark sexually. He's ecstatic with the way things have worked out; she feels sick every morning after a night of "love." Still, she knows she's got her man, and the idea that he might tire of her sends her into a cold sweat.

  Far from using sex as a natural expression of affection and pleasure, Marsha uses it as bait. Her self-esteem is so low she feels she has nothing else to offer a man so she never considers withholding sex from Mark despite the disgust their lovemaking inspires in her.

- *Mistaking sexual desire for genuine interest.* Isabel craves not sex but the need to be desired. Since reentering the sexual arena, she's become a notorious flirt, and if she leaves a party without having made a conquest, she is depressed. She never feels attracted to the men she goes home with, and she never experiences sexual pleasure during their encounters—it's solely their interest in her that turns her on and temporarily convinces her of her value.

Forced to confront their morning-after discomfort, each of these women might focus on sex itself as its cause, but in fact the problem is the low self-esteem that drives their behavior, not the behavior itself.

If you recognize yourself in any of these examples—if you consider yourself promiscuous, if you are perpetually involved with men who are wrong for you, or if you are participating in *any* sexual activity without enjoying it—try to see the sex itself as a symptom that both signals and obscures an underlying problem. Continuing the behavior is a sure way to reinforce feelings of self-disgust. But stopping the behavior, even if only temporarily, in order to see the underlying problem of self-acceptance more clearly can help you begin the slow process of recognition and change that's right for who you are.

SEX WITH THE EX

There's one more unhealthy use of sexuality that's cropped up time and again in my practice and interviews. This is the act that a patient usually confesses at the end of the hour in a whisper directed at her clasped hands in her lap. It happens much more often than most people suspect, and every time it happens for a divorced woman it means trouble—trouble she must handle before she can move on.

Sleeping with your ex-husband is the Ex-Wife Syndrome in its most distilled form, and it's all the more poisonous for being concentrated. When women do it they sense this and often keep the secret to themselves. For that reason, I have no precise estimate of how many people do it—there's never been a study of sexual relations among ex-spouses. It's not something women share freely with friends or even therapists—in my experience, many people will tell *everything* in therapy before they'll admit to this. Still, one on one the secret often will out, and I've come to recognize certain reasons for it.

- *"I just wanted things to be the way they were—if only fleetingly."*
  Loneliness and the yearning for intimacy fool us into making all

sorts of mistakes. The main reason women go to bed with their ex-husbands is the mistaken belief that they can quench these awful feelings by doing so. But in every case, what these women come out with instead of the emotional relief they seek is a worse set of feelings: a reminder of their initial loss of intimacy, a sense of rejection, a feeling of having been used and thrown aside. The first few moments of sexual activity may stir up an artificial sense of well-being, but this is always short-lived and quickly replaced by self-loathing.

For example, Suellen's sexual relations with Berry were the best part of their marriage. Even two years after their divorce, although Berry was engaged and involved in plans for a new life, time and again Suellen agreed to meet him in restaurants to work out some unresolved detail. She knew and he knew the dinner meeting would lead them to bed, and secretly she was exultant, for she antici-pated—if only for an hour—the escape of those old, self-obliterating feelings. Each time, staring up at the ceiling as Berry completed the act, she lay there crying and crying—with disappointment, with frustration, and with the emptiness already beginning to fill her.

If you still sleep with your ex, even occasionally—or are tempted to—your job isn't to talk yourself out of the longing for intimacy—that's a separate problem that can't be talked away. The real task is to remind yourself of what you already know: if you're looking for intimacy and the peace it can bring, you aren't going to find it there.

- *"I have to admit it—he's off limits now, and I just love the thrill."*

Like single women who protect themselves against true involve-ment by choosing only married men as sex partners, some divorced women love the illicit thrill of sleeping with their exes—once the men are married to somebody else. Sometimes thrill-seeking yields real excitement, but in this case, like the seekers after intimacy, these women find only those same awful feelings—loss, loneliness, and despair. I've never met a woman, in therapy or in my inter-views, who didn't regret her impulse to "have fun being bad" in this way.

- *"He's all I deserve to have."*

As I have shown, some women are linked to their ex-husbands by guilt at having initiated a divorce the men didn't want. In a small percentage of cases, these women see themselves as undeserving of the happiness they sought, as "bad" and in need of punishment. They are analogous to the small percentage of battered women recognized in the research literature as staying in or seeking out abusive situations because they feel they need punishment. In both cases, the ex-husband may collude in this destructive fantasy and reinforce the woman's sense of degradation.

When a woman is trapped by guilt into returning compulsively to her ex-husband, the psychological dynamics of their interactions can become seriously pathological. This is one of those red-flag situations in which psychotherapy is critically needed. Any woman who believes so fully in her need to be punished that she repeatedly sets herself up to receive pain is unlikely to recognize the problem. Loved ones reading this book can only urge—*very* diplomatically—that she seek professional help.

- *"We always had something special, and we always will—divorce or no divorce."*

If your sex life with your ex-husband was really terrific, you could misinterpret his desire to keep it going as "love." And you might even kid yourself with that common fantasy "He might be remarried, but I'll always be his *true* wife." But the reality is that while for an hour you might believe you are having an authentic intimate interaction, for him the encounter is probably just a "good screw." Remind yourself: later he will go home to his girlfriend or his wife while you are left to stare at the wall and deal with your unleashed feelings.

Nevertheless, when I point this out, some women, in an effort to turn the tables, retort, "I'm horny, and he's convenient." Gusto for sex is fine, but in the interests of eradicating the Ex-Wife Syndrome from the face of the earth, I highly recommend seeking out another man or masturbating with a hot new fantasy.

- *"I can't help it. He makes me do it."*

A recent *Playboy* cartoon shows a man in a bathrobe opening his hotel room door to a woman with her dress unzipped, breasts exposed. "The support check's in the usual place," he says with a leer, and there it lies, on his pillow.

Blackmail is probably the most potent motive behind sex between ex-spouses—she knows that the only way to get the court-ordered check, or extras for Annie's bike, or braces for Chuck, is to do this "one little thing." "What's the big deal?" he asks her. "We've been sleeping together for years."

Initially she may agree, but every woman who barters sex this way ends up feeling violated and trapped. If you find yourself in such a situation, take a deep breath and say no (and go back and read the section in chapter five on threats). If he's married, threaten to tell his wife.

Consider Brenda, who asked Ken to see her through to the end of the month with a loan of $250. He told her outright he'd consider making her the loan but that she would have to "earn it." She needed the money and went to bed with him, which she knew was what he had in mind. She came out with the $250—plus the feeling that she'd been a prostitute. And the feeling wasn't far from the truth—indeed, she had sold sex for money, and the bad taste stayed with her for many weeks afterward.

Soon Ken was calling Brenda on Friday afternoons and telling her he had just bought a bottle of her favorite wine, and could he come over that night to deliver it? This was his coy shorthand for saying he was ready for another roll in the hay. The third time she found the strength to say, "No, not tonight, and not ever."

"Why not?" said Ken, who had come to look forward to this unexpected uplift in his sex life.

"Because I'm not your wife anymore, Ken."

"That wasn't a problem last week," he said. He didn't have to add, "when you needed a little more cash."

"Yes, it *was* a problem last week, I just didn't have the nerve to tell you. But I hated it. Sleeping with you makes me sick."

He was furious now. "I can't believe you're so stupid," he told her. "You'll never get anything out of me again."

"If you don't leave me alone I'll call your wife and tell her what's going on. I don't have to worry about protecting my pride. It can only be uphill from here."

"You do that and I'll kill you."

"You won't have to kill me because we're never having sex again, so I won't have to call her, will I?"

With a bang, Ken hung up.

Two days later, Ken called her with an obnoxious informational call, but Brenda didn't mind. There was no mention of any bottle of wine, and she could tell by his tone of voice that he'd dropped the idea of ever getting her into bed again.

Brenda felt great about herself. She might become involved in power struggles with Ken later on, but she was better equipped to deal with them now. As with many difficult experiences, the payoff was that Brenda felt stronger and smarter for having won this battle for control.

SEXUAL PRIVACY

One cautionary note as you begin to contemplate the new life opening to you. Remember that self-disclosing to others is an invitation to intimacy; hence, self-disclosing to your former husband can reopen the way for an unhealthy connection to him. Privacy is a cornerstone of your new household, and privacy is the key to protecting your new sexuality.

A man inclined to maintain what control he can over his former wife may be tempted to suggest to their children when she is beginning to taste her sexual freedom that "Mommy's sleeping around." He might intimate that her interests in sexuality are unnatural or perverse, her habits "dirty," and her choices of men "cheap" and unworthy of her. Even if the woman has managed to clear away old attitudes toward sex planted in her by her mother, she must then face down her ex-husband's antiquated and judgmental ideas about sexuality and women.

Make it a rule, then, *never* to discuss your sexual activities with your ex-husband. And be careful—these exchanges can sneak up on you if you're not on your guard.

"Hey," says Al, "I hear you're going out with Jerry."

"Yeah," answers Pat. "Small town, isn't it?"

"He's a nice guy. I really like him."

"Yeah, he is. He's really nice."

"Slept with him yet?"

This is the critical point. If Pat answers yes Al could continue like this: "So how was it?"

"Great," she says, oblivious to what's coming. "Wonderful."

This is Al's cue to get hurt. He interprets Pat's message as "Better than you." In defensive anger, he starts thinking, "She's sleeping around already. She's behaving like a tramp," that is, dumping harsh judgments on her to deflect his sense of inadequacy. If Pat continues to date Jerry and perhaps others, this sort of exchange can escalate into a terrible argument. In the worst-case scenario, Al threatens to take the kids away because Pat's "sleeping around and acting so cheap."

Don't leave yourself open to these kinds of judgments and threats, even if they're empty. Disabuse yourself of any hope, wish, or fantasy that your ex-husband's inquiries about your sex life are expressions of interest in your happiness. Until it becomes second nature remind yourself to keep your personal business to yourself.

SUGGESTED READING

Barbach, Lonnie. *For Yourself.* New York: Doubleday, 1976.

Boston Women's Health Book Collective, The. *The New Our Bodies, Ourselves.* New York: Simon and Schuster, 1985.

Krantzler, Mel. *Learning to Love Again.* New York: Thomas Y. Crowell, 1977.

Lehrman, Nat. *Masters and Johnson Explained*. Chicago: Playboy Press, 1970.

Lyman, Howard B. *Single Again*. New York: David McKay, 1971.

Napolitane, Catherine, and Victoria Pellegrino. *Living and Loving After Divorce*. New York: Signet, 1977.

9

THE WIDOW
AS EX-WIFE

It's been four years since Barbara's fifty-eight-year-old husband died suddenly from a heart attack. The two had an up-and-down marriage that was basically strong, although they did have counseling twice during their twenty-six years together. As her family and friends inevitably note, Barbara is doing "remarkably well." She's energetic, healthy, and looks like she's taking terrific care of herself—and "she's absolutely *devoted* to those grandkids of hers."

What nobody knows is that every night Barbara goes to bed and talks with her late husband, often with tears streaming down her face. She tells him no man could ever take his place, understand her the way he did, or fulfill her needs so completely. Twice a month she visits the cemetery for more extended conversations. Though she lives alone, Barbara still stocks up on Bill's favorite foods. Bill's handkerchiefs are still in the top drawer of the bureau, and his chair still sits empty in the prime space in front of the television.

This isn't grief Barbara's playing out, but marriage still—four years after her husband was laid to rest.

Barbara is suffering from the Ex-Wife Syndrome. Most people would agree that, technically at least, a widow is an ex-wife.

Clearly, she too must come to grips with living alone; she must wrestle with questions pertaining to her sexuality and the role it will play in her new life. But, skeptics might point out, while a divorced woman must struggle to break an unhealthy connection to her ex-husband, the widow has that connection broken for her—painfully, but irrefutably. Right?

Wrong!

Intensive interviews with sixty-five widows and with the widowed women I have seen in my practice over the years has shown me that a widow often lives out her life after her husband dies almost as if nothing at all has changed. Moreover, studies reveal that while divorced women consistently experience a drop in economic well-being after marriage, widows tend to experience a drop in *personal* well-being, with chronic depression and loneliness the characteristic complaints. (Note that this does not mean that widows necessarily have a higher standard of living—in fact, one study shows 65 percent of widows to be living below the poverty level.)

GIVING UP THE GHOST

Think back on what I call in chapter two "the secret from the self," and remember that the essence of the Ex-Wife Syndrome is the *unacknowledged* connection sufferers maintain to their ex-husbands, a connection that tends to be largely psychological and emotional rather than actual. I hope I convinced you early on that the first step in curing the Ex-Wife Syndrome and moving on with life as an autonomous single woman must be perceiving and acknowledging the existence of this unhealthy and inhibiting connection.

Unfortunately, women whose husbands have died are not only in danger of nurturing an unbroken, terribly unhealthy connection to their late husbands but are likely to find the job of acknowledging the connection and its inherent destructiveness even more difficult than if they had divorced. Characteristically, widows with the syndrome have yet to say good-bye. To do so means ending the fantasy that their husbands are in some sense still "there" for them. They tend to cling to an idealized version of their late husbands, selectively remembering their best characteristics and blocking out the less pleasant, a tendency that is hard to dispel since there is no longer a real man to check against. Such selective remembering is not limited to women who have had good marriages. It is true that the stronger the love, the greater the loss, but even after mediocre marriages widows tend to focus on happy memories and their late husbands' best qualities.

The added difficulty for widows is that society itself impedes their recovery. Widows remain "married" to their dead husbands not only in their own eyes but in the eyes of society. There is a funeral to mark the end of the husband's life, but nothing—and usually no one—articulates the fact that *the marriage itself is over*.

In fact, on a subtle level, a widow gets the opposite message. To a certain extent, she is encouraged to pick herself up and begin to make a new life, but only to a certain extent: her active life, it is implied, is now finished. "The world seemed to say to me, 'You're old now. Be satisfied with what you've got because it's all you're getting,' " said Joan, an interviewee who had made a very healthy and productive adjustment to her husband's death. "I even felt I had to fight my children on this. They seemed to expect me to live my life as I did with Jack. When I told them I was going to look for a job, they talked as if I'd betrayed a sacred rule—*his* wish that I stay at home for him. And when they found out, about three years after Jack's death, that I was seeing a man rather seriously, my grown daughters stopped talking to me for six months."

In the Hindu practice of suttee, now outlawed, a wife voluntarily (under centuries' worth of social pressure, that is) threw herself onto her husband's funeral pyre, immolating herself as an expression of her devotion to him. We can be grateful that no such customs have been part of Western culture, but it's important that we be aware of the pressures exerted on widows to continue to "prove" the strength of their love and the health of the marriage after the fact, in an extension of women's conventional role of sole nurturer and caretaker of the relationship.

"I discovered a new twist to the double standard when I started going out with other men after those three years of widowhood," Joan told me. "It began occurring to me that if *I* had died and Jack was left, the kids—and all our friends—would have said, 'Come on, Dad, come on, Jack, get out and socialize. You can't sit in here and stew in your emotions. Have some fun out of life. Joan would have wanted it that way.' But it was me who was left, and what I was getting was 'Joan, so *soon?*' or just the sullen, angry faces of my daughters, not speaking. When you're a widow everybody's watching, and you'd better act the way they think he would have wanted you to or somebody's going to quit speaking to you."

Social pressure, then, is a significant factor, if not in keeping the ghost alive, then in keeping the wife a "good widow." But there's much more work to do when a woman finds herself unable to move forward five, ten, fifteen years after her husband dies. And those barriers to her development are exactly the same ones that impede the divorced woman. When the marriage itself reflected an imbalance of power, the stage is set for a full-blown case of the Ex-Wife Syndrome. Not only the external barriers to autonomy built into conventional marriage roles, but the internal barriers in the form of fantasies and wishes may have their grip on a woman's psyche so firmly that she never dreams of deviating from the familiar paths she's taken throughout her married life even years after her husband has died.

Though the Ex-Wife Syndrome binds widows and divorced women to the past, similarly the widow has perhaps even more reason to keep her affliction a secret. Six years after her husband's death, Diane said to me, "You know, people just don't want to know after a while. They get sick of hearing about it, and they want to see you perk up. But I hurt every day, I hurt every hour. And my only happiness is to sit with him. Yes, you'll laugh, but I sit and I watch TV with him, and I find myself thinking what he would say about a program, and then I answer him about it and pretty soon I'm talking out loud. If they knew I did that they'd have me in a rest home in a second."

So Diane keeps her secrets, as most widows keep their secrets. And because their secret lives with their dead husbands often seem to them more authentic, than the lives they have in the outside world, when they "put on a happy face," they often have very little incentive to give it up.

If you are a widow and have turned directly to this chapter because you think it might have some relevance to your life, turn to page one of this book and read straight through. Once you allow yourself to think consciously about whether you are nurturing an unhealthy connection to the past, it may be easier for you to read this chapter. I want to help you see that marriage to a ghost could be keeping you from entering the world of the living and that there's plenty in that vital world still left for you to do.

IT WON'T HAPPEN TO ME

Divorced readers who might be idly skimming this chapter should also take heed. If you are considering remarriage, you're considering the possibility of widowhood—whether you know it or not. Statistics show that three out of four women currently in marriages that do not end in divorce will be widows. Moreover, the median age at which widows begin their widowhood is *fifty-two*. Since the average life span for American women is now seventy-eight, that suggests potentially decades of pain for women caught in the Ex-Wife Syndrome. So if you're skimming this chapter and thinking, "It won't happen to me," slow down and consider. Particularly if you've already experienced the psychological distress of the Ex-Wife Syndrome in the aftermath of your divorce, you may discover here some facts about widowhood that you ought to know.

Helen's husband, Dave, died suddenly after forty-one years of a marriage Helen describes as "a forty-one-year love affair." Completely unprepared emotionally for the loss, Helen was absolutely devastated. Helen has two grown children and four young grandchildren. From the time of Dave's death she has been extremely concerned that her children pass smoothly through the stages of grief and mourning and emerge intact, enriched by memories of their father but unhindered by the inevitable depression and anxiety that accompanies unresolved conflict. In fact, Helen wants for her children what a good therapist would wish for Helen: a healthy, graduated period of mourning lasting from six to eighteen months, after which separation from the lost loved one is complete.

In our interview, Helen leaned back and admitted, "You know, Sandra, I've never told anyone this. Partly it's because they don't want to hear—they're tired of my sad story already—but partly I don't want to tell. I can't make a decision without mentally consulting Dave. For forty-one years he made the decisions! Sure, he talked about them with me, but he was smart about money, you know. And I let him, because I knew I would never catch up. I liked it—but *now*. I'm doing the money but I hate it. Luckily, he made his accountant coexecutor of his estate, so my decisions aren't everything. The accountant still has to decide before anything gets spent."

Luckily the accountant is coexecutor of the estate? This was a red flag for me. It meant that Helen was still being controlled, by proxy, financially—that even though she was a wealthy woman by virtue of her inheritance from Dave, her financial decisions still didn't carry full weight. So Helen, who still "consulted" with Dave, who "knew" she'd never find a man like Dave so never bothered to try, who always spoke of Dave in the present tense as "my husband," never "my late husband," was not only married to a ghost but was still being controlled by one. When I heard that strange word *luckily*, I realized that if Helen really wanted to shed her pain she had her work cut out for her.

What Helen had to see in order to change was that it was her *continued connection to Dave* and not Dave's death per se that was the source of her current pain, that pain she felt every day, every hour, but carefully hid away. Earlier I mentioned that when I ask patients in mourning whether they would like to see their lost loved one magically restored temporarily, after the first enthusiastic *yes!* they usually reconsider when they realize they'd then be facing the pain of loss again. It is precisely this pattern of losing and relosing that a widow experiences when she keeps up the rituals of her married life after her husband has died. Every time she sees the bathrobe hanging on the back of the bathroom door, every time she fantasizes herself into a conversation with him, every time she travels to the cemetery—as Helen did, for instance, bringing her daughter and her new baby so Dave could "see the baby"—reality strikes her down and she must reexperience her grief once again.

What I am describing is a recurrent interruption in the natural grieving process, which if allowed to play itself out, would lead, eventually, to acceptance of the loss. As I mentioned in chapter seven, pioneering psychologist Elisabeth Kübler-Ross has made a lifework of studying the grieving process and describing it in a clear and eloquent way that has benefited both professionals and lay-people. Her simple and elegant model of this process, which may take a psychologically healthy person in mourning anywhere from half a year to a year and a half to complete, is composed of five stages: shock/denial, confusion, anger, depression, and finally re-covery marked by acceptance of the reality of the loss. In this way the shock and psychological disruption the death provokes gradually gives way to a calm acceptance of its reality. Along the way, mood swings, sleep disturbances, and moments of uncontrollable crying are all natural and expected expressions of the pain of loss.

This process is as natural, as gradual, and as complete as the healing of a flesh wound. And interrupting this gradual process, by bringing the loved one "back to life" in fantasy and wish only to lose him again, is as traumatic and painful as it would be to inflict a new wound on the injured tissue. Keep this cycle going long enough and the pain becomes chronic.

Unresolved grief—which really means unaccepted loss—does not go away by itself, and if allowed to continue without resolution it causes increasingly acute distress. So when I suggest that a widow turn her attention inward to see that she is still connected to her dead husband in an unhealthy way, I do not mean she should not ignore the unfinished work of mourning or try to turn her back on the memories of forty-one happy years. Quite the contrary, I mean she must allow herself to continue through the grief process to acceptance and resolution and in that way liberate herself from her pain so she can *enjoy* her memories.

If Helen were in therapy I would see it as my number-one task to gently but persistently convince her that talking to Dave every night, going to the cemetery, and allowing the accountant to make her financial decisions were the things that were making her unhappy, hurting and rehurting her every single day. I would try to find a way to shape and reshape this message so that she could hear it: "What's making you miserable, Helen, is not living alone but rather *keeping Dave alive* and then beginning to miss him all over again."

A woman without a husband is *not* a married woman. This is a radical thought for a woman like Helen, who has nurtured a connection to her husband years beyond his death. But the fact remains: a woman who loses a husband—for whatever reason—is a *single woman* entering a new period of her adulthood.

THE FINAL GOOD-BYE

Do you remember how, as a child, when you went visiting your parents were always promising to leave but kept thinking of one last thing to say? I can recall waiting in the warm house of family friends all dressed up in a snowsuit while my parents *almost* said good-bye but kept on talking at the door, interminably. I remember just as clearly frustrating my own children in the same way. An incomplete mourning is not unlike such an endless good-bye. To put an end to it at last, each woman has to find her own way of completing her mourning, accepting her loss, and closing the door forever. Often a symbolic gesture or ritual makes the occasion memorable and the meaning concrete.

"I feel so *deprived*," Jean tells me. "I feel as if someone's grabbed away something I needed and won't give it back. I keep his clothes in the closet just as they were and sometimes I go in there to try to get the smell of him. At least I can have this much—but even the smell is fading now." Jean gives a broad clue as to how she could say the final good-bye—by finally getting rid of her late husband's clothes.

Claudia is one who visits the cemetery often. She goes there on every religious holiday and every important family occasion, and there for the past eleven years she's been updating Charlie on important family events. Here too is a clue to how she might say her final good-bye symbolically. If she can't quite disbelieve the fantasy that he is there participating in her one-sided conversations, and if she has perceived that the very fantasy has her imprisoned in her past, she could turn the power of her fantasy upon itself, going to the cemetery one last time to say, "Charlie, I won't be talking to you anymore. I've come to say my last good-bye." In doing so, she would be performing the role a judge plays in a divorce: articulating the end point, putting it into words.

One woman I treated actively fantasized for more than two years that her husband was on a business trip, that he was in the other room sleeping—he was always somewhere else, but never dead. Rather than try to grapple with the facts head-on, we focused on the symbolic nature of her wedding ring.

"What exactly does it symbolize to you?" I asked her.

"That I'm a married woman, of course."

Into the pause that followed floated a silent question: If you're a married woman, where is your husband? Is it possible to be married, truly married, to a man who has died? This was a very sharp woman who intuitively understood the questions buried in the silence. She grappled with the problem for some months, and one day she came in without her wedding ring. She held up her hand, but before I could speak, she said, "No, no, I haven't lost it, haven't sold it. I just decided to have it reset." After one of our pregnant pauses, she added, "I'm having the stones reset so it doesn't look so much like a wedding ring." She began to cry. "I designed the setting myself."

Three weeks later, she came into therapy with her hand outstretched. "My freedom ring," she told me. It was beautiful, and it marked the beginning of her new status as a mature single adult. May I add that we both understood without having to say so that the freedom she was celebrating was not from her late husband but from the fantasy of him that had kept her home night after night suffering loneliness and a sense of despair?

Take a cue from my patient. If you have remained attached to your late husband but are coming to face the fact that the marriage is over and you are now a mature single woman, you might make use of the ready-made symbol that is your wedding ring to make a gesture of separation. Move the ring to your right hand, put it in a drawer, or, like my patient, have the stones reset so it becomes something beautiful but different.

If the ring is too formal a symbol to work for you, give some thought to selecting something that truly represents the bond—and then change it. For example, take a picture of your late husband off the wall, or give an object of his that's been around the house to an adult child. The idea is to create a concrete ritual—however small—to symbolize the ending of the internal bond.

REFOCUSING YOUR LIFE

Many widows maintain their connection with their past and reinforce their old patterns by staying in constant touch with their in-laws and old married friends. But these social interactions are often no more than empty patterns functioning to impede progress. Like the divorced woman, the widow may find if she studies these relationships carefully, she has little in common with her married friends, who may even perceive her as a threat. In-laws, too, may be using her in the same way she is using them: to keep her late husband "alive" in their daily lives. In both cases, the social interactions are inauthentic and barriers to her progress. If you find yourself running in the same old circles you ran in with your husband, ask whether the *substance* of these relations is still there.

Simultaneously you must ensure a new social life for yourself. Seek out widowed friends, single friends, divorced friends. Without a social network, that dismal whine—"I'm alone, I have nobody"—becomes a self-fulfilling prophecy. With a social network, you have models to learn from, companions to go through the motions with until true enjoyment starts to take hold, and even the potential for the growth of new intimacy should you choose to cultivate it.

Saying good-bye to your late husband is a leave-taking, but it will be useful to mark the passage into your new single adulthood with another symbolic gesture. What can you do to please yourself, to make yourself more comfortable with yourself as a single woman, and to claim your life as your own?

One widow remarked to me, "I have such an empty house now. There's nobody there to enjoy it." Yet for many years this woman kept her house just as it was when her husband was alive, on the superstition that he, or his "ghost," would be dismayed at any change. Now, with the final good-bye said, it would be a liberating gesture, and undoubtedly a source of much pleasure, for this woman to redecorate her house or at least move things around to suit her new life, her own particular tastes. One patient of mine had always hated her bedroom set but considered it a betrayal of her marriage vows to change it. "We slept together in that bed for thirty years," she told me reverentially. I knew she was on her way when she finally sold the set.

Another woman in my practice had had a lifelong but undeveloped interest in extraterrestrial life. She read all the journals and kept up with new UFO sightings, but whenever she considered going to a lecture on the subject, her husband had pricked her balloon. It took her a long time after her husband's death, but eventually she took herself to a meeting of the Skywatchers' Club at the local planetarium, and soon she was an enthusiastic member.

Other widows may feel ready for a new life but self-conscious about their new single status. As Joan reminded me, though, "Now is the best time ever for single women. It used to be that a woman stayed home if she didn't have a husband or a date on Saturday night. Women just weren't seen together at a restaurant, play, or movie. Nowadays, nobody cares about things like that. For heaven's sake, there are so *many* of us. They'd *better* not raise an eyebrow!"

This is a time for *self*-appreciation, a time to discover or rediscover what it was in you that inspired your husband's love, yes, but also what you loved about yourself. This might sound like a cliché, but in fact one can and must cultivate appreciation of the self just as one can cultivate a love of music or art. To live a rich life on your own, you need to understand your own value, and if you are accustomed to measuring that value only in terms of your late husband's love for you and/or in terms of *his* achievements—that is, as Mrs. Doctor or Mrs. Lawyer—it is crucial for you to turn to yourself now and study and develop your strengths. Thinking about what might please you and finding a way to give it to yourself might well be a gentle way to start your course in self-appreciation.

AGAIN . . . TELLING THE CHILDREN THE TRUTH

Grandchildren are wonderful and a great source of pleasure and company, but widows who literally "live for their grandchildren" are carrying their involvement too far. If your interactions with your grandchildren are a way of keeping your late husband alive—by giving yourself an opportunity to extol his virtues, by doing what he would have you do, or by doing what you *think* he would wish you to be doing—then you are avoiding the work of completion so necessary to your psychological well-being. And too often, cheerful visits with the grandchildren are a way of masking the deepest secret of all—the degree of your pain. Are you being fair to yourself or honest with them if, with tremendous effort, you continually put off the moment when you must confront your own unhappiness and make the decision to end it?

The same is true for your adult children. In acting the sunny, well-adjusted widow for the sake of your children, you may be robbing them as well as yourself of the opportunity to move through the natural grieving stages to resolution. Appearances should be the last concern during this difficult transition—and yet for many widows I spoke with, appearances were their *first* concern.

Though both you and your children may have loved your late husband dearly, you can neither do the children's grieving for them nor protect them forever from the depth of your own. I'm not at all advocating that you drown them in your sorrows. Rather, I'm suggesting that it may be far more beneficial for both of you in the long run if instead of chirping brightly "Just *great*" when your child

inquires after you, you find a way to express the truth: "I'm struggling, honey," or "It's not so easy at the moment." Give yourself
a break from reassuring those around you. You'll find you need all
the energy and attention you can muster to face down fantasy and
move toward acceptance of the truth.

Once the recovery process is working, the need for truth does
not diminish with respect to your children. In fact, things can get
particularly bumpy at this point. A patient of mine, Lillian, found
that her adult children, a son and a daughter, seemed to unite against
her in voicing the "wishes" of their late father. When Lillian began
making arrangements to sell the house, they called an emergency
meeting of the family and insisted that she drop her plans. "Daddy
intended this house for you—he chose this house so that you would
be comfortable and safe. How could you even think of selling it?"
"But the house is much too large for me on my own," Lillian told
them. "I hate having to worry about the yard and everything. All
I want is a two-bedroom apartment close to my friends." The
children were furious, and her son began asking questions about
her financial arrangements. Soon he had arranged a meeting with
her, himself, and his financial planner, at which it quickly became
clear that the two men had worked out a plan for Lillian's money
and for her life. Some women, unfamiliar with or frightened by
finance, might have welcomed such interference, but Lillian saw
that she would lose the power to make her own decisions, to follow
her own interests and exercise her own preferences, just at the point
when she was starting to appreciate it. She had to face her children
firmly with this message: "Dad's gone, I'm the mother, and you're
the children. I know what's best for myself, dears, and I'll make
the necessary decisions."

Lillian quickly enrolled in a business course at the local junior
college called Managing Your Money. On a list of financial planners
and brokers the professor gave out she found one whose special
interest was in advising "reentry" women, and in a couple of meetings this young, savvy woman had armed Lillian with some very
sophisticated ideas about how to invest her money. Lillian spent
six months researching the city she had lived in all her life to

determine where she could afford to live and where she would enjoy living. In this way, Lillian made the transition from widow—"that dismal, dreary word; it sounds like an illness," she said—to mature single woman. Though her children were outraged at first, she did indeed sell her house for a very nice profit and did indeed make a comfortable, safe, pleasant home for herself. Since she chose and decorated the place with an eye to spending some high-quality time with her grandchildren there, her children soon found themselves thinking that even their father might have liked their mother's new home.

JEALOUS GHOSTS

Paul Gebhard's study on postmarital sexual interactions showed that 82 percent of his divorced subjects had experienced postmarital intercourse as compared with 43 percent of the widows. Why the discrepancy?

Consider Grace, whose husband, Ralph, took the opportunity during the long illness that preceded his death to talk to her about men. "They're out for two things and two things only, honey— money and sex. Maybe not in that order, but that's all they want." Was it a coincidence that he chose this time in his life to discuss such matters? Maybe, although one thing widows reported to me with a surprising consistency was their late husbands' absolute refusal to talk of their impending death explicitly. Because these men shied away from the reality of what was happening to them, most of the widows I interviewed reported that their husbands had not taken the opportunity to inform them of the practical matters they would soon face. Perhaps Ralph was attempting to protect his assets in a roundabout way.

Such pressures often merge in the widow's mind with whatever ghostly presence her fantasy conjures up to keep her on the "approved" path. A woman trying hard to break her attachment to her past and enter a new phase of life must confront these invisible pressures and face them down. When it comes to money, as Lillian's story demonstrated, there are steps she can take. The more educated she becomes not only in money matters but also regarding her newly emerging interests and preferences, the more concrete is her motivation to confront the ghost and act on her own behalf.

When a new man enters the picture, however, the ghost tends to rise up in all his idealized glory. "That man, that wonderful man," she thinks, as she carries on the sometimes awkward rituals of going out with someone new for the first time. "Who could ever measure up to Joe? What am I thinking of, going out with this guy?"

Children, often grown children, don't often help, at least at first. Frequently, their response to the first stirring of their mother's interest in the outside world, especially in another man, is, "But how could you do this to Daddy? How can you think of replacing him?"

If she's a realistic woman who has worked through her mourning and accepted her husband's death, she will have no intention of *replacing* their father but will be hoping to have a little fun, maybe dinner and the theater. But the widow still in the grips of the Ex-Wife Syndrome will cave in at this point: "They're right. What am I thinking? How can I do this to his memory?" The ghost in the next room can fold his arms and nod with satisfaction at that, for guilt at being the survivor can be a powerful inhibitor all by itself.

In therapy, when I work with a woman who is on the brink of beginning her own life as a single woman, I ask her to mentally turn the tables. Rather than imagining your late husband as suffering with jealousy at your ability to have a good time in the presence of another man, I suggest, imagine that it was *you* who died. Do you see yourself coming back from the grave to make sure he's still home suffering from your loss? Would you want him to spend his remaining years lonely and miserable? Many women have ambivalent feelings in response to this question at first, but if they loved the man and focus on their love, they invariably answer, "I would only want him to be happy." Why not give him the benefit of the doubt, I ask her, by assuming that he loved you that well himself?

* * *

Once you have made the passage into your mature single adult-hood, you may find that you love the freedom more than you ever expected. After all, when you were single before, as a young woman, the social pressure on you to marry may have been too great to allow you to enjoy yourself. Now, you have the chance to spread your wings and live out your own agenda, not a compromise path that sets others' priorities over yours. Just as the divorced woman has shed that dead-end word *ex-wife* and all its limbo-land connotations, you have wiped *widow* from your vocabulary and shaken off its gray insinuations that you're old and finished now. Freedom is your greatest asset and your newest discovery. The delicious work ahead becomes learning how to use it.

SUGGESTED READING

Brockman, Elin Schoen. *Widower*. New York: William Morrow, 1984.

Loewinsohn, Ruth Jean. *Survival Handbook for Widows*. Chicago: Follett, 1979.

Lopata, Helena Znaniecka. *Women as Widows*. New York: Elsevier, 1979.

Nudel, Adele Rice. *Starting Over: Help for Young Widows and Wid-owers*. New York: Dodd, Mead, 1986.

Nye, Miriam Baker. *But I Never Thought He'd Die*. Philadelphia: Westminster Press, 1978.

Yates, Martha. *Coping: A Survival Manual for Women Alone*. Engle-wood Cliffs, N.J.: Prentice-Hall, 1976.

Epilogue

It is important in concluding this book to remind you that my purpose in writing it was not to promise you happiness, fulfillment, or joy in your mature single life but instead to point to the *potential* for joy in it. When you have freed yourself from the Ex-Wife Syndrome, you have given yourself the opportunity to shape the rest of your life as you choose. That shaping process—the exploring, choosing, preparing, learning, and problem solving—may not be easy and may bring its own difficulties and obstacles. But my practice has shown me that every woman who recovers from the Ex-Wife Syndrome finds herself facing *forward*, and in that turnaround alone lies a wealth of possibilities.

This is the secret that no one who opens this book would believe at the outset: in the process of overcoming the Ex-Wife Syndrome, a woman not only finds her way out of limbo, she equips herself with skills for living that will serve her well no matter which direction she takes. She is not simply cured; she is stronger, more resourceful, more courageous, and more wary of the temptation to let another "take care of things" for her.

I have treated many, many women with this syndrome, and not all of them have come crying and hopeless into my office. A great

number of Ex-Wife Syndrome sufferers I have treated or interviewed have been extremely successful career women or strong
and outspoken mothers who gave the appearance of striding
purposefully and freely through life. But even these seemingly
well-equipped women, when they divorced or found themselves
widowed, discovered within themselves something that had never
grown up and had never been allowed independence. To their very
great surprise, they found their seeming strength undermined by
the loss of the men in their lives, and not until they had confronted
the secret they had kept from themselves—their stubborn and vital
dependence on sustaining a connection to these men—could this
childlike, dependent, secret part of their personalities come to light
and be brought to true strength and maturity.

THE CHOICE OF REMARRIAGE

Statistically speaking, 75 percent of divorced women and 80 percent
of divorced men remarry, although as Judith Wallerstein explains
very cogently, the actual distribution of remarriage among divorced
people depends greatly on their age. Nevertheless, remarriage for
both divorced and widowed women who have recovered from the
Ex-Wife Syndrome is not only a statistical possibility but a potentially fulfilling option.

Women in my practice who have married after ending therapy
begin their new families from a position of strength unprecedented
in their lives. Even the very small number of women who remarried
their former husbands were able to establish a new kind of connection.

If you have successfully recovered from the Ex-Wife Syndrome,
you will discern the extreme danger of going into a marriage with
less power and self-respect than your partner, and you will appreciate the value of a marriage in which spouses respect and value
each other. You will know that you need not give up any part of
yourself for the sake of the alliance. Your autonomy and freedom
will have been too hard-won and too fulfilling to sacrifice.

Still, the traditional concepts of marriage and sex roles die hard, and it's worth remembering that remarriage carries the danger of regressing and sacrificing newly won strengths, unless you remain alert to the temptation to slide into the old familiar patterns and are wary of its consequences: the loss of self-respect, your new husband's respect, and, ultimately, the loss of your freedom.

One more reminder to the woman considering remarriage: don't expect your prospective husband to help you build and keep your independence. Nurturing and maintaining your independence and sense of autonomy is *your* business. You've lost it before and, unless you stay alert and self-observant, you can lose it again. The great advantage of your position as one who has recovered from the Ex-Wife Syndrome is that you know the warning signs now.

Janet, a patient who had been through a grueling postdivorce experience, told me that when the man she was going out with jokingly called her a "ditz" one evening, she stopped on the street and turned to him very seriously. "I have to tell you," she said to him, "that's something I just can't take. I know you meant it as a joke, but it hurts me. I just don't like it." Janet's former husband had constantly ragged both her and their sons about "not being very bright." In fact, Janet was an extremely bright woman, and her sons were both creative artists; her former husband lacked confidence in his own intelligence, and he could only feel powerful at home if he made those around him feel dumb. Janet wasn't convinced that her new boyfriend lacked confidence in his intelligence, but she took the opportunity to nip a danger sign in the bud and to define one condition of the relationship. Her ability to see the sign and take the necessary action stemmed directly from her successful struggle with the Ex-Wife Syndrome.

Remarriage is one option open to the mature single woman, but certainly not the only one. The real bonus at the end of the struggle with the Ex-Wife Syndrome is *psychological health*. No amount of defining or explaining can convey the wealth of possibilities and good feelings contained in that phrase.

The notion of health contains within it the clarity of vision to *see* the multitude of choices open to each of us, and it contains as well the inner freedom to make those choices. But even more gratifying, and perhaps less frequently discussed, is the *eagerness*, the *enthusiasm*, to make life-defining choices that is experienced by the emotionally healthy, psychologically balanced human being. In undertaking the difficult work I have described in this book, you may well have discovered that struggling with the knotty problems of recovery has yielded a depth of understanding, a sense of accomplishment, and an outright joy you never dreamed of experiencing. If that is the case, your autonomy is now your greatest treasure. If it is not yet the case, take encouragement from the promise that these are the gifts that lie in store for every woman who truly wants them.

Selected Bibliography

Amato, Paul R., and Partridge, Sonia. "Widows and divorcees with dependent children: Material, personal, family and social well-being." *Family Relations: Journal of Applied Family and Child Studies*, Vol. 36, no. 3 (July 1987), pp. 316–20.

American Demographics. "The Divorced Generation." Vol. 8 (July 1986), p. 11.

Baber, Asa. "Custody Is a State of Mind." *Playboy* (August 1985).

Barbach, Lonnie. *For Yourself*. New York: Doubleday, 1976.

Becker, Lisa. "What Not to Say to a Widow." *U.S. Catholic* (February 1987), pp. 28–30.

Bell, Crystal; Kirkpatrick, Sue W.; and Rinn, Roger. "Body Image of Anorexic, Obese and Normal Females." *Journal of Clinical Psychology*, Vol. 42, no. 3 (May 1986), pp. 431–39.

Berman, William H. "The Role of Attachment in the Post-Divorce Experience." *Journal of Personality and Social Psychology*, Vol. 54 (1988), pp. 496–503.

"Births, Marriages, Divorces and Deaths for 1988." *Monthly Vital Statistics Report*. Vol. 37 (March 28, 1989). pp. 1–15.

Bohannan, Paul. *Divorce and After*. Garden City, N.Y.: Doubleday, 1970.

Bonkowski, Sara E.; Boomhower, Sara J.; and Bequette, Shelly Q. "What You Don't Know Can Hurt You: Unexpressed Fears and Feelings of Children from Divorcing Families." *Journal of Divorce*, Vol. 9, no. 1 (Fall 1985), pp. 33–45.

Boston Women's Health Book Collective, The. *The New Our Bodies, Ourselves*. New York: Simon and Schuster, 1985.

Bowlby, J. "Attachment Theory, Separation Anxiety and Mourning." *American Handbook of Psychiatry*, Vol. 6, S. Arieti, ed., New York: Basic Books (1975), pp. 292–309.

Brockman, Elin Schoen. *Widower*. New York: William Morrow, 1984.

Bulcroft, Kris, and O'Conner-Roden, Margaret. "Never Too Late." *Psychology Today*, Vol. 20 (June 1986), pp. 66–69.

Burks, Valerie K., et al. "Bereavement and Remarriage for Older Adults." *Death Studies*, Vol. 12, no. 1 (1988), pp. 51–60.

Byron, Ellen. "Will You Marry Me Again?" *Redbook* (February 1986), p. 90.

Casper, R. C. "Disturbances in Body Image Estimation as Related to Other Characteristics and Outcomes in Anorexia Nervosa." *British Journal of Psychiatry*, Vol. 134 (1979), pp. 60–66.

Cherlin, A. *Marriage, Divorce, Remarriage*. Cambridge, Mass.: Harvard University Press, 1981.

Chicago Sun-Times. "Marriage." May 4, 1989.

Cooney, Teresa M., et al. "Parental Divorce in Young Adulthood: Some Preliminary Findings." *American Journal of Orthopsychiatry*, Vol. 56, no. 3 (July 1986), pp. 470–77.

Crosbie-Burnett, Margaret, and Ahrons, Constance R. "From Divorce to Remarriage: Implications for Therapy with Families in Transition." *Journal of Psychotherapy and the Family*, Vol. 1, no. 3 (1985), pp. 121–37.

Diagnostic and Statistical Manual of Mental Disorders, DSMIII.

Doan, Michael, and Collins, Dan. "11 Million Widows—Here's How They Cope." *U.S. News & World Report* (October 28, 1985). pp. 56–57.

Dranoff, Linda Silver. "Joint Custody." *Chatelaine* (May 1987), pp. 54, 108, 109.

Edwards, Marie, and Hoover, Eleanor. *The Challenge of Being Single*. Los Angeles, Calif.: J. P. Tarcher, 1974.

Erez, Edna. "Intimacy, Violence and the Police." *Human Relations*, Vol. 39, no. 3 (March 1986), pp. 265–81.

Forward, Dr. Susan. *Men Who Hate Women and the Women Who Love Them*. New York: Bantam, 1986.

Freud, Anna. *The Ego and the Mechanisms of Defense*. New York: International Universities Press, 1946.

Freud, Sigmund. "Certain Neurological Mechanisms in Jealousy, Paranoia and Homosexuality." *Collected Papers of Sigmund Freud*, Vol. 2. ed. Ernot Jones. New York: Basic Books, 1959.
———. *Totem and Taboo*, ed. and trans. James Strachey. London: The Hogarth Press, 1955.

Friday, Nancy. *Jealousy*. New York: William Morrow, 1985.

Furstenberg, Frank, et al. "The Life Course of Children of Divorce: Marital Disruption and Parental Contact." *American Sociological Review*, Vol. 48 (October 1983), pp. 565–68.

Gardner, Richard. *The Boys and Girls Book About Divorce*. New York: Bantam, 1970.

Garland, Susan B. "A New Deal for the Children of Divorce." *Business Week* (September 7, 1987), p. 32.

Gathorne-Hardy, Jonathan. *Marriage, Love, Sex and Divorce*. New York: Summit Books, 1981.

Gebhard, Paul. "Postmarital Coitus Among Widows and Divorcees." *Divorce and After*. Garden City, N.Y.: Doubleday, 1970.

Gentry, Margaret, and Shulman, Arthur D. "Remarriage as a Coping Response for Widowhood." *Psychology and Aging*, Vol. 3, no. 2 (June 1988), pp. 191–96.

Ginsberg, Genevieve Davis. "Who Am I Without My Mate?" *To Live Again*. Los Angeles, Calif.: J. P. Tarcher, 1987.

Goode, William. *The Family*. Englewood Cliffs, N.J.: Prentice-Hall, 1964.

Gordon, Barbara. *Jennifer Fever*. New York: Harper & Row, 1988.

Greywolf, Elisabeth S. *The Single Mother's Handbook*. New York: William Morrow, 1984.

Hauser, Marilyn J. "Bereavement Outcome for Widows." *Journal of Psychosocial Nursing and Mental Health Services*, Vol. 21, no. 9 (September 1983), pp. 22–31.

Hinget, Ann G.; Hyman, Bruce M.; and Salmon, Joy L. "Male Children of Divorce Grown-up: Parental Bonding, Relationship Satisfaction, Commitment and Sex Role Identification." *Australian Journal of Sex, Marriage and Family*, Vol. 6 (February 1985), pp. 15–32.

Humphrey, Frederick. *Marital Therapy*. Englewood Cliffs, N.J.: Prentice-Hall, 1983.

Hunt, Morton. *The World of the Formerly Married*. New York: McGraw-Hill, 1966.

Jacobi, Marianne, and Wright, Rosalind. "Mothers Who Go to Jail for Their Children." *Good Housekeeping* (October 1988), p. 158, 234, 237.

Jong, Erica. "Is There Sex After 40?" *Vogue* (May 1987), pp. 304–5.

Kahn, Sandra, with Davis, Jean. *The Kahn Report on Sexual Preferences*. New York: St. Martin's Press, 1981.

Kaminer, Wendy. "The Divorce Industry." *7 Days* (February 22, 1989), pp. 24–30.

Kansky, Jacqueline. "Sexuality of Widows." *Journal of Sex and Marital Therapy*, Vol. 12, no. 4 (1986), pp. 307–21.

Kitson, Gay C. "Attachment to the Spouse in Divorce: A Scale and Its Application." *Journal of Marriage and the Family* (May 1982), pp. 379–93.

Kitzinger, Sheila. *Women as Mothers*. New York: Random House, 1978.

Koch, Mary A., and Lowry, Carol R. "Visitation and the Non-custodial Father." *Journal of Divorce*, Vol. 8 (1984), pp. 47–65.

Krantzler, Mel. *Creative Divorce*. New York: Signet, 1973.

———. *Learning to Love Again*. New York: Thomas Y. Crowell, 1977.

Kübler-Ross, Elisabeth. *Death—The Final Stage of Growth*. Englewood Cliffs, N.J.: Prentice-Hall, 1975.

———. *Living with Death and Dying*. New York: Macmillan, 1981.

———. *On Children and Death*. New York: Macmillan, 1983.

———. *On Death and Dying*. New York: Macmillan, 1969.

———. *Working It Through*. New York: Macmillan, 1982.

Leena, Linna. "The Mourning Work of Small Children after the Loss of a Parent through Divorce." *Psychiatric Fennica*, Vol. 18, (1987), pp. 41–51.

Leerhsen, Charles. "I Do, I Do, I Do." *Newsweek* (October 7, 1985), p. 81.

Lehrman, Nat. *Masters and Johnson Explained*. Chicago: Playboy Press, 1970.

Lewis, Alfred Allan, with Berns, Barrie. *Three Out of Four Wives: Widowhood in America*. New York: Macmillan, 1975.

Lindeman, Les. "On Your Own." *Plus* (November 1985), pp. 25–30.

List, Julie Autumn. *The Day the Loving Stopped: A Daughter's View of Her Parents' Divorce*. New York: Seaview Books, 1980.

Loewinsohn, Ruth Jean. *Survival Handbook for Widows*. Chicago: Follet, 1979.

Long, Nicholas, and Forehand, Rex. "The Effects of Parental Divorce and Parental Conflict on Children: An Overview." *Journal of Developmental and Behavioral Pediatrics*, Vol. 8, no. 5 (October 1987), pp. 292–97.

Lopata, Helena Znaniecka. *Women as Widows*. New York: Elsevier, 1979.

Lyman, Howard B. *Single Again*. New York: David McKay, 1971.

Maynard, Fredelle. "Ex-wives, the Long Hard Road from Homemaker to Breadwinner." *Chatelaine* (February 1988), p. 51.

Mead, Margaret. "Anomalies in American Post-Divorce Relationships." *Divorce and After*. Garden City, N.Y.: Doubleday, 1970.

Napolitane, Catherine, and Pellegrino, Victoria. *Living and Loving After Divorce*. New York: Signet, 1977.

Northcott, Herbert C. "Widowhood and Remarriage Trends in Canada: 1956–1981." *Canadian Journal on Aging*, Vol. 3, no. 2 (Summer 1984), pp. 63–77.

Norwood, Robin. *Women Who Love Too Much*. New York: St. Martin's Press, 1985.

Nudel, Adele Rice. *Starting Over: Help for Young Widows and Widowers*. New York: Dodd, Mead, 1986.

Nye, Miriam Baker. *But I Never Thought He'd Die*. Philadelphia: Westminster Press, 1978.

Parkes, C. M. *Bereavement Studies of Grief in Adult Life*. New York: International Universities Press, 1972.

Peale, Stanton, with Brodsky, Archie. *Love and Addiction*. New York: Taplinger, 1975.

Peters, John F. "A Comparison of Mate Selection and Marriage in the First and Second Marriages in a Selected Sample of the Remarried Divorced." *Journal of Comparative Family Studies*, Vol. 7 (1976), pp. 483–90.

Piaget, Jean. *The Language and Thought of the Child*. New York: Humanities Press, 1959.

Pietschmann, Richard J. "A Fond Farewell to the Nuclear Family." *Los Angeles* (August 1985), pp. 139–45, 382–83.

Priester, Steven. "Marriage, Divorce and Remarriage." *New Catholic World* (January/February 1986), pp. 9–11.

Rayburn, Carole A. "Loneliness and the Widowed Divorced." *Psychotherapy Patient*, Vol. 2 (Spring 1986), pp. 26–46.

Roha, Ronaleen R. "The Dollar Side of Divorce." *Changing Times* (May 1987), pp. 94–100.

Rodgers, Roy H., and Conrad, Linda M. "Courtship for Remarriage: Influences on Family Reorganization after Divorce." *Jour-

nal of Marriage and the Family, Vol. 48 (November 1986), pp. 767–75.

Rosemond, John. "When the Children Visit the Weekend Parent." *Better Homes and Gardens* (May 1987), p. 56.

Rubin, Zick. "Measurement of Romantic Love." *Journal of Personality and Social Psychology*, Vol. 16, no. 2 (1970), pp. 265–73.

Russianoff, Penelope. *Why Do I Think I Am Nothing Without a Man?* New York: Bantam, 1983.

Safron, Claire. "Unhappy Endings." *Ladies' Home Journal* (May 1986), pp. 96–101.

Saul, Suzanne C., and Scherman, Avraham. "Divorce Grief and Personal Adjustment in Divorced Persons Who Remarry or Remain Single." *Journal of Divorce*, Vol. 7, no. 3 (Spring 1984), pp. 75–85.

Scarf, Maggie. *Unfinished Business: Pressure Points in the Lives of Women*. New York: Ballantine, 1980, pp. 376–87.

Schiff, Sandra Gass. "Coping with the Single-parent Phenomenon." *Forecast for Home Economics*. (September 1985), pp. 34–42.

Schurenberg, Eric. "How to Cope after a Spouse Dies." *Money* (June 1988), pp. 101–8.

Schwartz, Lita Lizner, and Kaslow, Florence W. "Widows and Divorcees: The Same or Different?" *The American Journal of Family Therapy*, Vol. 13, no. 4 (1985), pp. 72–76.

Shaevitz, Dr. Morton H. *Sexual Static*. New York: Little, Brown, 1987.

Smos, B. G. *A Time to Grieve: Loss as a Universal Human Experience*. New York: Family Service Association of America, 1979.

Sowell, Carol. "Starting Over." *Modern Maturity* (June/July 1986), pp. 64–69.

Stark, Elisabeth. "Friends Through It All." *Psychology Today* (May 1986), p. 54.

Tagliacozzo, Rhoda. "The Legacy of Widowhood." *New York Times Magazine*, (October 1988), pp. 150–52.

Teyber, Edward. *Helping Your Children with Divorce*. New York: Simon and Schuster, 1985.

———, and Hoffman, Charles D. "Missing Father." *Psychology Today* (April 1987), p. 36–39.

U.S.A. Today. "Erroneous Assumptions about Bereavement." (December 1986), p. 5.

Victor, Ira, and Winkler, WinAnn. *Fathers and Custody*. New York: Hawthorn, 1977.

Viorst, Judith. *Necessary Losses*. New York: Ballantine, 1986.

Wallerstein, Judith S., and Blakeslee, Sandra. *Second Chances*. New York: Ticknor & Fields, 1989.

———, and Kelly, Joan Belrin. *Surviving the Breakup*. New York: Basic Books, 1980.

Warren, Nancy J., et al. "Children of Divorce: The Question of Clinically Significant Problems." *Journal of Divorce*, Vol. 10 (Fall/Winter 1986), pp. 87–106.

Webb, Marilyn. "The Debate over Child Custody." *Working Women* (May 1986), p. 162.

Weitzman, Lenore. *The Divorce Revolution*. New York: The Free Press, 1985.

———, et al. "Beneath the Surface: The Truth about Divorce, Custody and Support." *Ms.* (February 1986), p. 67–70.

Williamson, Murray, Marilyn. *Diary of a Divorced Mother*. New York: Wyden Books, 1980.

Women in Transition. A Feminist Handbook on Separation and Divorce. New York: Scribner's, 1975.

Wooley, Persia. *The Custody Handbook*. New York: Summit Books, 1979.

Yates, Martha. *Coping: A Survival Manual for Women Alone*. Englewood Cliffs, N.J.: Prentice-Hall, 1976.

Young, Jane. "The Fathers Also Rise." *New York* (November 18, 1985), pp. 50–75.

Zimerman, Dawn H., and West, Candace. "Sex Roles, Interruptions and Silences in Conversation." *Language and Sex Difference and Dominance*, ed. Barrie Thorne, and Nancy Henley. Rowley, Mass.: Newbury House, 1975, pp. 105–29.

SANDRA S. KAHN is a psychotherapist who has established a national reputation as an expert on topics related to sexuality, dynamics of the male-female relationship, depression, anxiety, and a variety of other issues. She has been in private practice since 1976 and is the author of *The Kahn Report on Sexual Preferences*. She is a past president of the Chicago Psychological Association, and lives in Chicago, Illinois.